THE NATURE
OF PROJECT LEADERSHIP

SVEIN ARNE JESSEN

THE NATURE
OF PROJECT LEADERSHIP

UNIVERSITETSFORLAGET, OSLO

Scandinavian University Press (Universitetsforlaget AS), 0608 Oslo
Distributed world-wide excluding Norway by
Oxford University Press, Walton Street, Oxford OX2 6DP

London   New York   Toronto
Delhi   Bombay   Calcutta   Madras   Karachi
Kuala Lumpur   Singapore   Hong Kong   Tokyo
Nairobi   Dar es Salaam   Cape Town
Melbourne   Auckland

and associated companies in
Beirut   Berlin   Ibadam   Mexico City   Nicosia

British Library Cataloguing in Publication Data
Jessen, Svein A.
Nature of Project Leadership
I. Title
658

ISBN 82-00-21516-4

Cover: Anne Cathrine Jansen
Illustrations: Bjørn Norheim
Printed in Norway by a.s Joh. Nordahls Trykkeri
Binding: Kristoffer Johnsens Bokbinderi

PREFACE

Project work is more than tools and techniques. This has been recognized for years. However, most modern project literature and project plans still concentrate on the technical aspects of project work, such as better organizational structures, better monitoring and control systems, better technical reports and better communication channels.

But project work is also a mental process, a strain for the human resources involved and a challenge that often goes well beyond the fulfilment of technical goals. Today's "project approach" in its modern, comprehensive form has in fact a rich blend of social and behavioural characteristics which exert great influence on the project participants and the whole organization.

One person who is particularly exposed and vulnerable in this context is the project manager. It is his or her ability to make other people work harder, perform better and with more energy that in the end engenders the project's success. How is this accomplished? Which forces make him or her do a better job? Which conditions coerce the ability to meet time and resource limits with the best go-ahead spirit and the right willingness and motivation?

To find possible answers to these and similar questions is the main topic of this book. However, as the title suggests, it is more. It is also a contention that in order to do the job as the main responsible person in the best way, the project manager must act and regard him- or herself as a project *leader*. There may be many similarities between being a manager and being a leader, but the best way to distinguish between the two may be that given by McGregor, who claimed that while a manager does "things right", a leader also does "the right things".

In general, leadership is a subject that has long excited interest among scholars and lay persons alike. More serious studies on leadership have, however, a short historical background. Moreover, studies of how *project managers* act as leaders are almost nonexistent. This is, in my opinion, unfortunate because the project manager often has to execute professional leadership far more wilfully than when performing traditional management.

In this book one aspect of project leadership will be given particular attention, namely the project leader's reactions in terms of variations in *motivation* in project developments. According to studies made and general knowledge acquired, it seems that Man's own interest in achieving and succeeding as an organizational member is a crucial parameter for most of his performance. But what also seems to be clear is that since the business environment itself is continually undergoing transformation due to rapid changes in markets and tools for business effectiveness, these changes have also increased the need for an understanding of human adaptiveness, in addition to requiring an increased understanding of how humans respond to responsibility and authority within an organization. The growth in the service industry has also changed the demand patterns and particularly focused on the human behavioural components in business environments. In general, these trends have given a deeper respect for the individual, enhancing factors such as security, participation, challenge and meaning of life as crucial parameters at the workplace. The evolvement of the project approach has additionally brought in a new dimension in organizational settings, in the sense that it has propagated the idea that some work is best executed under an ad-hoc or temporary policy, implying that instead og "living forever", which is the ultimate goal of the traditional organization, the project concept demands an attitude concentrating on "dying" or getting it over with.

The project concept has also challenged the traditional yearly cycle of the business organization following a division in 365 days and 12 months. In projects, individual time limits specific to each project have to be followed. In many organizations this has produced severe conflicts with regard to goal attendance, financial accounting and human resource assignments.

The often considerable uniqueness embodied in a project effort has finally required those involved to strike a healthy balance between the challenge it is to create new products and opportunities and the risk for punishment and disgrace they may meet if they fail.

As already contended, it is the project manager as a *leader* who is the most exposed person in this context, and the person who should be particularly well recognized and supported in his or her struggle for success. This book is for the most part based on my thesis, "The Motivation of Project Managers. A Study of Variation in Norwegian Project Managers' Motivation and Demotivation by Triangulation of Methods", submitted for the degree of Doctor of Philosophy at Henley, The Management College, UK. In this regard I extend special thanks to Professor David Birchall, my supervisor. Other sources have also been used, in particular *Prosjektadministrative metoder*, Universitetsforlaget, Oslo, which I wrote as a textbook for The Norwegian School of Management in 1986 and revised in 1992, and *Prosjektadministrasjon og Utredningsteknikk*, Tano Forlag 1985/1990, Oslo, written together with Leif Skare [†].

Finally, I would like to thank my wife, Gerd, for her support and intellectual stimulation during the many months it took to complete this book. Without her encouragement and patience, there would definitely not have been any book on this topic from my hand.

May 1992

Svein Arne Jessen

CONTENTS

1 THE NATURE OF PROJECT LEADERSHIP

"...an organization chart is not a company, nor a new strategy an automatic answer to corporate grief. We all know this; but like or not, when trouble lurks, we call for a new strategy and probably re-organize. And when we re-organize, we usually stop at re-arranging the boxes in the chart. The odds are high that nothing much will change."
(Peters and Waterman)

1.1 General

It seems fair to state that the "project approach" to problem solving has found general application in almost every corner of the world. In a survey carried out in the United States fifteen years ago,[1] it was found that 65 per cent of planning in the USA had a project emphasis compared with 50 per cent in Japan and that the trend was increasing. A similar survey made in Norway in 1990, based on interviews taken in more than 100 private and public organizations,[2] revealed that many of these organizations felt that almost "everything we do is project work". Undoubtedly, there is at present a very high degree of project work taking place in the "Westernized" world, particularly so in the Nordic countries where the project approach has become more or less the standard way of accomplishing both major and minor tasks when constraints are placed on the use of financial, technological or manpower resources.

There are many possible reasons for this development. An apparent one is that the "project approach" seems to coincide with typical trends in modern society: the often ad-hoc or "one-time" nature of problems occurring in organizations due to a rapidly changing environment, the development of more flexible organizational structures and the need for lateral networking and communication between semi-autonomous societal units.

Viewed from another angle, the "project approach" appears to be a term that is commonly used when the problem to be solved is identified reasonably well and the aim is to introduce limits to the combined problem-solving effort and apply simplified decision processes. By defining the problem within a "project" frame, it is generally noted that this generates challenges and opportunities for groups and individuals often lacking in the traditional organizational systems. In particular, its goal-directed effort and the immediate stimulation of innovation and creativity throughout the whole development and execution process seem to be the most appreciated characteristics.

On the other hand, critics have contended that projects may be quite risky and complex endeavours. Often they provoke undesirable interdisciplinary conflicts which result in frustration and project failures. The decision to solve a problem through the "project approach" does not necessarily guarantee success, it may even create more problems.

This mix of latent fortunes and misfortunes within the approach has caused both researchers and practitioners to engage in greater efforts toward a better understanding and amendment of the project concept. Different concepts have been tried out in these efforts. The most convenient way has been to describe the obvious and easily recognizable achievements and failures observed in practical project work and then evaluate the extent to which these may be seen as logical consequences of the way the project work has developed and thus affected the organization and its individuals. This procedure has also been successful in demonstrating and describing the most apparent advantages and disadvantages of the "project approach". This is the reason why many of them have become well known today.

1.2   The Project Approach and Its Recognized Advantages

Four advantages of the "project approach" seem particularly well known. One of these is its obvious *simplicity and efficiency* in managing limited resources and reaching predefined *goals* in non-routine operations.[3] The opportunity to limit our efforts to well-defined tasks or operations, following agreed and expedient routines, supports the seemingly basic desire for rational behaviour recognized among organizational members in general. It also helps to clarify the purpose of the effort.[4]

Another advantage is the project work's apparent *stimulating effect* on the people involved, if project "conditions" are right, or felt to be right. The achievement of goals and utilization of our capacity are generally recognized as major contributors to human motivation.[5]

A third advantage is its often *cross-disciplinary* orientation, combining different professional views and knowledge in one operational, goal-directed concept.[6]

The fourth advantage, recognized more recently, is that the "project approach" has properties and characteristics which may make it appropriate to regard it as a *professional discipline* in its own right,[7, 8] even if it at present is a rather general term for managing change and solving problems. But, as Lord and Birchall have argued,[9] "If nothing else, the diversity [of projects] has revealed the discipline's healthy tendency to propagate itself under different conditions".

Part of this increased attention and status is a natural consequence of the way the project concept has developed recently. Initially, the project "idea" was developed by practitioners for the fast and effective solving of mainly technical or construction-oriented, non-routine problems.[4] The apparent success of the approach was then recognized by cross-disciplinary theorists. They saw the project concept as a promising way of injecting alternative ways of thinking, performing and behaving into problem-oriented environments. As argued by Wilemon and Baker,[10] "one of the most significant developments in management thought and practice during the past two decades has been the accelerated emphasis on project management in administering complex tasks and programs". There should therefore be ample grounds for characterizing the "project approach" and "project management" as a well-established method for better problem solving in turbulent and fast-changing environments.

1.3   The Project Approach and Some Recognized Disadvantages

An increasing number of authors have found it necessary to point to some apparent *disadvantages* of the "project approach" also. Wilemon and Baker[10] have come to the conclusion, after studying a multitude of project management efforts, that "there…[seems to be]…no single panacea in the field of project management; some factors work well in one environment while other factors work well in other environments". This points to the interesting awareness, particularly among practitioners, that the "project approach" has many flaws which have rendered it an incomplete tool for many problem-solving efforts, particularly in the sense that disadvantages not previously observed, or observed but treated as infirmities of the human component and therefore not regarded as a weakness of the concept itself, have increasingly come to be seen as typical of the "project approach".

Among these are the tendency to *overrun* time and cost limits, the tendency that the project goal ends up as a *sub-optimization* of effort, in conflict with or highly inadequate in comparison with the expected overall benefit to the company or organization initiating the project, and that efforts on a new project seem to derive little benefit from knowledge gained in previous projects due to a *lack of effective transferability of knowledge* from earlier failures or successes. The increased application of the "project approach" to new problem areas, and thereby a greater cross-disciplinary usage of this approach, has also created interrelationships between factors and conditions within the project environment of a steadily more complex, more difficult, and apparently more disorderly nature.

1.4   Main Developments of the Project Approach in Recent Times

If we were to take a broader view on how the project concept has developed recently, we would start out by realizing that the partly encouraging, partly discouraging recognitions of the viability of a new methodology or concept, such as those that are currently observed for the "project approach", are common enough when developing new sciences. When they emerge, they often show a conglomerate of interrelated and interdependent functions. Forrester[11] described the outcome of such processes as hard to "translate into a common frame of reference from which they can be transferred from the past to the present...[and then]...effectively applied in new situations".

These are also factors which seem to have compelled both the theorists and the people in active project work to try to improve and extend their knowledge about the project concept. It was widely observed then that what they had to look for and deal with were some "new" and more "indirect" problems which most certainly were typical traits of project work, too. These traits or characteristics were less plainly discernible and less easily handled by the traditional methods of project management. But in practical project work they were increasingly regarded as commonly having a decisive influence on the successful outcome of project endeavours. "Professional" project management today may therefore also be said, although still in the process of being fully accepted as a separate discipline, to be a discipline in a state of unrest.

As already indicated, part of this present status of the "project approach" is a natural consequence of the way the discipline has developed in recent years. At a relatively early stage it was recognized that for this approach to work well and to be successfully implemented, it was necessary to define and include particular "project management" *methodologies* within the concept. Due to its "technical" origin, developments in such methodologies were accordingly focused mostly on technical improvements, i.e. how to better manage the technical procedures and the organizational structure of projects. This is why to begin with such special planning and monitoring techniques as PERT and CPM, developed in the USA in the middle of the 1950s for managing physical structures and large-scale technical developments, became almost synonymous with "project management".

The rapid development of the concept itself, however, continually made many of these earlier "quantitative" techniques and their applications obsolete, proving them unable to competently master the more integrated, non-technical sides of project management. This was partly overcome by replacing the old tools with more advanced techniques, often heavily computer-oriented, which gave more managerial control of physical and financial resources and an increasing ability to apply comprehensive decision-support systems for "optimum" goal attainment. But the ability of these techniques to handle the many "qualitative" sides of project management proved less successful.

Today, therefore, "project management" has become a discipline with many easily implementable techniques for fast and effective problem solving and many recognizable structural advantages, but also proved to be an arena for complex *human interplay* which, although it has led to success and personal achievement for many, has also led to frustration and disappointment, especially burdening those given the managerial responsibility for the project effort.

1.5   New Insights into the Workings of the Project Concept

The above observations makes it clear that despite the refinements and improvements of the project managers' possibilities of following up and monitoring the technical progress in greater detail, there is a growing realization among project executors that these techniques take care of only one or two functions within the life cycle of a project.

One important observation was that project work seemed to advance through steps or stages which differed in content and form and which seemed to constitute a certain "life-cycle" structure typical for projects.[12] What was also noted as significant was that the traditional project "methodologies", while working well in some project phases and in some projects, could fail catastrophically in others. They also described only a few of the many aspects of performing and managing project work.[13]

Another observation was that project work took place at different levels of authority. The "project management" level was particularly problematic due to its typical "middle-management" position – a position often regarded as being squeezed between other managerial layers of authority and therefore difficult to master and maintain satisfactorily.[14]

Within much project effort it thus came to be generally understood that it was not only important that those with project responsibility knew the details of the plan, the precise goal of the effort, and the technical and financial constraints during the project execution. It was also fundamental that they knew why the project was initiated, *how* and by which steps it was supposed to be socially performed, and *what* mission it should fulfil and for *whom* when completed, if a full understanding of the process was to be conveyed and total effectiveness obtained. These are items which strongly focus on the human behavioural aspects in project settings. In this context it has been increasingly accepted that projects also emphasize the need to understand how to communicate and deal with people, how to utilize know-how, how to motivate people to accept and implement effective monitoring systems, how to obtain consensus and convey agreements on policies and goals and how to inspire *project managers to utilize and develop their own capacity and capability* within their role of responsibility.[9]

Projects Are Not Only End Products

The consequence of these developments is that today project work is an effort no longer seen as limited to the production of an "end" *product*. A project today is more a "link-pin" to further developments, more a means to achieve future goals than a tool for fulfilling only one, particular goal. It is also thought of and applied as an important development *process*. This means that, besides having a technical, operational goal, the project effort also comprises the interaction with the environment and its enactors, creating new opportunities and inspiring to new directions for corporate prosperity and human growth. Through this process, project work creates a range of social and emotional interrelationships which have definite impacts on both the end product and on the whole enterprise or organization within which the project effort takes place. As reported by Morris,[15] at the March 1988 meeting of the UK Association of Project Managers it was agreed that "the traditional measures of project success –

on time, in budget, to technical specifications – have only limited application". And as also expressed by Ashley,[16] "technical skills can be acquired and updated; human skills must be developed".

It can be argued, therefore, that apart from the importance to satisfy a "technical" goal fulfilment, today's "project approach" in its modern, comprehensive form has a rich blend of social and behavioural qualities and characteristics. These have a major influence on the project participants and on the whole organization to which it belongs or addresses its work. A further study of the human component of project efforts is therefore likely to provide the most useful insight for improved project management. As part of this, it is worth considering that the project approach has a particular *psychological effect on people*. More insight into the behavioural outcome of motivation and demotivation of project efforts could therefore lead to a better understanding of the working of the total problem-solving mechanism embodied in the "project concept".

Projects As Behavioural Arenas

These thoughts have a close parallel to the increased interest in Western society in the area of human behaviour in organizational settings in general. That fact that human beings are not only motivated by technical, measurable quantities such as production output, salary, or the satisfaction of basic needs such as food, shelter and sex, has for years been recognized and discussed by philosophers, psychologists, sociologists and anthropologists.[17, 18, 19, 20, 21] It also seems fair to say, however, that although human motivation in work settings has been paid increasing attention by a wide range of researchers and theoreticians, the conclusions drawn so far are *not* unambiguous. What is important, though, is that there seems to be cross-disciplinary agreement that human behaviour and motivation are *caused* and are not the result of random influence.[22] Elster[23] goes as far as to declare causality in human endeavours to be the "cement of society". "Motivation" in project settings should therefore be worthwhile studying, provided those conditions that cause motivational reactions in such settings are possible to locate or trace.

This has to an increasing extent also become a problem area because there seems less agreement with regard to which forces and conditions are the *real causes* of different motivational reactions. Over the years several schools of thought have suggested a variety of explanations, ranging from the impact of personality[21] and reward,[24] to the impact of perception[25] and reinforcement,[26] to mention some of the more dominant directions. The effect of groups[27] and of the work setting itself,[28, 29] including how the organizational structure and the technological components influence human behaviour, have also been studied extensively and tried out in practice.[30, 31] The conclusion drawn by Elster[23] seems though to dominate, namely that "people have seriously incomplete information about each other's rationality, preferences and information". During the early 1960s "organizational behaviour" emerged as a new field of study, in an interdisciplinary combination of the three professions of psychology, sociology and anthropology. The main idea was to place the emphasis on the *interactions* of people and organizations in terms of organizational behaviour, and involved a systematic study of behaviour, the processes, and the structures found within organizations.

All these directions of thoughts have undoubtedly changed the traditional view on the merits and possibilities of the project concept, and also opened up for new problem areas to be solved by using the project approach.

1.6   The Change in Areas of Responsibility for the Project Manager

Though the general aim of the above efforts was to achieve a better understanding of the effects of organizations on people in a societal context, these studies focused increasingly on the *individual* in the organization. This trend was particularly noticeable in Western cultures, where the status of each individual human being became a main topic of interest not only among psychologists and anthropologists, traditionally occupied with the human mind, but also among organizational theorists and social scientists. From being a "theoretical" debate first arrived at in universities and schools, the importance and the rights of each individual to participate in decisions affecting their own future and well-being developed to social movements in the societies in general, inspiring new ways of organizing and administering human effort. Again, as argued by Elster,[23] "there are no societies, only individuals who interact with each other".

In line with this is the study done by Joynt[32] who contended that in observing more than 400 organizations from four different Western countries (Germany, Norway, Sweden and the United States), "the opportunity for independent thought and action" was ranked highest in all four countries, with "variety" or "the opportunity [for the individual] to do a number of different things" as second in the European cultures. Also "feedback" or "the opportunity to find out how well I am doing my job" ranked high in these cultures. The important discovery made from this and many similar observations is that the *individual's position*, which has received less direct attention among researchers in earlier studies of organizational processes, and particularly the *role of the manager*, increasingly became the focus of attention of a wide audience.[33] This role, initially covered by the impersonal term "the management" (for a body in charge of other people at the work place), now became a subject for deeper consideration, in terms of attitude, behaviour, and performance at the individual level. These studies revealed that managers perform a great variety of work, that they are constantly involved in activities that are characterized by fragmentation and brevity, and that they have a strong influence on the success of an organization.[33] In general, almost all the newer studies of the reasons why organizations succeed or fail point to the significant role played by their leaders.[22]

When looking at project work and settings typical for projects, and the role of the manager in such environments, and more specifically, when looking at *the stimuli and conditions guiding and affecting project leaders* in executing their project work, we realize that this must be a highly important area. Research into project management and leadership is, however, still young. But it seems fair to state that during the twenty to thirty years of research in this area so far the main focus has been on the technical project-goal description or end-product definition, and which efforts and structural improvements should be developed in order to better reach a final goal.[34] Another trend during the last ten to fifteen years is the focus on group processes and project team behaviour. This has caught wide interest,[12, 35, 36] and has naturally resulted in growing recognition of the "project approach" as an important social, managerial process. This has in turn provided valuable insight into which responsibilities may have particular positive or negative effects on the human mind in an *integrative social context*. Such observations may therefore help the project managers to increase both their own performance, the productivity of their staff, and the success of the company to which their projects belong.

1.7 The Importance of Leadership in Project Settings

The mix of technical ability and knowledge, together with a good social understanding, may make it relevant to suggest that it is the role of the project manager as a *leader* that is of particular interest, and how he or she acts in accordance with the "nature of leadership" in project settings. There may be similarities between being a "manager" and being a "leader", but the best way of distinguishing between the two may be that given by McGregor[25] who claimed that while a "manager" does "things right", a "leader" also does "the right things". In general, leadership is a subject that has long excited interest among both scholars and lay persons alike. Questions about leadership have also long been a subject of speculation, but scientific research so far has mainly concentrated on the technical determinants of leadership effectiveness.

Since the role of a project leader has become more and more commonplace in enterprises and organizations, we may question why this role has been given so little scientific recognition. One reason could be that the role has mostly been described and discussed by practitioners who have revealed their own, subjective experience from project work. These descriptions have often concentrated on the technical or formal obstacles they have met. This is so because these are observations that are most easily discernible, followed by a list of lessons they have learned in this respect so that they personally may avoid similar complications in future project work. These are important pieces of information. However, they indirectly assume that project success to a very large extent relies on the choice of appropriate project *structure* and tools, together with the relevant *rules* and manuals of instructions. The insight gained from newer research at the work-places where the projects are used appears to reveal what has already been suggested above; that for the project manager only to improve the project structural components is not enough. It is equally important to increase the knowledge-base on factors affecting the human component.[3, 8, 12, 37, 38]

This is why the scope of the research has been widened, and also the reason why behavioural scientists have attempted to discover which traits, abilities, behaviour, sources of power, or aspects of the situation determine how well a leader is able to influence his or her followers and accomplish objectives.[39] The most commonly used measure of leader effectiveness seems accordingly to be the extent to which the leader is able to make the group or organization perform its tasks successfully and thereby attain set goals. This demands the cross-disciplinary understanding of both the technical and behavioural elements prevailing in the problem environment. Today the definition of "leadership" is far from clear-cut, and terms such as "authority", "management", "administration" and "supervision", to mention a few, are used as alternative terms. Stogdill[40] concluded, after a comprehensive review of the leadership literature, that "there are almost as many definitions of leadership as there are persons who have attempted to define the concept".

Despite these problems, it is appropriate to argue that more emphasis should be given to "leadership" components in projects. Project managers are those people with responsibility for the whole project and therefore for the total work progress. They are thus the key persons on whom the performance of other project personnel largely depends and to whom they look for guidance.

Despite the indistinctiveness and lack of complete agreement as to which roles are the most typical for leaders in general, the project scope nevertheless appears to demand the need for a type of "management" which closely resembles what may generally be understood as "leadership". And the main reason is that the responsibility is given to an "individual" at a certain level in an identified organization with the authority both for defining precise goals and for accomplishing them through a combination of his or her own capability and other's efforts.

1.8   Conclusions on the Status of Project Management Today and Possible Constraints to the Role in the Future

In the turbulent environment that individuals and organizations operate today, and which they will experience even more so tomorrow, it seems fair to state that helping the project managers in their struggle to master their roles and responsibilities better will be of paramount importance. It should be clear, furthermore, that the "project approach" with its given organizational structure, its definite constraints, its agreed plan of progress and particular built-in leadership responsibility, makes the role of the individual holding the position of project manager more clear-cut than in many other organizational settings. This also makes the person in such a position more individually "visible" than in traditional organizations at a similar level. By observing the way problem-solving effort is executed by project managers, there should be every reason to believe that more insight can be gained into how managers generally behave and react, and by which factors they are particularly motivated to perform better or worse. Such research efforts have after all shown to be particularly rewarding in a wider context.[2]

Two main characteristics seem to be particularly embodied in this, namely:

1. That there are some concrete *general responsibilities* that project managers attend to, which may be direct functions of the way projects are "born", "fostered" and "disposed". It should be possible to discern these and from them draw conclusions of both general and project-particular value.

2. That the role of the project manager is particularly *visible*, and it is therefore easier to observe and examine the project manager as an *individual* in terms of the characteristics of this role compared to that of managers in general organizational settings. From this more information on how individuals react in special organizational settings could be learned.

The Problem of a Limited Scope

There are naturally also several constraints to these assumptions. We cannot expect a single project, limited in terms of time and personnel and of the relatively narrowed field outlined by it, to provide comprehensive and fully scientific answers, considering the vast range and number of projects carried out over the years. It is also a fact that the understanding of the project concept is still developing and constantly creating new empirical data which may alter the interpretation of existing historical records of project knowledge. However, much social scientific work consists of thinking up ideas about the nature of a not fully understood world, generalizing from observed facts to scientific "laws", and from there on developing logical "theories" or "models". If there exist some current properties of the project concept which particularly affect the way project managers do their job, and these can be extracted and represented in a simplified form, for instance through some project "models" portraying the interlinkages between objectives, rules and performance, and which also show reasonable consistency in time, any effort with the above objectives should still be a feasible and sound operation.

The Problem of Instability

Another obstacle, which is also one of the outstanding characteristics of the social sciences, is that the subject matter under study is rarely static. This makes attempts at precise measurement difficult. One way around this problem is to search through experiments or surveys for particular *cause-and-effect* relationships in the area of research and combine these with "good judgment" about the nature of the problem. The advantage of cause-and-effect observations is that they attempt to go beyond the assumption of the existence of an absolute association and try to determine if one variable can plausibly be said to cause another. It will be argued here that cause-and-effect relationships to a very large extent seem to exist in project matters, particularly on the human behavioural side. In this context the importance of managerial motivation as a predictor of managerial advancement and effectiveness has been observed and confirmed by many authors.[5, 41] One could therefore, perhaps, understand the nature of project leadership better by a *comparison in time* of variations in the project manager's motivation based on plausible cause-and-effect relationships to this motivation. This is a possibility not seriously studied previously, but should be a relatively simple operation since so much project work is actually taking place today and the gathering of data accordingly reasonably straightforward. Although this is not done in this book, it is perhaps one of the most interesting and worthwhile studies of tomorrow.

The Problem of Reward and Reinforcement

A third problem is related to the effects of reward and reinforcement of preceding behaviour. The effect of a reinforcement following some behaviour may not always be a simple "stamping-in" process. One person may perceive an event to be contingent upon his or her own behaviour, while another may perceive it as a result of the environment or the unpredictable outcome of forces outside his or her control.[42] This difference in "locus of control" may depend on personality, heredity or cultural background.[43] In a problem complex where "motivation" is a central issue, this is a worrying problem. To some extent, however, this may be solved by, on the one hand, concentrating on the project managers as "individuals" within a particular "culture" delimited by the project constraints and, on the other hand, including not only factors and conditions stimulating *motivation,* but also conditions enhancing the contrary, *demotivation.* Although motivation and demotivation may be two sides of the same coin, we should be aware that the demotivational impact of the "project approach" may be equally pronounced in modern project management as the motivational impact, since it cannot be assumed that projects always develop as desired or planned, and this may accelerate demotivation.

These observations, assumptions and arguments give room for many new thoughts about what is referred to here as "the nature of project leadership". And this gives a particular touch on the role of one individual, the project manager, in one role, namely as "leader". In the following chapters this is further elaborated and conclusions are drawn which will perhaps bring new guidelines for selecting, conducting, administrating and leading future projects successfully.

1.9   Features of This Book

CHAPTER 1. THE NATURE OF PROJECT LEADERSHIP

In this chapter the apparent main advantages and disadvantages of the "project approach" were surveyed briefly, and comments given on the importance and wide use of this approach to problem solving in Western society. The recognition today of the "project approach" as a discipline of its own was also focused upon.

Further, we have touched upon how this concept developed over time from being one that concentrated chiefly on employing the best tools and techniques for producing a specific end "product" to one that caters for newer trends, which also places considerable emphasis on the project as a "process" in itself. This implies a stronger focus on the human behaviour component in project work, and, consequently, a need to explore in particular the way the project manager performs his or her work, and by which conditions and needs he or she is particularly motivated or demotivated during the lifetime of a project. The extent to which project management is also a role-function incorporating a wider "leadership" responsibility was finally commented.

CHAPTER 2. THE PROJECT APPROACH AND PROJECT LEADERSHIP IN PERSPECTIVE

In this chapter we take a closer look at the forces behind the development of the current applications of the "project approach" as a management tool for organizations. This development is discussed relative to different perspectives of organizational theory in recent years. On the one hand, which forces in particular seem to have affected the way organizations have adapted these theories and, on the other hand, which forces have brought about new theories on the development of organizations? Two approaches are discussed: one which bases its view on "rational" and "natural" systems thinking combined with an "open" system and a "closed" system perspective; the other emphasizing the extent to which "growth" and "change" are typical traits of organizations, and if so how this may affect organizational behaviour. Both approaches are then compared to the way the project concept has been applied and implemented. The extent to which these developments have influenced project managers' motivation and demotivation has been the underlying issue, and thoughts about this are set forth.

CHAPTER 3. THE PROJECT MANAGEMENT SYSTEM

In this chapter we discuss the conditions that should preferably be focused upon in order to define a "project management system". Initially, this is debated by a brief review of current literature discussing the role of organizations in society, followed by an elaboration of the rationale for characterizing "organizations" as "systems". Based on the notion that a "systems approach" to organizations is valid, the recognition of "projects" as "systems" is then discussed. This discussion is followed by a review of the main characteristics that different authors have suggested as typical for projects, of which change-readiness, recognizable structure, process dependency, and goal-directedness are seen as especially important. From this a simple "project system" model is suggested, combining these elements into one logical project framework. Each of the elements of this model is then discussed separately with respect to the motivational and demotivational implications they may have in different project settings, and how they may vary at different stages or phases of a project "life". These thoughts are concluded by an exploration of the main implications of defining project efforts through a "project management system" perspective, and in particular features such as purposive temporality, the needed combination of rigidity and flexibility, and the special goal-directedness are examined.

CHAPTER 4: MANAGEMENT AND MOTIVATION IN RELATION TO PROJECT WORK

In this chapter we concentrate our discussion on the implications certain features of the "project management system" may have for the project manager's motivation.

The discussion begins by emphasizing some of the leading theories on motivation at work and is followed by a review of current thoughts on management and motivation related to project efforts. Also the importance of studying both motivation and demotivation in projects is discussed, particularly with regard to the leading motivation theories of today.

This is followed by a discussion of how those more specific characteristics of the "project management system" we have suggested may create variations in the project manager's motivation. This discussion is divided into four parts.

The first part focuses in particular on the motivational implications for project managers of being confronted with, and often associated with, the "change" desire behind the project effort, and how different authors have found that project managers cope with this. In this respect the combination of "uncertainty" and "opportunity" brought about by the change desire is discussed in relation to the effect this may have on project managers' motivation and demotivation. In addition, the different management styles applicable are debated, with special reference given to the "contingency approach".

The next item for discussion is the motivational implications for project managers of the "structural" components included in the "project approach". The interactive effect between the way the project manager behaves and performs, and becomes motivated, and the particular project structure chosen or enforced is the central issue here.

The third topic of discussion is the motivational implications for project managers of the different "processes" that continually take place in project endeavours, and the impact such processes may have on the motivation and demotivation of project managers. In this respect different motivational theories are also discussed.

The last item discussed is the motivational implications for the project manager of the project "goal" itself. Different "goal theories" are debated, and the conclusion drawn is that management generally reacts positively to a goal-directed atmosphere, and that the project concept should therefore have considerable motivational incitement.

Finally in this chapter it is suggested that a full understanding of managerial motivation in projects should comprise both the "systems approach" of organizations and the "contingency approach" of leadership, and that "change", "structure", "process" and the "final goal" are key elements which together form the combination of "stability" and "dynamism" that it is necessary to adopt in order to "understand" and master projects. These are also the keys to the variation in the project managers' motivation and demotivation over the project life cycle, and the elements included in a comprehensive computer-oriented simulation model of managerial motivation in projects. The model and its main findings and conclusions are presented.

CHAPTER 5. PRACTICAL CONSEQUENCES OF THE THEORETICAL ASPECTS OF PROJECT LEADERSHIP

In this chapter some practical conclusions on the nature of modern project management are drawn. In broad terms these comprise the way project work is defined and executed, the way the project goal is decided and constraints imposed, and the fact that the motivation of the project manager may vary from one project phase to the next due to specific causes and stimuli prevailing in each project phase. This in turn leads to the assumption that projects should perhaps be conducted by a certain leadership-style prototypical for project work. The style envisaged is a combination of a "path-goal" model of leadership and a "discontinuous" leadership model, in which the project leader, depending on the project phase, structures, supports and rewards the project enactors differently in order to reach the project's goal, and, on the other hand, that he or she adjusts the leadership style to the immediate situation as observed and interpreted by the project leader.

To obtain this a five step development procedure for project work is suggested, each with two mutually dependent sub-steps. The sequence of steps is also "dynamic" in nature in the sense that the outcome of one project phase may well affect parameters from the earlier phases and the succeeding phases. The project goal may, for instance, be allowed to change (within the given constraints) if the project execution signals that goal attainability is impossible or unreasonable. Similarly, the project plan may be altered due to unforeseen monitoring information, etc.

Conclusively, the project concept of today must be seen to inhibit a new type of problem-solving methodology for organizations and enterprises with a correspondingly new type of leadership style. Most important is perhaps the fact that the project approach introduces a problem-solving concept which challenges the traditional administrative system inherited from Medieval times and the Venetian book-keeping culture where the one-year cycle governed most of human activity (for example, the settling of company accounts, the filing of tax returns, the ordinary school terms, holidays, etc.). Similarly, the role of the "project manager" is changed to a "leadership" role in which his or her responsibility is no longer to merely do "things right", but also to do "the right things". In order to wield this appropriately, those in charge have to master both "structural" and "cultural" components and to understand and realize that project work is ad-hoc endeavours governed by humanly-imposed constraints to time and resource expenditures and that the task itself does not necessarily end up a success but could indeed bring dissatisfaction, misfortune and even disgrace to those involved. As betoken by Meredith and Mantel,[3] "Project management [and project leadership] is no place for the timid!"

1.10 References

1 Kono, T. 1976: Long Range Planning – Japan – USA – A Comparative Study. *Long Range Planning 9*, 5, 61–71.
2 Jessen, S.A. 1990: The Use of Projects in Public and Private Norwegian Organizations and Enterprises. Unpublished paper based on student surveys in 103 Norwegian companies in July–August 1990.
3 Meredith, J.R. & S.J. Mantel Jr. 1989: *Project Management. A Managerial Approach.* (Second edition.) John Wiley & Sons. N.Y.
4 Gray, C.F. 1981: *Essentials of Project Management.* Petrocelli Books Inc. Oregon.
5 McClelland, D.C. 1971: *Assessing Human Motivation.* General Learning Press. N.Y.
6 Baumgartel, J.S. 1963: *Project Management.* Richard D. Irwin, Homewood. Ill.
7 Wideman, R.M. 1988: The Basic for a Profession? The Project Management Body of Knowledge. *Proceedings of the Ninth World Conference on Project Management.* Glasgow. 1225–1231.
8 Lord, A.M. 1989: An Investigation into the Role of the Project Manager. (Draft thesis.) Henley, The Management College, Henley.
9 Lord, A.M. & D. Birchall 1988: The Choice of Management Structure and Staffing the Team during Project Initiation. *INTERNET Proceedings.* 189–196.
10 Wilemon, D.L. & B.N. Baker 1983: Some Major Research Findings Regarding the Human Element in Project Management. In D.I. Cleland & R.W. King (eds.): *Project Management Handbook.* Van Nostrand Reinhold Co. N.Y.
11 Forrester, J.W. 1961: *Industrial Dynamics.* M.I.T. Press. Cambridge. Mass.
12 Cleland, D.I. & R.W. King (eds.) 1983: *Project Management Handbook.* Van Nostrand Reinhold Co. N.Y.
13 Butler, A.G. Jr. 1983: Project Management – Its Functions and Dysfunctions. In D.I. Cleland & R.W. King (eds.): *Project Management Handbook.* Van Nostrand Reinhold Co. N.Y.
14 Locke R. 1985: The Relationship Between Educational and Managerial Cultures in Britain and West Germany. A Comparative Analysis of Higher Education from an Historical Perspective. In P. Joynt & M. Warner (eds.): *Managing in Different Cultures.* Universitetsforlaget. Oslo.
15 Morris, P.W.G. 1988: Initiating Major Projects – The Unperceived Role of Project Management. *Proceedings of the Ninth World Conference on Project Management 1.* Glasgow. 801–813.

16 Ashley, G. 1988: The Art of Management of Human Resources: Generation and Implementation of Human Capital. *Proceedings of the Ninth World Congress on Project Management 1*. Glasgow. 87–95.

17 Bentham, E. 1789: *An Introduction to Logic*. Menston, 1967. (Oxford 1773).

18 Comte, A. 1844: *Om positivismen*. Gøteborg 1979. *Discours Préliminaire sur L'esprit Positif.* Paris.

19 James, W. 1890: *The Principle of Psychology* Vols. I and II. Henry Holt. N.Y.

20 Freud, S. 1915: *Collected Papers of Sigmund Freud. Vol. IV, The Unconscious.* Hogarth. London

21 Maslow, A.H. 1943: A Theory of Human Motivation. *Psychology Review 50*, 370–396.

22 Cherrington, D.J. 1989: *Organizational Behavior*. Ally & Bacon. Mass.

23 Elster, J. 1989: *The Cement of Society. A Study of Social Order.* Cambridge University Press. Cambridge. Mass.

24 Lewin, K. 1951: *Field Theory in Social Science: Selected Theoretical Papers.* Harper & Brothers. N.Y.

25 McGregor, D. 1960: *The Human Side of Enterprise*. McGraw-Hill. N.Y.

26 Skinner, B. 1953: *Science and Human Behavior*. Ally & Bacon. Mass.

27 Schein, E. 1968: Organizational Socialization and the Profession of Management. *Industrial Management Review 9, 2.*

28 Mayo, E. 1945: *The Social Problems of an Industrial Civilization*. Graduate School Business Administration, Harvard University, Boston. Mass.

29 Cummings, L.L. 1977: Emergence of the Instrumental Organization. In P.S. Goodman & J.M. Pennings (eds.): *New Perspectives on Organizational Effectiveness.* Jossey-Bass. San Francisco. Cal.

30 Burns T. & G.M. Stalker 1961: *The Management of Innovation*. Routledge, Chapman & Hall. Tavistock. London.

31 Lawrence, P.R. & J.W. Lorsch 1967: *Organization and Environment: Managing Differentiation and Integration.* Graduate School of Business Administration, Harvard University. Boston. Mass.

32 Joynt, P. 1985: Cross-Cultural Management: The Cultural Context of Micro and Macro Organizational Variables. In P. Joynt & M. Warner (eds.): *Management in Different Cultures.* Universitetsforlaget. Oslo. 57–68.

33 Mintzberg, H. 1973: *The Nature of Managerial Work*. Harper & Row. N.Y.

34 Roberts, E.B. 1981: A Simple Model of R&D Project Dynamics. In E.B. Roberts (ed.): *Managerial Applications of System Dynamics.* M.I.T. Press. Cambridge. Mass.

35 Thorsrud, E. 1969: A Strategy for Research and Social Change in Industry: A Report on the Industry Democracy Project in Norway. Mimeo.

36 Belbin, R.M. 1981: *Management Teams: Why They Succeed or Fail.* Halsted Press. UK.

37 Martin, M.D. & S.D. Owens 1985: Project Management and Behavioral Research in an International Context. *Proceedings of the Eighth INTERNET World Conference May 19–24 1985.* De Doelen, Project Management. Clarity for the Nineties. Rotterdam.

38 Jessen, S.A. 1988: Can Project Dynamics be Modelled? In *Proceedings of the 1988 International Conference of the System Dynamics Society.* La Jolla. Cal. July 5–8

39 Yukl, G.A. 1989: *Leadership in Organizations.* (Second edition.) Prentice-Hall. Englewood Cliffs. N.J.
40 Stogdill, R.M. 1974: *Handbook of Leadership. A Survey of the Literature.* Free Press. N.Y.
41 Jessen, S.A. 1990: The Motivation of Project Managers. A Study of Variation in Norwegian Managers' Motivation and Demotivation by Triangulation of Methods. Thesis submitted for the degree of Doctor of Philosophy, Henley, The Management College and Brunel University. August 1990.
42 Miner, J.B. 1973: *The Management Process. Theory, Research, and Practice.* The MacMillan Company. N.Y.
43 Rotter, J.B. 1966: Generalized Expectancies for Internal Versus External Control of Reinforcement. *Psychological Monographs: General and Applied 80,* 1.
44 Hofstede, G. 1985: The Interaction Between National and Organizational Value Systems. *Journal of Management Studies 22,* 4.

2 THE PROJECT APPROACH AND PROJECT MANAGEMENT IN PERSPECTIVE

2.1 General

"The secret is to have your project team behind the project, rather than in front acting as roadblocks."

In this chapter we use existing literature and other relevant sources as a basis to take a closer look at the forces behind the development of the modern "project approach". Our main assumption is that there are structural components in project efforts which may have a special impact on the way project managers perform and act and thus the way they execute their project "leadership".

The review is performed by regarding the characteristics of the "project approach" relative to what has characterized the development of modern organizations in our time according to some of the leading theories in this field. The increasing interest in the impacts of change on organizations as they grow is given special attention using different sources of literature as references, together with a discussion of how the "project approach" has developed and found its particular form in this context. In addition, we will focus on the way "projects" appear to have become a means of solving some of the problems growth, decline, and rapid change have caused for modern organizations and for society in general.

In conclusion we will discuss some of the main characteristics of the "project approach" in its modern form and the extent to which such characteristics may be regarded as components and interactions of a special management system called the "project management system".

2.2 The Project Approach as a Management Tool

"You can't light a fire with a wet match."

As many authors have observed, the "project approach" seems to require the occurrence of some particular managerial responsibility.[1, 2, 3] If, after studying the increasing amount of literature dealing with "projects", we should wish to make a simple statement to describe what "project management" is all about, we could say that it is: "the total effort of managing every task and every responsibility entailed in the 'project approach'". While this is a very wide definition, and far from adequate in capturing the diversity of project efforts and the many managerial burdens and incentives that challenge project managers during their project assignments, it is also quite a "perfect" description of the role of the project manager, implying that the project manager's total responsibility is very diversified and difficult to fully comprehend.

The term the "project approach" itself has undergone quite a few changes since it was first launched in 1954 as a tool for improving the decision process in the US military bureaucracy, initially connected to the development of the Atlas missile program. The success of the approach accelerated its use, and it was promoted even further with the development of computer-aided planning and scheduling techniques such as CPM (Critical Path Method) and PERT (Program Evaluation and Review Technique) by Du Pont Company and the United States Navy, respectively, together with Lockheed and Booz, Allen & Hammilton. Although many project efforts may still have their base within construction and production,[4, 5] the project approach as a specific management tool has found widespread application in almost all areas of organized human activity, including finance and economics, development of organizations, environmental studies and social research, to mention a few. From being an effective and rational aid in reducing costs and saving time in large-scale technical endeavours, the "project approach" today seems to have become a general management tool or organizational "system" for handling almost any specific goal-directed effort involving human participation initiated within or outside a traditionally structured organization. Projects therefore take a wide variety of shapes and forms, and few will question the conclusion that project work today plays an integral part in organized human activity in our society.

In spite of its increasing usage, however, the "project approach" has also confused many project enactors, particularly the project managers, in the sense that they have realized that traditional techniques, well adjusted to the progress of "rational", technical concepts, do not always fit in so well in more turbulent organizational structures and environments, and in situations where the human component is less "programmable". Also the managers have come to realize that in order to be effective, it is necessary to re-interpret prevailing norms and ideologies throughout the organization, their commercial sector and society in general to reinforce their role.[6]

One must therefore look more closely at the development of the project concept and its organizational implications. One way of doing this is to compare its development with the way management efforts in general have been organized in modern societies in recent decades. Theorists appear to have found some societal "megatrends"[7, 8, 9, 10, 11] typical for our time and which may explain many of the developments that lead managers and employees to perform and act the way they do, including applying the "project approach". The flavour of these trends is discussed in the following paragraphs.

2.3   Trends in Organizational Development in Modern Time

"It's a long road that has no turn."

If we were to point to one general observation of the "history" of "organizational development", it would be that there have been significant changes in what society has expected of its institutions and what managers have believed are their proper roles. A typical example is that the depression of the 1930s and the activist movements of the 1960s and 1970s both seem to have stimulated mounting criticism of business behaviour, but in different ways. This criticism was directed against the view that business should pursue profit single-mindedly, with little or no consideration of social needs. In the 1980s a gradual erosion of the traditional system of Caveat Emptor ("Let the buyer beware") appeared to take place, and new ways of "making contracts" between business and society evolved. Stoner and Wankel[12] state that many people, including managers, are increasingly, and correctly, aware of their responsibility to society in addition to their responsibility toward the organization they serve. Others, such as Friedman,[13] the Nobel Prize winner in 1976, have slightly opposed this view and have criticized a development in which managers devote corporate resources to pursuing perhaps misguided notions of the social good. In his view business should, both now and in the future, produce goods and services efficiently and to the full benefit of the customer, and leave the solution of social problems to government agencies and concerned individuals. These are views well worth noticing when areas of project work shall be identified and given priority.

In this respect two important areas of study may serve as a frame of reference for a better understanding of how much and by which incentives the project concept has developed into a managerial tool.

One approach chosen here is to look at what kind of organizational megatrends have taken place in recent years and compare these to the general development of the "project approach".

The other approach chosen is to look at the impact the general increase in size and complexity of business and communications over recent years may have on members of organizations, and the extent to which such trends may be said to foster a "project approach" solution to problem solving.

2.3.1 Trends in Theoretical Views on Organizational Development Compared to Developments of the Project Concept

"It's the buzzing bee that gathers the honey."

General Trends

The change in perspectives on organizational development in recent years is provided in a particularly lucid way by Scott.[14] In his view, which is based on the theory of organizational "paradigms" or "models from which spring particularly coherent traditions of scientific research",[7] four paradigms on organizations seem to have dominated organizational thinking this century. These paradigms have created special managerial approaches which have influenced the way managers have dealt with problems and how efforts in research on organization and management have been directed. The four perspectives are the "rational" systems perspective, the "natural" systems perspective, the "closed" systems perspective and the "open" systems perspective. They are defined by Scott as follows:[14]

> Viewed as *rational systems,* "organizations are collectivities oriented to the pursuit of relatively specific goals and exhibiting relatively highly formalized social structures".

> Viewed as *natural systems,* "organizations are collectivities whose participants share a common interest in the survival of the system and who engage in collective activities, informally structured, to secure this end".

> Viewed as *closed systems,* "organizations are coalitions of specific groups aiming at well-defined goals and their structure is little influenced by environmental factors".

Viewed as *open systems,* "organizations are coalitions of shifting interest groups that develop goals by negotiation; the structure of the coalition, its activities, and its outcomes are strongly influenced by environmental factors".

By interlinking these perspectives, Scott was able to construct a matrix of system models covering four time periods within which each period had its own representative organizational theorists. Without defining it more specifically, he himself included the term "closed system" for a more "introvert" perspective on an organization as something which can be separated and studied completely isolated from its environment. Perhaps his reason for omitting a closer definition of the "closed system" was that this term had already been the backbone of almost all earlier organizational analyses. A good description of it is the one by Thompson,[15] contending a "closed system" to be entirely "independent of its environment...(i.e.) autonomous, enclosed, and sealed off from the outside world". Or, as suggested by Daft,[16] a closed system having "all the energy it needed, and it could function without the consumption of external resources".

Scott's cross-classification of all these classes of models and their leading theorists is illustrated in a simplified version in table 2.1. As can be seen, all theories within the "Closed Rational System Models" portray organizations as tools designed to achieve preset ends. All of them also ignore or minimize the perturbations and opportunities posed by connections to a wider environment. The theories within the "Closed Natural System Models" view organizational structure as more complex and flexible, recognizing diffuse and conflicting goals and participants endowed with multiple interests and motives. Most of the work within this tradition confines the attention to the inside of the organization, emphasizing interpersonal systems of power, status, communication and friendship and their impact. The theories of the "Open Rational System Models" revert to regarding organizations as rational systems, but with more recognition of the variable nature of the challenges posed by tasks and environments. Since organizations face environments of varying complexity, the idea is that they must adjust their internal decision-making apparatus to these variations. An underlying assumption is that organizations are striving to develop effective and efficient structures, and in this effort they continually adapt their structures to the environmental requirements. In this process they also try to efficiently organize their structure so as to reduce the transaction costs, or the costs of exchanging goods or services between

	CLOSED SYSTEM MODELS	OPEN SYSTEM MODELS
RATIONAL SYSTEM MODELS	Time period: 1900–1930 Weber: Bureaucratic Theory (1904–05) Taylor: Scientific Management (1911) Fayol: Administrative Theory (1919) Simon: Decision Making (1945)	Time period: 1960–1970 March & Simon: Bounded rationality (1958) Lawrence & Lorsch: Contingency Theory (1967) Blau: Comparative Structure (1970) Williamson: Transition Costs (1975)
NATURAL SYSTEM MODELS	Time period: 1930–1960 Barnard: Cooperative Systems (1938) Mayo: Human Relations (1945) Whyte: Human Relations (1959)	Time period: 1970– Strauss et al.: Negotiated Order (1963) Weick: Organizing (1969) Miller & Rice: Socio-technical Systems (1967) March & Olsen: Ambiguity and Choice (1976) Pfeffer & Salancik: Resource Dependence (1978) DiMaggio & Powell: Institutionalist Theory (1983)

Table 2.1 Some dominant theoretical models and representative theorists for four time periods and four perspectives on organization and management
Source: Scott 1987: 100–101

persons or across boundaries, these costs being necessary for carrying out these adaptations efficiently. The theories of the last perspective, the "Open Natural System Models", place greatest emphasis on the importance of the environment in determining the structure, behaviour and survival chances of organizations.

It is clear that the assumption that organizations behave as rational systems is strongly challenged by Scott's thoughts. Other authors have made similar statements, e.g. that actions often precede rather than follow goals,[17] and that decision outcomes are strongly influenced by their contexts. For this reason, it is important to know how the decision has been defined, what interests are brought into play and by what "rules" individual choices are aggregated to produce an organizational decision.[18] The statement that social reality is a human construction, being created in social interaction, and as such organizations may try to imitate other

	CLOSED SYSTEM MODELS	OPEN SYSTEM MODELS
RATIONAL SYSTEM MODELS	Time period: 1950–1970 The traditional project concept	Time period: 1980– The prevailing project concept of today
NATURAL SYSTEM MODELS	Time period: 1960–1980 More emphasis on the human factor in project work	Time period: 1990– The emerging project concept of tomorrow?

Table 2.2 Some dominant trends in the use and performance of the project approach for four time periods and four system perspectives on organization and management

organizations to "uniform" themselves, especially when confronting uncertainty,[19] is also important.

Project Trends

If we look at project work from a similar angle of systematization, it will here be contended that the project concept seems to have followed a pattern of development in time parallel to that of organizations in general. This can be seen by examining the achievements and frustrations prominent authors in this field have observed and recorded over the years as typical for the performance of projects and for the attitudes of project managers.[1, 2, 3, 4, 20, 21, 22, 23, 24, 25, 26, 27, 28] A summarized outline of what these opinions and observations may cover is given in table 2.2.

The general contention is that when the project approach was launched in its modern form in the 1950s, it followed a strict "Closed Rational System" perspective, basing the managerial effort on typical measurable qualities found in "operational research" methods such as network programming and statistical minimalization of cost and time. They also only focused on the project internal environment. A change toward an emphasis on the human component came in the 1960s and 1970s when project team thinking and more flexible organizational setups for projects were introduced. This is typical for the "Closed Natural System" perspective, where improvements in human effort primarily tend to take place within the boundaries of one's own organization. A different perspective on "project management" seems to be more predominant today, where project work is still seen as dependent on the existence of a basic structure and fundamental, operational rules for managerial performance, but also dependent on a high degree of flexibility and an ability to adjust goals and performances to suit external forces operating outside the project's formal boundaries. These are typical features of the "Open Natural System" thinking.

Seeing these trends in the perspective of Scott's "paradigmatic" developments in organizational thinking in recent years, it may be appropriate to state that the *project management concept has followed the general trend of organizational theories, but with a time lag of 10 to 20 years.* When the "Closed Natural System" perspective had its strongest supporters, the project management concept prospered due to its "Closed Rational System" perspective on rationality, effectivity and efficiency. When the "Open Rational System" began to influence the way writers and managers regarded organizations in general, the "Closed Natural System" perspective with its emphasis on teamwork optimalization and collective goal-precision started to dominate project work. Today, when the "Open Natural System" view excites managers and theorists, "good" project management tends to be conceived as one following a typical "Open Rational System" view in which basic structures are fundamental, but where flexibility toward external and environmental changes and uncertainties is crucial for effective and successful project management. This may eventually give way to a new project concept, with more emphasis on traits typical of the "Open Natural System" perspective, although these implications cannot be observed today due to the suggested time-lag in the evolution of the "project concept".

The most important observation from this, however, is that although organizational theorists launched new ideas on how to organize and manage business enterprises, these ideas were not necessarily brought into practice. As argued by several authors,[29] many theories never left the scientific laboratories and their application came slowly. It is quite possible therefore that the "project approach" has developed as a mixture of two trends. One in which the project concept has continually been formed as a protest or *reaction* to recognized inadequacies in the theoretical recommendations of "new" organizational thinking, and as such may be described as a *conservative* or "safe" alternative to some leading, but not yet fully adopted, organizational theories at any point in time. The other trend may be seen as the first application of new theories to see if they work, and thereby being in the *forefront* in terms of the possible practical applicability of new organizational theories. Said in a different way: *the project approach has continually been applied as a means of filling the gap between the initial theoretical acceptance of new, advanced organizational theories, and their general practical application in modern organizational development.*

For many managers who need tools and co-operational forms they feel they can trust, and which also seem to be in line with "current common sense" and which are therefore more readily accepted among staff and superiors, the "open system" thinking combined with strong "rational" elements should thus be an appropriate answer to such precautionary thinking today. This may be the reason for the continuing popularity and widespread use, particularly today, of the "project approach" despite its recognized shortcomings.

2.3.2 Perspectives on Evolution and Change as Organizations Grow

"One time a mistake: two times a purpose."

When contending that the development of the "project approach" can best be understood by comparing it to the shifting views among theorists and practitioners on what organizations are and how they should best be handled, it is also important to regard projects in view of the fact that many managerial researchers have recently come to the conclusion that organizations more often than *not* behave rationally and follow predictable patterns of development. Burns and Stalker[30] and March and Olsen[18] found that informal roles played an important part in the way decisions are taken, and Lawrence and Lorsch[31] and later Joynt[32] found that successful innovative organizations often changed from individual integrators to more diffuse behaviour, emphasizing group integrators and committees. March,[33] as partly quoted by Obtòy and Joynt,[34] concludes that:

1. Organizations are continually changing, routinely, easily, and responsively, but change within them cannot ordinarily be arbitrarily controlled. Organizations rarely do exactly what they are told to do.
2. Changes in organizations depend on a few stable processes. Theories of change emphasize either the stability of the process or the change they produce, but a serious understanding of organizations requires attention to both.
3. Theories of change in organizations are primarily different ways of describing theories of action in organizations, not different

theories. Most changes in organizations reflect simple responses to demographic, economic, social and political forces.

4. Although organizational response to environmental events is broadly adaptive and mostly routine, the response takes place in a confusing world. As a result, prosaic processes sometimes have surprising outcomes.

These and similar arguments on the seeming unpredictability of organizational behaviour led authors to look for other parameters operating within the organizational frame and which also were parameters of organizational life. One important angle of study was to try and perceive the *process* by which organizations seem to *grow* and *change*. The most prominent of these views are discussed in the following.

2.3.3 Possible Impacts of Growth on Organizations

> "Growth is seldom a chance of occurrence. It is the result of conscious managerial decisions."
> *(Robbins 1983)*

The idea that organizations have to *grow* to be profitable probably stems from the early recognition by Adam Smith in his *Wealth of Nations* that by division of labour into separate operations in which each worker could specialize, total productivity would "multiply geometrically".[12] The larger the organization, the more it could subdivide labour and benefit from the combined effort.

The "evident" correlation between prosperity and size has been questioned by many authors in recent years as the number of large, and very large, organizations has increased and opened up for more comprehensive knowledge on organizational behaviour.[35] Parkinson[36] claimed early on that large organizations are overbureaucratic, devoting a disproportionate amount of their staff resources to administration. Rushing[37] found that the administrative component of an organization is not a unitary structural element but rather, in his words, a "heterogenous category" composed of varying participants performing quite different and necessary functional roles. Also Kimberley[38] found in his quite extensive studies that the causal status of size in relation to structure was problematic. Freeman and Hannan's[39] findings supported this view, but they found that correlation was dependent on whether the organization was in a period of growth or decline. Meyer[40] advocated similarly that longitudinal studies of organizational development were necessary to understand such relationships, and concluded after examining data on 249 finance agencies in fifty US states over the last 100 years that there was a positive correlation between formalization and the number of levels in the hierarchy. Chandler,[41] on the other hand, studied four large US companies and concluded that market opportunities, not internal connections, determined a company's strategy, which in turn determined the size and structure of the company's organization. Mainiero and Tromley[35] have criticized this view and suggested the opposite: that structure and size can play a critical role in influencing corporate strategy. A positive correlation between size and centralization has also been looked for and disputed. Hage[42] found such a correlation to exist while Child[43] came to the opposite conclusion.

One study which has given particular focus to the impacts of organizational growth is that done by Starbuck,[44] who found five key features thought to be essential to the understanding of which reactionary patterns in time developed in organizations. They were:

1. The age of the organization,
2. The size of the organization,
3. The stages of "evolution" or of modest but steady growth,
4. The stages of "revolution" or of substantial turmoil in the organization's life, particularly when affecting management practices, and
5. The growth rate of the industry to which the company belongs.

Greiner[45] and Quinn and Cameron[46] have followed the same line of thought, contending that organizations when they grow develop through phases characterized by a certain dominance of some of the above characteristics, representing a sort of "differentiation in time". This brings in some particular qualities in each phase. The most clear-cut ones being a high degree of creative evolution in the first phase, an effective specialization in the second phase, a greater responsibility through delegation in the next phase, good coordination and the establishment of efficient formal procedures in the penultimate phase, and strong interpersonal collaboration and flexible team organizing in the final phase. However, they leave this last phase more open-ended, implying that in the future new knowledge regarding even larger organizations, for instance of a multinational or global character, might bring in new phases and new knowledge of the growth process at these levels.

What Starbuck[44] contended as problematic, though, is that although each phase has "evolutions" which may be characterized by a management style promoting growth, each phase also tends to have "revolutions" which are characterized by some dominant management problem. In the first phase the dominant problem is the *leadership* crisis, in the second phase an *autonomy* crisis is developing, in the next phase a *control* crisis will soon take over, and in the subsequent phase a *red tape* crisis develops in the sense that the proliferating of systems and programs begin to exceed their usefulness. Although Starbuck has not fully examined the last phase himself, Mainiero and Tromley,[35] who have also argued for the existence of such growth development phases in organizations, have anticipated this last phase to contain a lack of *psychological saturation* among employees, in the sense that they become emotionally and physically exhausted by the continual intensity of teamwork and heavy pressure for innovative solutions. They have portrayed the above descriptions of organizational growth in a simplified graph form (figure 2.1).

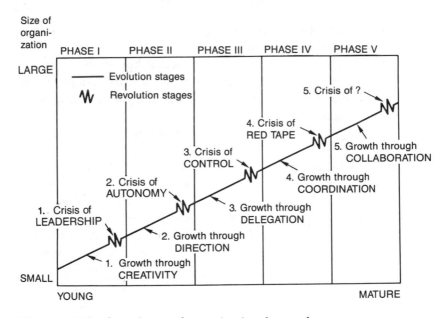

Figure 2.1 The five phases of organizational growth
   Source: Quinn and Cameron 1983: 33–51

The important conclusion drawn from these thoughts, as also suggested by Mainiero and Tromley,[35] is that many private companies and public organizations have reached a "phase 5" development stage, and they now need to solve their "revolutionary" problem with a "new structure and programs that allow employees to periodically rest, reflect, and revitalize themselves".

The important notion after this is that they suggest that companies may do this problem solving by developing *dual organizational structures:* a "habit" structure for getting the daily work done, and a "reflective" structure for stimulating perspective and personal enrichment. Employees could then "move back and forth between the two structures as their energies are dissipated and refuted".[35] This is a thought which has many resemblances to the rationality behind the "project approach", being a reaction to insufficiencies in existing organizations, particularly when they have reached "mature" stages of development.

A similar view, when applying the former "differentiation in time" as an organizational design device regardless of size but with a focus on the "revolutionary" problems above, is in this respect the one of the collateral organization[47] or *parallel organization.*[48] The parallel organization is supposed to be a flat and flexible organizational structure, forming an organic mechanism for managing change and building environmental responsiveness into bureaucratic structures on a continuing basis. The parallel organization is suggested to be composed of a set of pilot (project) groups, each with a steering committee and possibly an advisory group. Employees should be strongly involved, since a major purpose of the parallel organization is to "energize the grass roots". Kanter[9] who has strongly advocated the use of parallel organizations suggested that if applied it had to be "loose enough to allow for flexibility and some trial-and-error, yet connected enough to the line organization that the lessons learned could easily be seen as relevant to the larger setting and ultimately incorporated into ongoing operations."

It will be suggested here that both the observations by Starbuck[44] and the views by Mainiero and Tromley[35] on how organizations experience different kinds of problems when they grow, and the recommendations on what organizations have to do to cope with these problems,[9, 47] comply well with what seems to have been the characteristic features of the "project approach" in recent years. The ad-hoc structure of projects fits in well with the requirement for rest and revitalization after completing a demanding task. "Projects" also encourage rapidity and flexibility in dealing with external influence, by establishing an additional project organization to the existing, less flexible parent organization.

It will therefore be argued here that the "project approach" fits in very well with the needs of those organizations which have got the impression that they have reached a certain "unhealthy" growth stage and level relative to their environment, and which now need to solve important problems by temporary, organizational structures avoiding excessive bureaucracy, enhancing autonomy, flexible control and visible leadership.

2.3.4   Possible Impacts of Change on Organizations

"If things were to be done twice, all would be wise."

When studying the evolution and growth of modern organizations, it is also necessary to take into account the implications of *change*. Many authors have stated the need for organizations to increase their flexibility in order to cope with the constantly turbulent business environment observed in developing societies. Barnard[49] suggested more than fifty years back that once established, organizations change their unifying purpose, tending to perpetuate themselves, and in the effort to survive may change the reason for their existence.

A focus on the organizational forces in a change-oriented environment could thus yield valuable insight into employee behaviour, and thereby increase the understanding also of the managerial reactions. Many such efforts related to change in organizational environments are today referred to as *organizational development* (OD) techniques, combining the basic principles of behavioural science to improve the effectiveness of individuals, groups or the entire organization. One of the fundamental axioms of OD is, according to Cummings and Huse,[50] that people's readiness for change depends on their creativity and their felt need for change. Another important parameter is that its implementation needs special structures for managing the change process to be created, and that particular "process consultants" should be appointed to lead the change process.[50]

Weick[17] explained this same phenomenon in an organizational development process, and concluded that from starting out with "loose" structures and high flexibility, organizations tend to stabilize themselves and therefore successively lose their ability to be innovative and behave in a change-oriented manner. This "change resistance" affects the organizational members themselves, who end up behaving similarly to the organizational structure around them. Aldrich[51] refers to this as "structural inertia", while Selznick[52] and Berger and Luckmann[53] have described it as habit-forming attitudes ("Cognitive traps") and developed this into the "Institutionalist Theory" as typical for how humans cope with society.[19] This "cognitive" view was, however, disputed by Harrison,[54] who argued that human beings give priority to their own growth and development at the expense of the organization they belong to in exposed positions.

An interesting way of classifying organizational thinking in relation to change adaptiveness has been proposed by Aldrich.[51] He claims that the earlier views of "unitarism" of organizations is today in a process of being replaced by the "differentiated school" of thought and the "ambiguity school" of thought. "Unitarism" is by him defined as the "airport-bookshop view", which regards organizations as entities that can solve their change problems by improving their internal efficiency only, as their productivity or their "culture", by appropriate, unitary means. Foremost in these thoughts are traditional OD-supporters such as McGregor,[55] Peters and Waterman,[56] Mainiero and Tromley,[35] etc. The "differentiated school" is defined by Aldrich[51] as a school of thought that suggests that change can be mastered by allowing many cultures to exist simultaneously in the same organization, or, as he puts it, "islands of clarity in a sea of ambiguity". Typical representatives of this school of thought are Emery and Thorsrud,[57] Lawrence and Lorsch[31] and Trist,[58] to mention a few. The "ambiguity school" then takes according to Aldrich[51] a third view, which states that "meaning" is constantly to be negotiated and that the best way to handle organizations is from a "messy cultural view". Typical representatives of this school are Cyert and Marc[59] and March and Olsen.[18]

Relating these thoughts to the project concept, and assuming that the job of the project manager is to create within the project organization processes which facilitate the best accomplishment of the project goal, it may be relevant to suggest that the "project approach" was initially developed to manage those parts of the organizational work that could be "unitarily" defined, but that the inflexible system structure this created has increasingly been challenged by the need for more flexible and dynamic managerial systems in project endeavours. These are thoughts which also comply with the earlier "historic" review of the development of the project concept (table 2.2).

Perhaps the most illuminating modern contribution to the understanding of the impact of change is the study by Peters and Waterman,[56] in which, after collecting information on structures, innovation and management philosophies of forty-three of the most prominent US companies, they arrived at eight characteristics of successful, excellent organizations. One of the (many) interpretations of the practical wisdom which may be extracted from these characteristics was made by Lange,[60] and is displayed in table 2.3.

ATTRIBUTES OF EXCELLENCE	PRACTICAL CONSEQUENCES
BIAS FOR ACTION: A preference for doing something – anything – rather than sending an idea through endless cycles of analyses and committee reports	A need for project groups and ad-hoc efforts, task-oriented communication and learning and experimenting
STAYING CLOSE TO CUSTOMER: Learning his preferences and catering to them	Main efforts directed toward market and customer service
AUTONOMY AND ENTREPRE-NEURSHIP: Breaking the corporation into small companies and encouraging them to think independently and competitively	A need for decentralization
PRODUCTIVITY THROUGH PEOPLE: Creating in all employees the awareness that their best efforts are essential and that they will share in the rewards of the company's success.	An emphasis on the human resources and smaller organizational units
HANDS-ON, VALUE DRIVEN: Insisting that executives keep in touch with the firm's essential business and promote strong corporative culture	An emphasis on value-oriented leadership
STICK TO THE KNITTING: Remaining with the business the company knows best	An orientation toward the company's niche, building on own strengths
SIMPLE FORM, LEAN STAFF: Few administrative layers, few people at the upper levels	Avoidance of bureaucracy and "double work", and concentration on small units
SIMULTANEOUS LOOSE-TIGHT PROPERTIES: Fostering a climate where there is dedication to the central values of the company combined with the tolerance of all employees who accept those values	A management approach based on operational autonomy and easily visible units of control and performance

Table 2.3 A comparison between the eight "attributes of excellence" for modern organizations and derived practical consequences
Source: Lange 1989.

As can be seen, most of the attributes on the left side of the diagram, such as loose-tight control of properties, all imply the necessity to adopt "change" as a central parameter for survival and success. The other striking observation is that the practical consequences mentioned in the right column most directly match the typical traits of the "project approach".

It will be argued here, therefore, that the "project approach" embodies characteristics which may be of great importance to a better understanding and management of organizational "change" in the future. There is therefore a need to understand how new desires and directions expressed through this approach affect managerial performance, how project managers react to the changes brought about by projects, and how project managers adjust to, or resent, established or self-imposed, new project structures and procedures for accomplishing given tasks. "Change" clearly has many motivational effects on managers, but may also create many demotivational situations for people with managerial responsibilities.

2.4   Conclusions

> "The accuracy of our understanding depends on our sensitivity to differences in people."

However varied the conclusions and views on size and change of organizations may be, it seems fair to say that organizations in general, and especially organizations which are large in size and budget, have a tendency to encourage bureaucracy,[61] and to "copy" prevailing organizational trends as a means of risk minimization.[62] Others[63, 64, 65] hold the view that there are rational grounds for aiming at a bureaucratic structure since it promotes precision, reliability and efficiency, and that the bureaucratic structure exerts constant pressure on officials to be methodical, prudent and disciplined, maintaining a high degree of conformity. This may be highly advantageous in many situations. Business organizations are, however, also confronted with increasingly turbulent environments, and have therefore to accept and react positively to change. As stated by Grønhaug and Kaufmann:[66]

> ... the need for organizational flexibility is accelerating...imposing new requirements on organizational design and management.... In order to keep the business organization viable, the question of how to balance the need for innovation and flexibility with the requirements for certainty and planning has to be emphasized – and research should be devoted to this problem to bring forth workable solutions.

Consequently, it will be concluded here that the "project approach" has come as a natural response to, on the one hand, inadequacies in the shifting recommendations given by current theorists on how to "optimally" manage organizations, and, on the other hand, the ever new insights gained both by practitioners and theorists into the way organizations grow and change.

These developments have shown needs which are particularly well taken care of by the "project approach", and have become the background for the particular characteristics which today are generally used in the definition of "projects". The same new theories have brought increased insight into organizational behaviour and have increasingly brought the human component to the centre of focus. It seems therefore fair to conclude that many of these project characteristics have particular effects on managerial performance and on the managerial motivation in project work.

This leads to the realization that those who are responsible for the managerial effort embodied in such developments are of central interest. Realizing that organizations usually can define the managerial part of them as a sub-system in itself,[67] a search for an identifiable "project management system" should therefore be of special interest. The next chapter will elaborate on these thoughts and discuss, with support from current literature, the extent to which characteristics of such a managerial system may be seen as part of some recognizable "project sub-system". Assuming that such a sub-system can be identified both by its sub-components, or its "sub-structure", and by the way these components work together, its "sub-processes", a review of literature also on resulting variations in project managers' motivation and demotivation caused by changes in these structures and processes seems to be a possible and worthwhile effort. This is also the topic of the succeeding chapter.

2.5   References

1 Stuckenbruck, L.C. 1981: *The Handbook of Project Management: The Professional's Handbook*. Addison-Wesley Inc. Mass.
2 Cleland, D.I. & R.W. King (eds.) 1983: *Project Management Handbook*. Van Nostrand Reinhold Co. N.Y.
3 Meredith, J.R. & S.J. Mantel Jr. 1989: *Project Management. A Managerial Approach*. (Second edition.) John Wiley & Sons. N.Y.
4 Lord, A.M. & D. Birchall 1988: The Choice of Management Structure and Staffing the Team during Project Initiation. *INTERNET Proceedings*. 189–196.

5 Morris, P.W.G. 1988: Initiating Major Projects – The Unperceived Role of Project Management. *Proceedings of the Ninth World Congress on Project Management 1.* Glasgow. 801–813.

6 Lord, A.M. 1989: An Investigation into the Role of the Project Manager. Draft thesis. Henley The Management College, Henley.

7 Kuhn, T.S. 1962: *The Structure of Scientific Revolutions.* University of Chicago Press, Chicago. Ill.

8 Drucker, P. 1964: *The Concept of Corporation.* New American Library, Mentor. N.Y.

9 Kanter, R.M. 1977: Work and Family in the United States: A Critical Review and Agenda for Research and Policy. *Social Science Frontiers 9.* Russell Sage Foundation. N.Y.

10 Toffler, A. 1980: *The Third Wave.* Morrow. N.Y.

11 Naisbitt, J. 1982: *Megatrends.* MacDonald. London.

12 Stoner, J.A.F. & C. Wankel 1986: *Management.* (Third edition.) Prentice-Hall International. N.Y.

13 Friedman, M. 1963: *Capitalism and Freedom.* University of Chicago Press. Chicago. Ill.

14 Scott, W.R. 1987: *Organizations: Rational, Natural and Open Systems.* (Second edition.) Prentice-Hall International Editions. N.Y.

15 Thompson, J.D. 1967: *Organizations in Actions. Social Science Based on Administrative Theory.* McGraw-Hill. N.Y.

16 Daft, R.L. 1989: *Organization Theory and Design.* (Third edition.) West Publishing Company, St. Paul. Min.

17 Weick, K.E. 1969: *The Social Psychology of Organizing.* (Second edition.) Addison-Wesley. Reading. Mass.

18 March, J.G. & J.P. Olsen 1976: *Ambiguity and Choice in Organizations.* Universitetsforlaget. Bergen.

19 DiMaggio, P.J. & W.W. Powell 1983: The Iron Cage Revisited: Institutional Isomorphism and Collective Rationality in Organizational Fields. *American Sociological Review 48,* 147–160.

20 Marquis, D.G. 1969: A Project Team + PERT = Success or Does It? *Innovation 5.*

21 Sapolsky, H. 1972: *The Polaris System Development.* H.U.P. Cambridge. Mass.

22 Cleland, D.I. & R.W. King 1975: *Systems Analysis and Project Management.* (Second edition.) McGraw-Hill Book Co. N.Y.

23 Gray, C.F. 1981: *Essentials of Project Management.* Petrocelli Books Inc. Oregon.

24 Kertzner, H. 1982: *Project Management: A Systems Approach to Planning, Scheduling and Controlling.* Von Nostrand Co. N.Y.

25 Spirer, H.F. 1983: Phasing out the Project. In D.I. Cleland & R.W. King (eds.) *Project Management Handbook.* Van Nostrand Reinhold Co. N.Y. 222–264.

26 Adams, J.R. & S.E. Barndt 1983: Behavioral Implications of the Project Life Cycle. In D.I Cleland & R.W. King (eds.): *Project Management Handbook.* Van Nostrand Reinhold Co. N.Y. 245–264.

27 Might, R. 1983: An Evaluation of the Effectiveness of Project Control Systems. *IEEE. Transactions on Engineering Management 31,* 3.

28 Augustine, N.R. (ed.) 1989: Managing Projects and Programs. *Harvard Business Review.* Mass.
29 Prodi, R. 1984: Europas økonomiske situasjon – Sannsynlig innvirkning på lederfunksjonen. In S.A. Jessen (ed.): *Organisasjon og ledelse,* FOB 85, TANO. Oslo.
30 Burns, T. & G.M. Stalker 1961: *The Management of Innovation.* Routledge, Chapman & Hall. Tavistock. London.
31 Lawrence, P.R. & J.W. Lorsch 1967: *Organization and Environment: Managing Differentiation and Integration.* Graduate School of Business Administration, Harvard University. Boston. Mass.
32 Joynt, P. 1985: Cross-Cultural Management: The Cultural Context of Micro and Macro Organizational Variables. In P. Joynt & M. Warner (eds.): *Management in Different Cultures.* Universitetsforlaget, Oslo. 57–68.
33 March, J. 1981: Footnotes to Organization Change. *Administrative Science Quarterly* December 1981. (Referred to in K. Obtòy & P. Joynt: An Empirical Study of Innovative Behaviour in Poland. In P. Joynt & M. Warner (eds.) (1985): *Management in Different Cultures.* Universitetsforlaget. Oslo.)
34 Obtòy, K. & P. Joynt 1985: An Empirical Study of Innovative Behaviour in Poland. In P. Joynt & M. Warner (eds.): *Management in Different Cultures.* Universitetsforlaget. Oslo.
35 Mainiero, L.A. & C.L. Tromley 1989: *Developing Managerial Skills in Organizational Behavior.* Prentice-Hall. Englewood Cliffs. N.J.
36 Parkinson, C.N. 1957: *Parkinson's Law and Other Studies in Administration.* Houghton Mifflin, Boston. Mass.
37 Rushing, W.A. 1966: Organizational Size and Administration. *Pacific Sociological Review 9,* 100–108.
38 Kimberley, J. 1976: Organizational Size and the Structuralist Perspective: A Review, Critique and Proposal. *Administrative Science Quarterly 21,* 571–597.
39 Freeman, J.H. & T.M. Hannan 1975: Growth and Decline Processes in Organizations. *American Sociological Review 40.*
40 Meyer, M.W. 1979: *Change in Public Bureaucracies.* Cambridge University Press. Cambridge. Mass.
41 Chandler, J.P. Jr. 1962: *Strategy and Structure. Chapters in the History of American Industrial Enterprise.* M.I.T. Press. Cambridge. Mass.
42 Hage, J. 1965: An Axiomatic Theory of Organization. *Administrative Science Quarterly 10,* 289–320.
43 Child, J. 1972: Organizational Structure. Environment and Performance: The Role of Strategic Choice. *Sociology 6,* 1–22.
44 Starbuck, W.H. 1965: Organizational Growth and Development. In J. March (ed.): *Handbook of Organizations.* Rand McNally. N.Y.
45 Greiner, L. 1967: Patterns of Organizational Change. *Harvard Business Review 45,* 3, 119–130.
46 Quinn, R.E. & K. Cameron 1983: Organizational Life Cycles and Shifting Criteria of Effectiveness: Some Preliminary Evidence. *Management Science 10,* 1, 1–22.
47 Zand, D.E. 1974: Collateral Organizations: A New Strategy. *Journal of Applied Behavioral Science 10,* 1, 63–86.

48 Stein, B.A. & R.M. Kanter 1980: Building the Parallel Organization: Toward Mechanisms for Permanent Quality of Work Life. *Journal of Applied Behavioral Science 16*, 3, 371–388.

49 Barnard, C.I. 1938: *The Functions of the Executive.* Harvard University Press. Cambridge. Mass.

50 Cummings, R.G. & E.F. Huse 1989: *Organizational Development and Change.* (Fourth edition.) West Publishing. University of Southern California, LA. Ca.

51 Aldrich, H. 1990: From Traits to Rates: An Ecological Perspective on Organizational Foundings. Paper presented to the 1989 Gateway Conference on Entrepreneurship, St. Louis University, St. Louis, Missouri. Also notes from a meeting with him at the Norwegian School of Management, March 1990.

52 Selznick, P. 1949: *TVA and the Grass Roots.* University of California Press, Berkeley, Cal.

53 Berger, P.L. & T. Luckmann 1967: *The Social Construction of Reality.* Doubleday. N.Y.

54 Harrison, R. 1966: A Conceptual Framework for Laboratory Training. Unpublished manuscript.

55 McGregor, D. 1960: *The Human Side of Enterprise.* McGraw-Hill. N.Y.

56 Peters, T.J. & R.H. Waterman 1982: *In Search of Excellence.* Harper & Row. N.Y.

57 Emery, F.E. & E. Thorsrud 1969: *Form and Content in Industrial Democracy.* (First published in 1964.) Tavistock. London.

58 Trist, E. 1981: The Evolution of Socio-Technical Systems as a Conceptual Framework and as an Action Research Program. In Van De Ven & Joyce (eds.): *Perspectives on Organization Design and Behavior.* John Wiley & Sons, Wiley-Interscience. N.Y.

59 Cyert, R.M. & J.G. March 1963: *A Behavior Theory of the Firm.* Prentice-Hall. Englewood Cliffs. N.J.

60 Lange, K. 1989: Unpublished notes prepared for students in "Organisasjon og ledelse II" (Organization and Management) at the Norwegian School of Management, BI. Oslo.

61 Veblen, T. 1928: *The Theory of the Leisure Class.* Vanguard Press.

62 Swatez, G.M. 1970: The Social Organization of a University Laboratory. *Menerve: A Review of Science Learning and Policy 8*, 36–38.

63 Parson, T. 1951: *The Social System.* Free Press of Glencoe. N.Y.

64 Merton, R.K. 1957: Bureaucratic Structure and Personality. In R.K. Merton (ed.): *Social Theory and Social Structure.* Free Press of Glencoe. N.Y.

65 Weber, M. 1970: In H.H. Gerth & C.W. Mills (eds.): *Essays in Sociology.* Routledge & Keagan Paul. London.

66 Grønhaug, K. & G. Kaufmann 1988: *Innovation: A Cross-Disciplinary Perspective.* Norwegian University Press. Oslo.

67 Mintzberg, H. 1983: *Structure in Fives. Designing Effective Organizations.* Prentice-Hall. Englewood Cliffs. N.J

3 THE PROJECT MANAGEMENT SYSTEM

3.1 General

"When people talk about fairness, they mean fairness of distribution rather than fairness of contribution."
(Jon Elster)

The aim of this chapter is to give a more specific characterization and description of the "project approach" as a specific "management system". This is initially done by comparing its "system" features with those of established systematization efforts carried out by leading theorists and practitioners. Such a comparison is found viable, and such a system can obviously be defined. A further review of current literature is therefore carried out with regard to the extent to which this seems to have been taken into practical use in organizations at the individual, or more specifically, at the project management level.

One important task in this respect is to look at the basic characteristics of management systems in general, why they may be best operationalized in organizations from a "systems" point of view, and why projects may be best defined and studied as "organizational systems" in their own right. The extent to which such characteristics can be defined as either "structures" or as "processes" has also been elaborated on, since this is particularly important from a "project management system" point of view.

Special focus is also given to the extent to which one can find specific traits and components that are related to the initial project desire to *change* something, related to *structure* and static conditions, related to project *processes* and their dynamic components, or related to the *goal-directed* effort as such.

3.2   The Role of Organizations in Society

"The big gap is in the way human beings are being utilized – or more accurately, under-utilized."
(Robert H. Guest)

Daft[1] has stated that organizations are so common in our everyday life that they are taken for granted. However, according to Mintzberg,[2] it is "often…hard to describe the structuring of organizations exclusively in words", because though they are "formed to capture and direct systems of flows and define interrelationships among [many] different parts … these flows and interrelationships are hardly linear in form". And, as Mintzberg has also argued, organizational structures are a mix of formal and informal structures, intertwined and often almost completely indistinguishable. To study organizations means therefore to be particularly sensitive to the complex nature of their social systems. This is probably why Perrow[3] proposed that because organizations have a direct causal impact on politics, social class, economics, and even religion and family, they are the key phenomenon in existence today. Similarly, Daft[1] argues that "since we are truly a society of organizations, the systematic study of organizations can enable us to better understand and control this important aspect of our environment".

Organizations as Systems

Realizing the complexity of organizations, it is important to note that Perrow also argued that to understand the whole organization, one should preferably view it as a system. The term "system" originally had an engineering emphasis, which is defined as any "set of facts, principles, rules, etc. classified or arranged in a regular, orderly form so as to show a logical plan linking the various parts".[4] The biologist Bertalanffy[5] suggested that individuals, groups, and organizations were dependent on their environment and therefore also formed "systems" to cope with it. This view gives an operational approach to social phenomena and introduces "reason" as an important element in the process of how organizations are born. Boulding,[6] as an organizational theoretician, also promoted the systems view of organizations, and defined a system as composed of interrelated and interdependent parts whether it was a mechanical, biological, or social system. Forrester,[7] originally a physicist and mathematician, defined a "system" in a social sense as "a grouping of parts that operate together for a common purpose". In order to try to classify social systems more precisely, Johnson, Kast and Rosenzweig[8] defined "open systems" as systems which exchange information, energy, or material with their environment. Hunsaker and Cook[9] also distinguished between "systems" and "open systems", defining the latter as one "that interacts with environmental forces beyond the permeable system boundary", while Leavitt[10] and Scott[11] also included the environment in the general definition (see chapter 2).

Although these are broad definitions of organizations as social systems, they all include three common denominators: "people", "(physical) parts", and some "purpose" or "reason" enforced by or enacted relative to the environment. This may also explain the increasing focus on "systems" in our time: a search for some orderly structure and some explicit meaning in the relationship between Man and his environment, whether the latter is man-made, such as technology or organizational structure, or not, such as nature itself. In general, the search for order, for cause-and-effect relationships, and for a theory to explain "system" behaviour, gave way at times to a belief in random, irrational causes. Without a structure with which to relate facts and observations, it was found difficult to use the past to provide lessons for the future.

The Notion of a Systems Theory

It was probably also the recognition that "systems" were entities that could be defined and studied closely in order to enhance the well-being of their human components that inspired researchers to develop a "systems theory" which could be deliberately applied to societal phenomena as well. However, due to the comprehensiveness of social life, such a "system" inevitably had to be large, complex and difficult to operationalize in its full sense. Researchers and theorists have therefore continually struggled to find features and facts that could describe not all, but some of the most dominant characteristics of such social systems, and then use these findings to draw realistic conclusions about complete relationships in real-life situations.

The first detailed applications of systems theory specifically to the functioning of organizations appear to have been made in the late 1950s by Stogdill.[12] During the 1960s this approach achieved widespread acceptance within the management field.[13, 14, 15, 16] Despite the many new attitudes to systems and organizations that this activity entailed, Miner's[12] extensive study of research in this area concluded that: "although statements regarding the defining characteristics of organizations vary somewhat in specific detail, there remains considerable agreement. Thus definitions consistently refer to a combining of individual efforts in pursuit of certain common purposes or organizational goals".

Hunsaker and Cook[9] have later used a more comprehensive definition, claiming that an organization is "a collection of interacting and interdependent individuals who work together toward common goals and whose relationships are determined according to a certain structure". Cherrington[17] has suggested "a group of people with a common goal who are all working together" as a typical definition given by students and laymen, but then he has also criticized this definition to some extent as being misleading since neither "a group", "a common goal", nor "working together" are precise or appropriate terms. Members may have their own motives, not necessarily equivalent to a "common goal"; "working together" may contradict the idea of a division of labour; and to distinguish between those who are "in" and those who are "not in" the organization overlooks the open nature of organizations relative to their environment. These are the same arguments recognized in the earlier definitions of "systems" versus "open systems" by Hunsaker and Cook,[9] which make it plausible to suggest that an appropriate definition of "organizations" which would comply with today's use of the concept for operational purposes, is perhaps the one given by Cherrington:[17] "an organization is best described as an open social system that consists of the patterned activities of a group of people that tend to be goal-directed".

This is also a definition that is almost identical to the one given by Katz and Kahn[18] in their extensive research on patterned activities of organizations ten years earlier, and which they used for social psychological purposes.

Organizations and People

One basic observation following this definition of an "organization" is that it clearly includes the word "system" and the component "people" in its definition, and thereby concludes that organizations are systems of people which may be studied and evaluated from a systems point of view. This is also confirmed by Daft[1] and many other modern organizational authorities. The presence of the human component makes it reasonable to suggest that this component is strongly affected by the way this "system" is constructed.

Another important observation is that the definition contains four key elements, which are all recognizable and which may have operational characteristics, and which may well affect human behaviour and motivation in organizational settings as well. They are:

1. An organization seems to have some direct or indirect *purpose* behind its existence,
2. An organization seems to be characterized by some recognizable *structure*, which may consist of some patterned activities,
3. An organization seems best to function as an open social system, characterized by some human behavioural *processes*, and
4. An organization aims at fulfilling a purpose, or attaining a main objective or a *goal*.

The "purpose" implies that the organizational system is an intended, human-related effort. "Structure" or patterned activities imply the presence of relatively stable and predictable events that continue to occur with regularity within an organization. And the classification of organizations as "open social systems" means that an organization exists within a social environment that may require it to change and adapt to new demands in order to survive. Behavioural "processes" states that human activity is the dynamic backbone of all organizational behaviour. The "goal" attainment statement implies that the total "system" has some end state or final objective to strive for, and that this gives meaning and direction to the effort.

3.3   The Recognition of Projects as Organizational Systems

"I'm developing a new system of human relations – if you can't beat 'em, cooperate 'em to death!"
(Charley Brown in "Peanuts")

In order to gain a better understanding of the traits and behaviour of "projects", it is essential that there is general agreement among authors that one of the typical traits of projects is that they are *deliberately* "*organized*" *efforts.*[19-30] Parameters and traits characterizing organized efforts and their behaviour and structure in general should therefore be applicable to projects as well.

The first recognition that supports this is that there seems to be general agreement that a project needs a clear *purpose* in order to be identified. This purpose is normally converted to a distinct project *goal*. The goal-directed notion is in fact one of the earliest observations of characteristics fundamental to project work.[28]

Next, there seems to be general agreement that projects need some organized effort or *structure* if the required resources are to be utilized effectively, environmental changes interpreted with sobriety in order to produce desired outputs, and internal activities controlled and coordinated in order to mend unhealthy impacts of environmental disturbances and uncertainty.[24] And these elements clearly point to the presence of several behavioural *processes* in projects as well.[31]

This leads to an initial suggestion that "projects" may be handled as "organizational systems" in their own right, and, subsequently, that features characterizing "systems" and "organizations" in general could be discernible and operationable for "projects" too. However, when classifying these aspects from a more *detailed* systems point of view, conclusions are less apparent. Many properties comply very well with those of "closed system" thinking, in the sense that once given enough energy or resources, projects may function very well as autonomous, enclosed, internally designed bodies. Yet, since projects must continually change and adapt to their environment it would also appear appropriate to apply the "open system" paradigm. This is a paradox which has already been dealt with indirectly in the preceding chapters, and which has also been brought into the debate by modern project authorities.[25, 28, 31, 32, 33] From this it seems natural to suggest at this stage of thought that the "closed system" view fits the "project approach" well in its traditional fashion, but that it may well be necessary to include "open system" thinking as well, both for sub-components of the concept and perhaps limited to certain phases or stages of its development. A closer look at projects from both a "closed" and an "open" systems perspective therefore seems a relevant avenue of review.

3.3.1 Projects as "Closed Systems"

The general need for coordination, standardization, and order in forms of organizations is perhaps best stated by Mintzberg:[2]

> Five coordinating mechanisms seem to explain the fundamental ways in which organizations coordinate their work: mutual adjustment, direct supervision, standardization of work processes,

standardization of work outputs, and standardization of worker skills. These should be considered the most basic elements of structure, the glue that holds organizations together.

The observation that organizations are characterized by some inner structure holding them together is clearly also transferable to the "project approach", which gained much of its initial academic and managerial credibility through its systematization of the planning and monitoring functions through using such techniques such as CPM and PERT.[34] Pfeffer[35] has also argued that the systemized planning reflected the project "paradigm consensus". It should therefore be appropriate to claim that structure and patterned activities are typical characteristics of projects also. This means that they must conform to some kind of cooperation and conduct, that they must have some orderly or planned set-up, and that some presumably quantitative measurement rules for progress and achievement exist or are discernible. These are typical traits of the "closed" system perspective.

3.3.2 Projects as "Open Systems"

The "project system's" inability to exist without human participation is similar to the main conclusion arrived at about organizations as systems. And the human component, too, seems to be strongly dependent on its full environment in its struggle to survive.[36] This implies that projects must be incredibly complex, since Boulding,[6] who analyzed many types of systems, concluded that they can be arranged in order from simple to complex, and that the social system is the most complex system of them all. As also stated by Daft,[37] "the social system incorporates forms of complexity beyond machine and biological systems", and:[1]

> The sources of this complexity are characteristics found only in human groups: norms and values appear and are intangible and hard to detect; cultural dimensions such as music and art appear; system elements (the humans) display self-awareness; the structure of elements and roles continuously changes; and information is processed through abstract forms of language, symbols, and meaning systems.

This points clearly to a classification of projects as "open systems", and that features characterizing this systems "view" should guide the way project leaders perform and act in project work.

3.3.3 Conclusions

From the above reviews and discussions it seems relevant to suggest that though projects may well be regarded as "systems" and operated under a systems point of view, they cannot so easily be categorized as belonging to one particular school of thought or one "system" of classification only. They are very complex endeavours, and a practical study of their behaviour should probably best be done by concentrating on a limited but highly representative number of features recognizable in project work, regardless of which "system" thought they might spring out of. Further, since the main topic of this book is to reveal possible variations in the behaviour of project leaders, the features that enhance this are the most interesting ones to observe. Therefore, it is suggested here that it may be a feasible endeavour if such features as mentioned above, and which assume both an "open" and a "closed" system point of view to be viable, are combined or interlinked in a systematization specific to projects, and with an easily discernible and operational internal logic. Such an effort is here made by combining the former key elements of projects as "systems" into a simplified "model" structure as shown in figure 3.1.

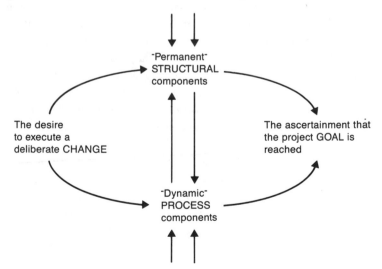

Figure 3.1 The simplified project system model with its suggested main components

The basic idea is that projects "move horizontally" from an initial "desire" towards a final "goal" attainment in a "closed system" perspective. This process is, however, disturbed by a "vertical interaction" between the internal more permanent components of the "structure" and the "process" components within projects, and both of these two sets of components again interact with external environmental components. These are thoughts which fit an "open system" perspective. Projects of this type comply with both a "closed" an "open" systems perspective. This is a philosophy which in many ways is similar to the difference between the two basic lines of thought within the social sciences, the "homo economicus" and the "homo sociologicus".[38] The former is supposed to be guided by instrumental rationality, while the behaviour of the latter is directed by social norms.[34] The notion is that rationality is essentially conditional and future-oriented. Its imperatives are hypothetical, that is, conditional on a future we want to realize. The imperatives expressed in social norms are generally unconditional[39] or, if conditional, they are not future-oriented.[34] In the latter case, norms make the action dependent on past events.

This model also points to the assumption that projects are systems created in order to achieve some predefined purpose in the most efficient and effective way. The same rational "motives" that hold systems together should then also apply to projects. It will be argued here that since many of the features above tend to optimize the extent to which goals are achieved, this is also an important reason for studying the "project approach" from a "systems" point of view. Additionally, their effectiveness and success should be measurable in relation to the degree of fulfilment of the project goal. But since projects easily create norms, one should also try to find the "social" components of the project management concept. As stated by Elster,[34] "it will become abundantly clear that social norms offer considerable scope for skill, choice, interpretation and manipulation". For this reason particular aspects both of outcome-oriented and non-outcome-oriented actions embodied in the project concept are further elaborated in the following.

3.4   Project Characteristics

"In fact, there is a possibility...that the only thing of real importance that leaders do is to create and manage culture."
(Edgar H. Schein)

The above project "model" bears of course many similarities to organizational endeavours in general. It is important therefore to make a review of the characteristics that may be said to be specific to projects.

Meredith and Mantel[31] have suggested that: "In the broadest sense, a project is a specific, finite task to be accomplished. Whether large- or small-scale or whether long- or short-run is not particularly relevant. What is relevant is that the project be seen as a unit."

One important issue must then be to locate those elements that distinguish project "units" from other ongoing efforts, and which may have clear resemblances with projects, such as "programs", "task forces", and "work packages", to mention some. The literature is not clear on this point, but as argued by Mantel and Meredith,[31] one "generally uses the term 'program' to refer to exceptionally large, long-range projects or a group of similar projects. Projects [may] further be divided into 'tasks', which are, in turn, split into 'work packages' that are themselves composed of 'work units'. But exceptions to this nomenclature abound".

This author has also reached the conclusion that "projects" are difficult to define in a fully comprehensive way, but it seems fair to state that "projects" can usually be defined as sub-components and often driving forces to "programs", in the sense that while "programs" are more open-ended and have more "ideal" aims, a "project" has, or is supposed to have, an operational goal and clearly defined constraints.[40, 41] This relationship is illustrated in figure 3.2.

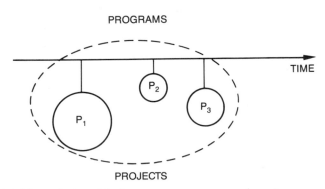

Figure 3.2 The relationship between programs and projects

That "task" and "work" endeavours in turn are regarded as sub-components of projects can further be confirmed by the way such elements are described and through the way they are technically combined. It is probably at this operational level project methodologies have become more easy to develop, and have thus become fundamental aids to project management. An example of such a methodology is the "Work Break-down Structure" (WBS), the purpose of which is defined by Stucken-bruck[25] breaking "the total project down into sufficiently small subdivisions to permit accurate cost estimates, and to permit adequate visibility and control".

Another technique is that of the "Linear Responsibility Charts" (LRC), which as Cleland and King[28] state "reveal the task-job position couplings (in projects) that are of an advisory, informational, technical and speciality nature". The LRC-idea is also the backbone of the so-called PSO-technique launched by Andersen et al.[65]

From these descriptions it seems relevant to state that such techniques cater particularly for the "structural" components of project work.

Lord[42] has stated that "the essential difference between a project and any other production or construction facility is the fact that it is temporary and directed towards the achievement of certain objectives". This ad-hoc nature, together with the aforementioned needs for some orderly "system" of activities, and a need for some stated, recognizable aim, has been contended by many other authors also.[24, 28]

The further literature study of project characteristics has used these descriptions as a basis, and then tried to find additional characteristics that are of a more "process"-oriented nature. This literature analysis is done in a two-step procedure:

1. Distinguishing which structural components different authors and researchers have portrayed as typical of the total project concept, and then each of these are studied separately. This has ended up in an identification of some typical project "structure" components generally recognized in all project efforts.
2. Analyzing the more "compound" effect of these components together, or groups of them together, also with relevance to the human reactions, with bases in current literature. This has identified important "process" features in projects.

Two characteristics may be easily distinguishable from the literature.[24, 28, 32] They are:

1. That projects are deliberate structural efforts, characterized by their *given limits* in time, their limited financial and physical resources, and their specific quality of performance defined by the end *goal.*
2. That projects are composed of *human* effort components which are combined in interlinked, *dynamic* processes.

From these generally agreed characteristics, additional traits have been suggested by many others. Meredith and Mantel[31] have stated that there are a multitude of attributes that today are combined in project efforts. The most prominent of these attributes are:

Uniqueness; in the sense that every project seems to have some elements that are unique. Even though it is clear that for instance construction projects are usually more routine than research and development projects, some degree of customization seems to be a characteristic of a project.

A particular structural base; in the sense that like organic entities, a project is often recognized by a certain "life-cycle" structure which from a small beginning progresses to a build-up of size, then peaks, begins a decline, and finally terminates. (And like other organic entities, projects often resist this termination too.) The life cycle also carries the typical characteristic of being limited in time, in resource expenditure, and in quality of performance.

Interdependencies; in the sense that projects always interact with some parent's standard, ongoing operations or organizations, and often also interact with other projects being carried out simultaneously by their parent organization. (That the project internal components also seem to interplay interactively, and often in a cross-disciplinary manner, has already been suggested.)

Conflict; in the sense that projects almost always compete with functional departments for resources and personnel. As stated by Meredith and Mantel:[31] "The members of the project team are in almost constant conflict for the project's resources and for leadership roles in solving project problems.... Individuals working on projects are often responsible to two bosses at the same time, bosses with different priorities and objectives. Project management is no place for the timid."

The Widening of the Project Scope

The project features described above constitute the most important characteristics of project work, and they will have many implications linked to management and managerial efforts. What is particularly important, however, is that by these characteristics the project concept itself has widened its scope considerably, and new areas for the application of the "project approach" have emerged.[31] Today "projects" therefore mean far more than engaging in special physical constructions. Equally often observed is the use of the "project approach" for efforts aimed at examining a possibility, or in clarifying a particular problem area, using the expression "we have a project dealing with this". Such projects may still remain "projects" in their full sense, the "end product" though being not a physical fabrication, but perhaps a decision support document or a report. This is often the case in public or governmental project endeavours, characterized by critical deadlines and very limited personnel allocation, even with less than one person in full-time engagement. Another type of commonly recognized projects is R&D (research and development) projects, characterized by a reasonably clear research purpose but with less emphasis on time and strict resource allocation. But it must also be abundantly clear that by this widening of the project scope and its definition, "projects" may also be handy ways of excusing oneself from really doing a job!

Subdividing "Projects" and Managerial Implications

We can also classify different kinds of projects in sub-groups, which has to some extent been done by, for instance, the World Bank, which operates with a set of pre-project studies being treated as "projects" in their own right. Examples are "feasibility" studies, "pre-feasibility" studies and even "pre-pre-feasibility" studies, when the subject of interest is very loosely defined or the risk of failure during the real project execution is high.[43]

It is a central fact that projects in general today must be managerial endeavours which presuppose that good coordination and skilful leadership take place. Good management will naturally involve also the selection and implementation of a wide range of technical and administrative tools, as well as a capacity and a behavioural instinct for handling the human component. It seems natural therefore to review the literature more closely to establish whether the following elements are mandatory in all project endeavours:

- To elaborate on the effect of organizational *change*, particularly in relation to project work, and possible variations in the project manager's motivation and demotivation caused by these changes.
- To elaborate on different kinds of organizational *"structures"* and "systems", and particularly those applied in project management, and the extent to which these have caused variation in the project manager's motivation and demotivation.
- To take into consideration research which has focused on which *"processes"* seem to be dominant in organized activity in general, and the extent to which similar processes may be present in project work and have thus caused variation in the project leaders motivation and demotivation.
- To study what characterizes *"goals"* in an organizational sense, and which connections there may be between general goal efforts and project goal effort. The extent to which goal-directed effort such as that found in projects may cause variation in the project leader's motivation and demotivation is then of particular interest.

3.4.1 Views on Organizational "Change" in General and Possible Transferability to Project Efforts

"Change" is defined by Webster[4] as "any variation or alteration in form, state, quality, or essence; or, a passing from one state or form to another". "Change" is therefore generally a measurement relative to something which exists or has been existing. For an organization, a change process therefore inevitably means the alteration of some established relationships existing within the organization. "Change" may thus easily lead to organizational conflicts if the change is felt or believed uncomfortable or inappropriate relative to an existing state.

Many authors have suggested different means for handling organizational change in order to minimize conflict and turmoil. The reason is that a deliberate change process will presumably lead toward the attainment of some overt or covert goal which may solely be desired by those instituting this process. Thomas and Bennis[44] have argued that when important changes are necessary in organizations, the process of change should be managed in an orderly manner or *planned* in order to ensure the change process is understood and accepted properly by all those involved or affected by the change. Earlier Lewin,[45] and later Schein,[46] suggested that a three-step sequential model of the process of change should be used, involving "unfreezing" the present behaviour patterns, "changing" or developing a new behaviour pattern, and then "refreezing" or reinforcing the new behaviour. This process would create an equilibrium between the driving and restraining forces for change (the "force-field" theory). If changes are substantial, the management should even aim at changing the whole *organizational culture*, that is, as Sathe[47] has defined it, "the shared understanding of norms, values, attitudes, and beliefs of an organization" in order to ensure the "change" is effective.

To facilitate such processes, it may be necessary to appoint particular "change agents". The term change agent is defined by Cherrington[17] as "the person or persons who serve as a catalyst facilitating an OD (Organizational Development) intervention". These agents of change may be members of the organization or they may be consultants brought in from outside. They are the key factors in the so-called "action research model", in which the OD effort is made in a well-planned and structured way, mandatorily involving processes of problem identification, data gathering, feedback of the data to the client group, data discussion and diagnosis, action planning, action, and re-evaluation. These processes are recycled as needed to increase organizational effectiveness.[17] Clearly most efforts to effect change, whether they take off from people, technology, structure or task, must deal with the others. As stated by Leavitt: "Human relators must invent technical devices for implementing their ideas, and they must evaluate alternative structures, classing some as consonant and some as dissonant with their views of the world. Structuralists must take stands on the kinds of human interaction that are supportive of their position, and the kinds that threaten to undermine it, etc."[10]

A comprehensive description on how to successfully master organizational change processes, using a project approach, may after this be expressed by the following seven steps:

1. Establishing the project
2. Assessment and goal setting
3. Identifying a solution
4. Preparing for implementation
5. Implementing the project
6. Reviewing progress and problems
7. Maintenance and institutionalism

The essence of this procedure is that project managers should be motivated to manage and master change. Their roles could in many ways be seen as similar to those of *"agents of change"* in organizations, because they are the individuals responsible for *taking the leadership* in managing processes of change in organizations.[48] But as already contended, the "project approach" is in reality an even wider concept. It may mean anything from erecting a new physical structure, developing a new product, reorganizing a company, investigating organizational behaviour, implementing a new administrative procedure, or creating background material for further decisions of a physical, financial or organizational nature. The human resource input may thus also vary considerably, from thousands of people, as for instance at huge off-shore oil-platform constructions, to even less than one person, for instance in part-time engagement in a public or private problem-solving effort.

The suggestion from OD that a "process consultant" or that a "change agent" is needed is also in line with one of the basic necessities of "the project approach", where a qualified project manager or leader is mandatory. The important issue is that the change effort most certainly has special constraints and conditions. It seems therefore natural to argue that investigation of the main principles of "organizational change" in relation to project leadership provides a relevant background for studying the variation in the motivation and demotivation of project leaders.

3.4.2 Views on Organizational "Structure" and its Possible Relation to Project Efforts

As revealed earlier in this book, managers have for a long time been looking for better ways of deciding how to create confident organizational stability in a rapidly changing environment. Subsequently, they have been searching continually for both some kind of intermediate flexible structure complementary to the established, traditional structures, and for structures that can withstand turmoil and ambiguity. If one should comprehend the different views prevailing today, figure 3.3 perhaps gives some of the main indications of preferred labels.

As suggested, the project approach perhaps fits best in an unstable but centralized environment. This should not, however, prevent project structures from being created in other environments.

Salapatas[49] has stated that: "In the past, companies involved in the management of projects placed little importance on the organizational implications of this new form of management. A company merely decided

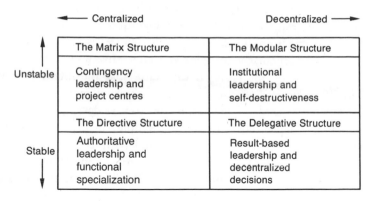

Figure 3.3 Prototypical organizational structures in different kinds of environments.

to take on a project, appointed a project manager, assigned personnel, and staked a claim on project management."

According to Morris,[30] systems thinking has shown how projects may work as successfully regulated organizations, benefitting from the existence of some internal structural interconnections. In his view, "it has been increasingly realized that all projects share a common pattern of interfaces derived from a common pattern of subsystems interaction. This is true no matter what the type of project, be it a theater production or an aid program, an election or a major capital investment program".

It will be suggested here that these arguments make it worthwhile to try to define typical project structures, or components of such structures, which have a special impact on the project leader's motivation and demotivation.

3.4.3 Recognizable Project Structures

"Structure" in an organizational context is simply defined by Davis and Newstrom[89] as "the formal relationships of people in organizations". Thompson[15] tried early to distinguish between different kinds of interdependencies in projects, and concluded with the following three: "pooled", "sequential" and "reciprocal", each requiring its own type of structure. In his view, the main differences between the categories were their requirements of rules or standards, and "reciprocal" interdependency was the most complex with its dependency on "mutual adjustment" between the parties. Morris[30] followed the same idea, and claimed that "in project terms, subsystems which are in continuous interaction require liaison in order to achieve the necessary integration".

We should assume from this that project "structure" is a relatively clear entity, but with a particularly complex and interactive way of operating. This seems also to be the case, in the sense that the importance of establishing clear project organizations to fit current requirements has been generally recognized.[30] What seems then to have developed is a great variety of operational project systems, from "simple liaison personnel who carry messages unobstructed across forbidden department boundaries",[25] to complex project systems where the project manager controls the project effort through an integrated network of distributed authority and responsibility.[50]

Approaches for Managing Project Structures

If any simplification of this variety should be made from the current literature, it should be that project leaders seem to employ two main types of organizational approaches in managing project structures:

- One is to use *formal* organizational structures and established influence sources such as authority, reward, and punishment in order to master the project effort.
- The other is to focus on the needs of the team members in the project and get their best support, and in addition rely on different types of *informal* influence if necessary.

Both these approaches seem to have one thing in common, namely that they establish open lines of communication and reinforce liaison relationships between project people and their parent "home" departments.

Many authors have studied project organizations from this angle. Morris[30] argued that liaison of the type mentioned above was imperative, and would be particularly well taken care of in "matrix organizations" because they "provide for maximum exchange, management coordination, and resource sharing". Many other authors have also declared the matrix organization to be particularly powerful in project contexts.[23, 25, 51, 52] Massie[50] went further and argued that to initiate what he called the "management of change", the matrix structure only would be insufficient, and suggested that three project structural models be used instead:

1. The "matrix approach" to the organization of the project,

defined as the identification of subsystems of a complex organization, each with its appropriate strategy for planning, control, reward, and boundary negotiations. The subsystems could vary from total dependence on hierarchical concepts to autonomous units or projects.

2. The pure "project approach", which was to tailor joint efforts to a particular mission or goal, and to coordinate actions and predefined resources toward the completion of the final goal while retaining the advantages of functional specialists. The structure accommodates the ideas of classical thinking, together with team and participative ideas.

3. The "grid organization", which attempts to assign responsibilities to one of the following designs: grouping of functional specialists, geographical groupings, or product groupings. This type of structure would be particularly important for huge, international endeavours and complex projects where there are substantial benefits from such rationalization.

This view, that projects could be organized in different manners and still maintain a "project structure", has also been advocated by this author after studying a multitude of Norwegian project efforts during the last 20–30 years.[40, 41] The most prominent forms were found to be:

1. The project organization which is established with no change in the parent organization's basic structure. This is often used when the project is completely allocated within an existing department or division in the parent organization, i.e. the project is *fully incorporated*.

2. The project organization which is established without any change in the parent organization's basic structure, but where a special high-level line authority is introduced to control and support the project work. This is a project structure often used in public enterprises and organizations, and where the project is governed by a specially appointed *steering authority*.

3. The project organization where the project members are partly fully, partly "fractionally" allocated to the project, and where the participants are recruited from different parts of the parent organization. This is a structure which fits well when project work and "line" work in the parent organization have to be done simultaneously, and the project members have to share

their time between the two. This is an organizational structure which comes close to the "matrix organization" described earlier, and which is recognized by a *split authority* of management.

4. The project organization which is organized completely outside the parent organization. The only formal connection in this case is established through special steering committees or advisory boards, as well as through some basic administrative functions if necessary. This is a structure which is most commonly used when the project effort is huge or particularly complex, and where the problem solving has limited resemblance to the line operations of the parent organization. The project management in this case can be recognized by its *full authority* over project operations.

Classifying Project Structures

Other ways of classifying project efforts have also been suggested. Kolltveit[33] recommended a focus on the internal structure of projects. He concluded in his research on three major off-shore projects that a more "organic" (or "soft") structure would be highly beneficial in the conceptual development phases, and a more "mechanistic" (or "hard") structure be more suitable in the implementation phases. This is an important observation in the sense that it questions the establishment of only one particular organizational form over the whole project lifetime. It says little, however, about the importance of the project environment. It is also rather simple in its view of organizational characteristics of projects.

Kolltveit's view has similarities with Burns and Stalker's[53] general view, where they distinguish between two main organizational systems: the "mechanistic" and the "organic":

- In a *mechanistic* system, the activities of the organization are broken down into separate, specialized tasks. Objectives and authority for each individual and each unit are precisely defined by higher-level managers. Power in such organizations follows the classical, hierarchical chain of command.
- In an *organic* system, tasks and activities are combined in a mixed blend, and individuals are more likely to work in group settings than alone. There is less emphasis on taking orders from a superior or giving orders to subordinates.

Studies by Burns and Stalker,[53] and later Lawrence and Lorsch,[54] have suggested that a mechanistic system is best suited to a stable environment, whereas organic systems are best suited to a turbulent one. They have further suggested different types of structures as appropriate for different units or departments in the same organization.

Etzioni[55] concluded that: "The structuralist point of view recognizes fully the organizational dilemma; the inevitable strains – which can be reduced but not eliminated – between organizational needs and personal needs; between rationality and non-rationality; between discipline and autonomy; between formal and informal relations; or between management and workers." This view was also supported by Thompson[15] and Aldrich,[56] who argue that many different structural perspectives must be present at the same time in organizations, but that they differ in strength and appearance in one part of the organization compared to another at different time intervals.

There is therefore probably no one best structure which fits every kind of project. But project leaders seem to be given different opportunities to choose between a set of structural possibilities depending on the nature of task at hand and his or her need of authority. It may also be appropriate to emphasize the effect of different structures within the same project, realizing that a project may change in time and may pursue different human and organizational objectives depending on its stage of development. (There is also the possibility, however, that the project leader may work through one particular project structure enforced upon him or her by higher managerial authorities, or a structure instituted as "company policy".[28] The motivational or demotivational implications of this are a worthwhile topic of deeper studies.)

3.4.4 Organizational Life-Cycle Development and the Transferability to Projects

Another way of regarding organizations from a structural point of view has come with a shift of focus from the "task content" to the "time development" of projects. The basic observation behind this is that, in line with today's turbulent business environment, organizations seem to run through a particular *life cycle*, which may be defined by a certain point of "birth", and another particular point of "dilution". Any organization should in this context be regarded as a temporary body going through some typical life-cycle development, the "temporality" though being for most organizations and corporations defined within quite a long-term perspective. Aldrich[56] argued that if organizations are regarded from a "demographic" point of view, one can clearly distinguish between their (1) founding or birth, (2) their transformational period, and (3) their dilution or the period in which they die. Quinn and Cameron[57] studied a wide range of organizations and integrated nine life-cycle models of organizations into one summary model with *four basic stages*:

- The first is the *entrepreneurial* stage, which emphasizes innovation, creativity, and the acquisition of necessary resources.
- The second, the *collective* stage, emphasizes cohesiveness, commitment, cooperation and a personal form of leadership.
- During the third stage, that of *formalization and control*, the organization becomes more conservative; the emphasis is on efficiency and on developing rules and procedures to enhance stability and control.
- In the final stage, consisting of *structural elaboration and adaptation*, the organization focuses more of its energies on monitoring and adjusting to the external environment. At this stage, the structure becomes decentralized and it is necessary to strike a balance between differentiation and integration.

Several authors have found that, when they develop, projects run through a similar kind of life cycle structure.[24, 28, 32, 33, 58, 59, 60, 61, 62] The major difference being that while an "ordinary" organization has as its primary objective to "survive", "projects" aim at *not* surviving, but at "dying". Because of this their life-cycle structure is even more pronounced than in organizations in general. In fact, many authors have declared that the life-cycle process is one of the *fundamental* characteristics of projects.[24, 27, 42, 63, 64, 65, 66] Also the World Bank is using a phased project classification comprising identification (pre-feasibility), preparation, appraisal (feasibility), negotiation, implementation, operation, and evaluation when describing its international project engagements. Although no research seems to have been directed specifically at proving this to be a universal characteristic, there does seem to be an agreement that a division into four to seven "physical" phases of a life cycle is typical of project development, and that the following phases are the most common:[27]

- The project conceptualization or initiation phase
- The project planning phase
- The project implementation or execution phase, and
- The project termination phase

Many authors have also reflected on the extent to which this can affect the project development, and in particular such problems as may be caused by shifts of responsibility and lack of concentration during different stages or phases of project development. Many of the requirements prevailing during the similar project phases may also be possible to discern:

- Structures that promote innovation, creativity, freedom and openness may be most important to cater for during project initiation;
- Structures that promote systematization, order and clarification are presumably most necessary, and should accordingly be given most attention during project planning;
- Structures that strengthen leadership, control, know-how and communication are presumably particularly important during project execution; and
- Structures that lead to conclusiveness and goal fulfilment are most probably the crucial parameters during project termination.

More comprehensively, these four life-cycle phases of projects and the effect they may have on the project participants, including the project leader, may be defined as follows:[27, 41, 67]

1. The project *initiation* phase comprises the very early steps of project formulation. At this stage the project idea is elaborated, it is given enough priority to be selected for further and more detailed study, the potential project manager is often contacted, and the first framework of a project plan made. The process is innovative and creative, the setting loose and open, and the process often consumes far more calendar time than it consumes labour (i.e. money and human effort). This is a view supported by Burbridge,[68] who argued that "during the conception stage most of the decisions are made which will dictate the success or failure of the project".

    This phase often creates a rich blend of opportunities and challenges, as well as possibly fostering insecurity and discomfort for the people involved, part of this directly related to the often "open" structure indicative of this phase.

2. The project *planning* phase comprises the first decisive step of the project process. The complete project goal is normally fully

developed early on in this phase. The tasks and efforts necessary to complete the project goal are then laid out in special diagrams, usually involving different project planning techniques such as PERT, CPM, etc. and their computer applications, often involving advanced software packages. Decisions are taken about the project organization, as well as about the project communication system, and the phase formally concludes with the project executors and the client agreeing on a contract.

This phase tends to reinforce the need for structure and stability, and is thus perhaps more related to a "rational" structure. The project plan also reduces uncertainties and makes participants more comfortable as to the attainability of the project goal. As such it has both motivational and demotivational implications for the people involved, to an extent which naturally depends on the match between the preferences of the people involved, and the plan for the project.

3. The project *execution* phase is the major and most comprehensive phase, encompassing the performance of the planned and ad hoc work and the planned and ad hoc decisions that are necessary. In an organizational context this is also often referred to as "adhocracy".[2, 69] External forces normally strongly affect the project in this phase: i.e. the client, the participants, the superiors, and colleagues in the parent organization, as well as the social environment such as "public opinion". This phase is also an arena for all kinds of endeavours performed in order to monitor and control the project properly. The effect of the monitoring becoming more and more sophisticated and computerized in line with the rapid developments in this field, and in line with the advancements in project planning tools, also affects the participants.

Project execution usually provides a multitude of motivational and demotivational responses related to the kind of executing and controlling structure imposed, and the way the participants "open up" and communicate and work together.

4. The project *termination* phase is the scene for all kinds of concluding efforts: the "wrapping up" of documents and procedures, the conveying of results and of contact with the client, and of possible new engagements for participants and enactors. Project termination also comprises the "un-freezing"

of commitments and the "selling" of the project end "product" to the project environment. This may also imply negotiations concerning extras and discussions about claims.

Whether the project has been a success or not will naturally have an impact on the motivation of the enactors during this phase, particularly with regard to the "closing-down" procedure of the project structure adapted, and the "rationality" executed in reaching the project goal.

A natural conclusion to draw from this is that the more diversified the phased project development is, the more varied the managerial attitudes need to be. It must therefore be assumed that projects in general offer different motivational opportunities and obstacles within each phase. This imposes a demand for a high degree of flexibility and ability on managers. We will argue here that this should also lead them to apply alternative organizational structures as projects develop in order to better adjust to new conditions and new challenges. This also requires them to understand when projects advance from one development phase to another. In general, this makes project management to some degree a "discontinuous process", which is probably best executed in a sort of *discontinuous management* style which allows for swift changes in roles and attitudes as projects develop. This opens up for the possibility that there are different motivational impacts prevailing at different stages of the project development process, and that a discernible variation in the project leader's motivation and demotivation will occur.

3.4.5 Views on "Processes" Operating within Project Developments, and the Consequences of These for the Project Leader

The increasing dependence of people on one another, and a trend towards organized societies have increased the importance of the search for some fundamental "processes" governing social life. For the project participants process decisions mainly aim at establishing a ranking of priorities, which in turn affects decisions about structural priorities. Structural priorities then affect decisions about process priorities through workload commitments and the availability of personnel in given time periods. Process priorities, in turn, affect decisions concerning the allocation of process resources, and assignment of process responsibilities to user and project personnel. The one range of components, those related to the "structural" side, could thus, as we have discussed earlier be described as components enhancing *stability* and institutionalism, while the others, those related to the "process" side, stand more for flexibility and *dynamism*. Foremost in today's turbulent climate seems to have been the appearance of a multitude of different "flexibility approaches" to organized activity. McLennan[70] suggested that the following four main groups of factors tend to be the most important for the way a modern manager chooses to organize his or her work:

1. The degree of change and uncertainty assumed to take place,
2. The type of task and technology,
3. The nature of the people in the organization, and the environment within which the organization operates, and
4. The objective of the effort.

Though these factors may be closely interconnected in a project context, as we have already suggested in the earlier simplified project "model", the subdivision above also points to an assumption that such factors may differently affect the managerial effort, and may also have different weight in different project phases. In particular, the relationship between "structural" decisions and "process" decisions seems important.

Yukl[71] used a similar notion related to leadership behaviour, defining some processes as "initiating structure" and some more devoted to that of "consideration": consideration being the degree to which a leader acts in a friendly and supportive manner, while initiating structure is the degree to which a leader defines and structures his or her role toward the attainment of formal goals. In Yukl's view consideration and initiating structure are relatively independent behaviour categories, but "causality operates in both directions, from behavior to outcomes, and vice versa".

In this respect he recommends varying use of "situational theories".[71] "Situational theories examine how the situation enhances or nullifies the effects of selected leader behaviors or traits, rather than taking a broader view of the way traits, power, behavior, and situation interact to determine leadership effectiveness."

This is also a view which has been contended in research done by this author, and which is based on the prevailing status of the project approach in our societies today. According to the literature also, the conclusion seems to be that the challenge to be focused on by the project leader in order to match the situation is that of striking a balance between the achievement of the necessary degree of strictness, conformity and structure, and the need to develop and maintain an adequate personal attitude and a resulting behaviour. Assuming that it is this combination of "static", stabilizing forces and the ambiguities, "dynamism", and disorder of human behaviour which are the essential ingredients in project leadership, authors have suggested that project leaders have to perform some kind of "interface management" between these two "dimensions" in order to comply. Archibald[34] defines "the basic concept of interface management [to be] that the project manager plans and controls (manages) the points of interaction between various elements of the project, the product, and the organizations involved". Stuckenbruck[25] defines interface management as consisting of "identifying, documenting, scheduling, communicating, and monitoring interfaces related to both the product and the project". The problem of the overall project interface is also thoroughly discussed by Cleland and King[72] who point out the complementary nature of the project and the functional or discipline-oriented organization. This leads, according to Stuckenbruck,[25] to the fact that project leadership involves at least three types of interface processes:

1. Processes related to "organizational interfaces"
2. Processes related to "system interfaces"
3. Processes related to "personal interfaces"

From this it seems reasonable to state that there are a multitude of "processes" operating within the project organization, and that these processes will naturally affect project leadership in different ways. This also points to the fact that a major function of the project leader is to serve as a catalyst to motivation in order to cope with the strong possibility that such processes may develop unfavourably and thus create demotivational attitudes among both the people constituting the project organization and those representing the project stake holders.

As already stated, project execution may involve the management of large amounts of money, people and material, but may also be done with a very limited use of resources and by only a few participants. It seems therefore important to suggest that, on the one hand, part of this execution should conform to some rules or structures in order to keep constraints and guarantee adequate performance (which should best be defined as "to manage") and, on the other hand, that the project execution should also open up for a flexible and dynamic approach in order to cater for the impact of the many interactions between different kinds of elements apparently operating within its scope (which could best be defined as "to lead"). These are issues which obviously also have particular motivational implications for those involved, especially for the "project leaders".

3.4.6 Views on Organizational "Goals" in General and Possible Transferability to Project Leadership Efforts

The close relation between "planned change" and "goal setting" in an organizational context has already been contended. Perrow[3] suggested that organizational goals are "broad statements about what the organization should be doing, the reason it exists, and the values that underlie its existence". Daft[1] stated that, "the purpose of official goals is to gain legitimacy for an organization". In general, it seems fair to state that organizations are purpose- or goal-directed devices, and that to manage organizations well, the management needs to be confident about the type of goals used within the organization and the process by which goals are chosen.

Cummings and Huse[73] have suggested, with reference to Perrow,[3] the following steps for implementing organizational goals:

1. *Diagnoses,* which shall provide information about specific goals and the kinds of feedback and support needed to monitor and achieve them.
2. *Preparing for goal setting,* which involves preparing the managers and the employees to engage in the goal setting. Specific action plans for implementing the program are also made.
3. *Setting goals,* involving the setting of specific, difficult goals that employees perceive as feasible.
4. *Review,* involving the assessing of the goal-setting process so that modifications can be made if necessary. This includes assessing the goal attributes to see whether they are energizing and directing appropriate behaviours. It also involves assuring that employees are receiving timely and relevant performance feedback, and that managers are coaching and counselling employees.

This process shows a close similarity with the way *project goals* are defined and used, in the sense that project goals have to be well-defined, well-structured, and be the dynamic steering mechanism for the manager of the project effort. In this way the goal also produces the necessary background for an understanding of how and by which forces project procedures are executed. Since the implications of changes in goal definitions throughout the project lifetime may have shifting motivational implications, the understanding of the main principles and practices of "organizational goal setting" is also fundamental. In addition, project goals are more precisely described than the strategic or tactical objectives of organizations in general, from which project goals are derived, or should be derived. This also helps the project participants, and particularly the project leader, to know exactly when the work responsibility is completed, which is meant to be when the project goal is fulfilled. This puts a particular strain on those responsible for the project goal definition, and in the next round on those responsible for the project execution. As Stuckenbruck stated: "A specific objective (of a project) is not described by such 'weasel words' as shortest possible, maximum, minimum, justifiable, allowable, desirable, reasonable, lowest, highest, or optimum. In addition, each job-related objective should be simple, understandable, challenging, job related, achievable, measurable, and above all, verifiable."[25]

This puts project "goal" definition and its attainment in the very centre as one of the characteristics that will particularly affect the project leader's motivation and demotivation.

3.4.7 Conclusions

There are several conclusions that might be relevant to draw from these arguments on project organizational characteristics and their impact on the managerial effort. The "change" issue emphasizes the importance of the project manager taking on a "leadership" role and operating as a "change agent" in relation to the organization. The "structural" issue stresses the "life cycle" of projects as fundamental, and recommends a "discontinuous management" style. The "process" issue advises that some kind of organizational "interface management" take place. And the importance of the project "goal" underlines the need to have project aims well defined, well structured, and operational in a wider organizational context.

Together this gives a very complex and diversified area of responsibility for the project leader, as well as pointing to the project as an organizational breeding ground for a multitude of motivational implications to consider.

3.5   Project Management as a System

"In a decentralized, customer-driven company, a good leader spends more time communicating than doing anything else."
(Jan Carlzon)

Over the years scientific research and field observations have given rise to many definitions and explanations of the term "management". The definition given by Stoner and Wankel[48] seems to include what has generally been adopted as typical for the managerial activity, i.e. "the process of planning, organizing, leading, and controlling the efforts of organizational members and of using all other organizational resources to achieve stated organizational goals." This definition clearly indicates the comprehensive nature of managerial work, and also complies well with the inherent mechanisms in project efforts. It also points to the fact that if one really wants to achieve something, and one cannot manage to do so with one's own input alone, one must also engage and systemize the effort of other people in the achievement process, and subsequently "manage" those people in order to obtain the desired outcome. The definition above is also supported by much behavioural science research, while at the same time having its origin in thoughts from traditional, classical management scholars. It indicates that managers use all the resources of the organization – its finances, its equipment, and its information as well as its people – to attain their goals.

Psychology and religion are disciplines which tried at an early stage to describe the existence of particular interactions between systems and people. Later, when people began to "organize" more and more of their effort in order to cope with the increasing complexity of the "systems" nature offered and the "systems" of technology, economy and structure they created themselves, "management" became a topic it was necessary to try to systemize due to its great importance to Man and his need to operate through a recognizable and operational frame of reference. There have been many attempts to define management in this context. One definition which clearly points to management in a systems perspective is suggested by Forrester: "a system of people for allocating resources and regulating the activity of a business in a purposeful way."[7]   Daft[1] has more precisely argued that "management is a distinct subsystem, responsible for directing the other subsystems of the organization". The fact that "projects" may well be regarded as organizational sub-systems has already been contended, and it seems therefore sensible to search additionally for components and characteristics that define the "project management system" as an organizational sub-system of projects. This is a thought argued by many authors,[7, 24, 31] defining "systems" as "wheels within wheels within wheels".

Due to the complex nature of systems in general, and the close connection between a project and its parent organization, we may also assume that since organizational systems and their sub-systems generally need to have a complex and overlapping flow of authority between them, then the interaction between the project organization and its parent organization will also be complex and difficult to discern. The need for considerable managerial competence and coordinating skill is obvious. It is therefore reasonable to suggest that project leaders also need to operate through some kind of "project management system" in order to meet their responsibilities, and that defining the components of such a system is a challenging but feasible endeavour. Two "system" features observed by many authors seem of particular importance for the description of a "project management system" in this respect. They are:

1. That all the parts of a system are related to one another and to the whole.[11] This implies that it is not only each single factor in isolation, but also the combination of factors, which defines a system. The desire, and the goal, are not the only keys to an understanding of its nature and its functioning, no more than only its participants, its technology, or its structure are.

   This may point in particular to the importance of establishing some temporary structure or "stability" in projects in order to make components and relationships more recognizable, which thereby supports the human need for logic, for order, or for a "system" to which the human can relate activities and observations.

2. That the whole is greater than the sum of its parts.[9] This is an observation adapted from biology, in which the simultaneous, "synergetic" effect of separate agencies together tends to create a greater total effect than the sum of their individual effects. In general, this points to an interest to steadily include new elements into established settings in order to increase the total output.

   This may particularly enhance the importance of "dynamism" in projects, which therefore highlights the human need for newness and change, for progress and development, for self-actualization, for achievement, and similar "process"-oriented constellations.

3.5.1   Elements of a "Project Management System"

As contended earlier, it seems natural to conclude that for this "system" to work, it will have to depend on its *human component*. Using this as a criterion, and with reference to the preceding discussion on "systems" and "structure" in a project context, a "project management system" should probably include the same features as suggested by Argyris[74] as mandatory for success in organizational systems in general. They are:

1. A human desire to perform a "change" effort in relation to an existing, established structure or process,
2. The existence of some "structured activities", in order to allocate and regulate the desired human effort in a rational way,
3. A "managerial effort" to be executed, in order to maintain the necessary dynamic combination of people, structure and process in the goal attainment procedure,
4. A "goal" to strive for, which satisfies the human preference for some measurable entities or product output.

These are all components which are typical for project endeavours. The combination of a "desired change", the achievement of an end objective or a predefined goal under some environmental influence, implies a need for the project leader to establish some *policy* agreements in order to obtain the necessary resources from the project environment and some needed activity from the project enactors. This need for a policy also links the goal attainment to the human component and the structural issues in the definition above, and combines the different characteristics above into one operational concept.

Combined, these features may in simple terms be said to comprise the following key issues in project leadership:

1. A "purpose" behind the effort
2. A "process" to facilitate the effort
3. A "policy" to guide the effort

Assuming that project environments generally have limited resources, this also accentuates the importance of project organizations being efficient and effective. "Efficiency" is in this context perhaps best defined as "the ratio of effective work to the energy expended in producing it".[4] For a "project management system" this implies that some work measurements and some production or output measurements are important to define.

"Organizational effectiveness" is defined by Argyris[74] as "an integration of the three effectiveness scores: namely the degree of energy needed to carry out the (following) three core activities in relation to output: maintaining the internal system: adapting to the external environment, and achieving objectives.

It may be pointed out here that the literature is not consistent on the definition of these issues. Argyris' description of organizational *efficiency*, for example, has by others been defined as organizational *effectiveness*, in the sense that an effective organization also ensures that the objectives are properly defined. This is also concluded by Joynt,[75] who distinguishes between "efficiency" and "effectiveness", claiming "effectiveness" to be the degree to which a goal is obtained, while "efficiency" is a measurement of how well resources are utilized.

It will here be assumed that by expanding on Argyris' definition of effectiveness with that of a proper goal description also, thus suggesting that his "change" desire be transformed to an operational entity, the above criteria together can be used directly to define the proper components of an effective and efficient "project management system", and also to measure its performance.

Relating this to project efforts, to obtain the "project goal" in some "best" way would naturally be to apply a "project management system" together with the above criteria for effectiveness and efficiency. And in accordance with the general demands for "systems" to work, this also implies the need for both some recognized structural components to be present and some process components be operating.

3.5.2 Implications of Special "Project Leadership" Features

There are several implications of Argyris' aforementioned features of a proper "project management system". First, that any project work is based on an initial decision to execute a "change", which is also supposed to be desired in a relevant perspective. The way this change desire is defined will naturally affect both how the subsequent project process will develop and by what structure it will be executed. Also the attainability of the final project goal depends on how and by which means the initial desire is concretized and transformed to an achievable and desirable goal for those involved, and for the "project management system" accordingly to operate in an effective and efficient way.

Next, although Argyris' definition has been criticized for its limited "operationality",[48] the term "structured activities" points to the possible existence of some underlying *structure* in projects too as a necessity for them to function. Such existence has been debated, but although suggestions have been put forward by researchers and practitioners regarding whether such structural features are necessary and, if they are necessary, which ones may be the most important for projects to work, it seems relevant to suggest that some "project structure" is a prerequisite for a proper "project management system".

The third element in Argyris' definition leads to a focus on the style of leadership in projects. To comply with the responsibilities of changing conditions and demands, of coordination and of integration, and of shifting processes and demands at different project phases or stages, it is reasonable to philosophize on the degree to which the "project management system" should adopt a management style which varies to suit the different "structures" and "processes" demanded during the phased project development. This coincides with more recent management theories, of which contingency theory has already been mentioned, which advocate that the management style should be varied to suit the circumstances. A "contingent" management style may therefore, as already suggested, be assumed to be a natural feature of the "project management system".

And lastly, the definition focuses on the need for a close link between the goal and the management system perspective. To achieve objectives and reach intended goals is by many theorists assumed to be one of the fundamental traits of human behaviour.[76, 77, 78, 79, 80, 81, 82] As Powers[83] has stated, "the purpose of any given behavior is to prevent controlled perceptions from changing away from the reference condition". These and other, similar definitions which suggest that purpose implies goal, indicate that the goal of any behaviour may be defined as the reference condition of the controlled perception. The fact that the project effort is particularly goal directed, and that managers use many operational features recognizable in systems operations in general to attain the project goal is then an important indication that for projects the well-functioning of the "project management system" depends on its proper goal description.

This leads to the assumption that the above characteristics combine parts of an organizational philosophy for projects which could well be given the general label the "project management system". The main content is that for projects to function, they need to establish a temporary, flexible, goal-oriented sub-organization in addition to the often more traditional, "bureaucratic" parent organization. When combining this into one concept, the resulting project management system may benefit both from the stability and security inherited from or enforced by the parent organization, and the flexibility and challenge offered by the project organization. This balance between the need for stability and the need for change, seems to be a basic trait of human nature, and is also reflected in the historic review of organizational development in recent years (chapter 2). Accordingly, these should be natural components both when directing and when manipulating project organizational structures and when affecting the attitude and behaviour of the people involved. It is also reasonable to assume that such a system contains specific parameters and variables which, by different measurement procedures, can be used to test out particular system features affecting the project leader's performance under different conditions typical for projects.

The above reflections on the essentials of the "project management system", together with the conclusion arrived at from the literature studies described earlier, lead to the realization that the "systems approach" of bringing together the pertaining parts of subsystems in an orderly and efficient manner to accomplish some predetermined goal[84] is of paramount importance for the project leader. It further emphasizes the fact that a good way to understand and handle the management of projects is to regard them from a "systems" point of view. By identifying, evaluating, and adjusting the interactions between components of this subsystem, the performance of the total project system may be optimized. It is the project leader who has the responsibility to integrate the activities of the different disciplines with respect to costs, schedules and output so that the best overall achievement is sought. The project must also be executed and tested to provide feedback for evaluating and improving the performance. These features are, according to the literature, particularly well taken care of by a specific "project management system".

3.5.3 Derived Aspects of "Project Management System" Features

In this context, two aspects of managing projects have been observed as particularly problematic. One relates to the importance of the integration of efforts, the other to the project internal relations.

The complexity of the project work states the need for a systematic way of integrating all the efforts necessary in projects. Stoner and Wankel[48] have suggested that special "integrative roles" should be established when a specific product, service or project that spans several organizational units requires continuing coordination and attention from one single individual.

This is the generally accepted rationale for introducing special managerial supervisory functions into coordinative organizational work. When the coordination is of a particular cross-disciplinary character, Lawrence and Lorsch[54] have proposed that well-planned "integration" be instituted in order to designate the degree to which members of various departments should work together in a unified manner. Merlo[85] has brought these thoughts further into the project concept, and concluded that:

> it is imperative that Project Management recognize the various systems that exist within any given project and that, to make the whole of them operate effectively, their respective input requirements, inherent work processes and coordination of the outputs be understood. It is the decision-making process that directs the coherent operation of these systems which constitute the general work process of the project.

Further, accepting that the human component in projects is central and that human beings need to cooperate closely to be organizationally effective, it may also be necessary to design a proper "system" for such cooperation in the particular setting in which project management systems operate. Kolltveit[33] has suggested that "lateral relations" is one efficient way of improving this needed coordination between all the parties involved in the project effort. Lateral relations have been explained as processes overlaid on an existing system to increase the flow of the available information, and to improve the interplay between groups.[86, 87] Williamson,[88] however, takes the contrasting view that lateral relations increase the number of levels of management and should not be used unless substantial benefits can be guaranteed. Nevertheless, some coordinating system seems important to establish in project efforts.

Both these aspects place a substantial degree of strain on the project management effort, hence the effect on the project leader's motivation and demotivation could well be considerable.

3.6   Conclusions

"If you are like a wheelbarrow, going no farther than you are pushed, then do not apply for work here!"
(Sign at a US factory employment gate)

The main objective of this chapter was to study, with reference to current literature, the extent to which the "project approach" may conform to some particular structure or systematic order which in turn affects the way project leaders behave and perform. This was done by briefly reviewing the way organizational theory seems to have developed in modern time, and comparing this development with typical traits of the "project approach" in the same time period.

The review revealed that projects seemed, on the one hand, to create ad-hoc, problem-solving efforts to facilitate a "safe" and "reliable" structure comparative to the shifting theoretical views in time on how best to handle organizations and their human resources, and to facilitate temporary stability and structure in turbulent environments, and, on the other hand, to serve as a testing-ground for new and appealing theories not yet fully accepted in organizational settings in general. Particularly important, however, was the fact that projects tend to be created to enhance flexibility, "mobility", and personal achievement for the people involved. The "project approach" may therefore be described as a "system" with many components, which are of different types, in the sense that some are "soft" and some are "hard", and which interact with each other in different, often complicated ways.

The reasoning that "projects" can be recognized as "systems", led to the assumption that also a "project management system" as a sub-system should be possible to define, together with its main components and characteristics. For this system to work, the major components of the overall project system had to be identified properly in terms of the extent to which such components were present in the pertaining project management sub-system, especially features connected to change-desire, to the preservation of a "static" structure, to the support of a "dynamic" interplay between different "process" parameters, and to features promoting "goal" fulfilment.

The conclusion is thus that it is possible to identify such a "project management system", that its main components and features seem discernible, and that their interplay is of major importance for effective project leadership and for the project leader's motivation and demotivation.

3.7   References

1 Daft, R.L. 1989: *Organization Theory and Design.* (Third edition.) West Publishing Company, St. Paul, Min.

2 Mintzberg, H. 1983: *Structure in Fives. Designing Effective Organizations.* Prentice-Hall. Englewood Cliffs. N.J.

3 Perrow, C. 1979: A Framework for the Comparative Analysis of Organizations. *American Sociological Review 32,* 194–208.

4 Webster, N. 1983: *Webster's New Universal Unabridged Dictionary.* (Second edition.) Dorset & Baber. N.Y.

5 Bertalanffy, L. von 1951: General Systems Theory: A New Approach to the Unity of Science. *Human Biology* (December). 302–312.

6 Boulding, K. 1956: General Systems Theory: The Skeleton of Science. *General Systems, Yearbook of the Society for the Advancements of General Systems Theory 1,* 11–17.

7 Forrester, J.W. 1968: *Principles of Systems.* M.I.T. Press, Cambridge, Mass.

8 Johnsen, R.A., Kast, F.E. & J.E. Rosenzweig 1967: *The Theory and Management of Systems.* McGraw-Hill. N.Y.

9 Hunsaker, P.L. & W.C. Cook 1986: *Managing Organizational Behavior.* Addison-Wesley Publishing Company, Boston, Mass.

10 Leavitt, H.J. 1964: *Applied Organization Change in Industry: Structural, Technical and Human Approaches.* In Cooper, Leavitt & Shelly (eds.): *New Perspectives in Organizational Research.* John Wiley & Sons. N.Y. 55–71.

11 Scott, W.R. 1987: *Organizations: Rational, Natural, and Open Systems.* (Second edition.) Prentice-Hall International Editions. N.Y.

12 Miner, J.B. 1973: *The Management Process. Theory, Research, and Practice.* The Macmillan Company. N.Y.

13 Katz, D. & R.L. Kahn 1966: *The Social Psychology of Organizations.* John Wiley & Sons. N.Y.

14 Miller, E.J. & A.K. Rice 1967: *Systems of Organization: The Control of Task and Sentiment Boundaries.* Tavistock. London.

15 Thompson, J.D. 1967: *Organizations in Actions. Social Science Based on Administrative Theory.* McGraw-Hill. N.Y.

16 Voich, D. & D.A. Wren 1968: *Principles of Management – Resources and Systems.* Ronald. N.Y.

17 Cherrington, D.J. 1989: *Organizational Behavior.* Ally & Bacon. Mass.

18 Katz, D. & R.L. Kahn, 1978: *The Social Psychology of Organizations.* John Wiley & Sons. N.Y.

19 Baumgartel, J.S. 1963: *Project Management.* Richard. D. Irwin, Homewood. Ill.

20 Goodman, R.M. 1967: Ambiguous Authority Definition in Project Management. *Academy of Management Journal,* December.

21 Steiner, G.A. & G.W. Ryan 1968: *Industrial Project Management.* MacMillan. N.Y.

22 Hed, S. 1970: *Handbok i Prosjektadministrasjon.* Eget Forlag. Täby.

23 Butler, A.G., Jr. 1979: Project Management: A Study in Organizational Conflict. In Hill & White (eds.): *Matrix Organzations and Project Management.* Michigan Business Papers, #64, Division f Research, University of Michigan, Ann Arbor. Mi.

24 Gray, C.F. 1981: *Essentials of Project Management.* Petrocelli Books Inc. Oregon.

25 Stuckenbruck, L.C. 1981: *The Implementation of Project Management: The Professional's Handbook.* Addison-Wesley Inc. Mass.

26 Sayles, L. & M. Candler 1982: The Project Manager: Organizational Metronome. In Tushman & Moore (eds.) *Readings in Management Innovation.* Pitman Publishing C. Marshfield. Ma.

27 Adams, J.R. & S.E. Barndt 1983: Behavioral Implications of the Project Life Cycle. In D.I. Cleland & R.W. King (eds.): *Project Management Handbook.* Van Nostrand Reinhold Co. N.Y. 222–244.

28 Cleland, D.I. & R.W. King (eds.) 1983: *Project Management Handbook.* Van Nostrand Reinhold Co. N.Y.

29 Burger, R. 1985: Project Organizations Models. Rules and Methods for the Set-Up and Review. Paper presented to the World Congress on Project Management. Rotterdam.

30 Morris, P.W.G. 1988: Initiating Major Projects – The Unperceived Role of Project Management. *Proceedings of the Ninth World Congress on Project Management 1.* Glasgow. 801–813.

31 Meredith, J.R. & S.J. Mantel Jr. 1989: *Project Management. A Managerial Approach.* (Second edition.) John Wiley & Sons. N.Y.

32 Stephanou, S.E. & C. Obradowich 1985: *Project Management. System Development and Productivity.* Daniel Spencer Publishers, Malibu. Ca.

33 Kolltveit, B.J. 1988: *The Technical Concept and Organizational Effectiveness of Offshore Projects.* Henley The Management College. March. Henley.

34 Archibald, D.R. 1977: *Managing High-Technology Programs and Projects.* John Wiley & Sons. N.Y.

35 Pfeffer, J. 1978: *The External Control of Organization. A Resource Dependent Perspective.* Harper & Row. N.Y.

36 Elster, J. 1989: *The Cement of Society. A Study of Social Order.* Cambridge University Press, Cambridge. Mass.

37 Daft, R.L. 1980: The Evolution of Organization Analysis in ASQ 1959–1979. *Administrative Science Quarterly 25,* 623–635.

38 Gambetta, D. 1987: *Did they Jump or Were They Pushed?* Cambridge University Press. Mass.

39 MacIntyre, A. 1988: *Whose Justice? Which Rationality?* University of Notre Dame Press. Notre Dame. Ind.

40 Jessen, S.A. & L. Skare 1984: *Prosjektadministrasjon og Utredningsteknikk.* Tanum Forlag (TANO). Oslo.

41 Jessen, S.A. 1986: *Prosjektadministrative metoder.* Universitetsforlaget. Oslo.

42 Lord, A.M. 1989: An Investigation into the Role of the Project Manager. Draft thesis. Henley The Management College, Henley.

43 The World Bank 1987: *The Twelfth Annual Review of Project Performance Results.* Operations Evaluation Department. Washington DC.

44 Thomas. J.M. & W.G. Bennis 1972: *The Management of Change and Conflict.* Penguin, Baltimore, p. 209.

45 Lewin, K. 1951: *Field Theory in Social Science: Selected Theoretical Papers.* Harper & Brothers. N.Y.

46 Schein, E. 1980: *Organizational Psychology.* Prentice-Hall, Englewood Cliffs. N.J.

47 Sathe, V. 1983: Implications of Organizational Culture. A Manager's Guide to Action. *Organizational Dynamics 12,* 2, 5–23.

48 Stoner, J.A.F. & C. Wankel 1986: *Management.* (Third edition.) Prentice-Hall International. N.Y.

49 Salapatas, J.N. 1981: Organizing the Project Management. In L.C. Stuckenbruck: *The Implementation of Project Management: The Professional's Handbook.* Addison-Wesley. Cal. 51–68.

50 Massie, J.L. 1987: *Essentials of Management.* (Fourth edition.) Prentice-Hall International, Englewood Cliffs. N.J.

51 Davis, M.S. & P.R. Lawrence 1977: *Matrix.* Addison-Wesley. Reading. Mass.

52 Kolodny, H.F. 1979: Evaluation to a Matrix Organization. *Academy of Management Review 4,* 4, 543–573.

53 Burns, T. & G.M. Stalker 1961: *The Management of Innovation.* Routledge, Chapman & Hall. Tavistock. London.

54 Lawrence, P.R. & J.W. Lorsch 1967: *Organization and Environment: Managing Differentiation and Integration.* Graduate School of Business Administration, Harvard University. Boston. Mass.

55 Etzioni, A. 1964: *Modern Organizations.* Prentice-Hall Inc. Englewood Cliffs. N.J.

56 Aldrich, H. 1990: From Traits to Rates: An Ecological Perspective on Organizational Foundings. Paper presented at the 1989 Gateway Conference on Entrpreneurship, St. Louis University, St.Louis, Missouri. Also notes from a meeting with him at the Norwegian School of Management, March 1990.

57 Quinn, R.E. & K. Cameron 1983: Organizational Life Cycles and Shifting Criteria of Effectiveness: Some Preliminary Evidence. *Management Science 29,* 1.

58 Cox, B. & M.W. Dale 1987: The Management of Finance. In H. Darnell (ed.): *Total Project Management.* Book 2. The Asset Management Group of the British Institute of Management.

59 Westhagen, H. 1984: *Prosjektarbeid.* Universitetsforlaget. Oslo.

60 Anderson, S.D. & R.W. Woodhead 1987: *Project Manpower Management. Decision-making Processes in Construction Practice.* Wiley-Interscience Publication, John Wiley & Sons. N.Y.

61 Thyness, P.A. 1987: *Prosjektundervisning.* Tano Forlag. Oslo.

62 Baker, B.N. 1988: Lessons Learned from a Variety of Project Failures. *Proceedings from the Ninth World Congress on Project Management 1.* Glasgow. 113–118.

63 Parkin, A. 1981: *Systems Management.* Edward Arnold. London.

64 Reve, J. & T. Levitt, 1984: Organization and Governance in Construction. *Project Management 2,* 1.

65 Andersen, E.S., Grude, K., Haug, T. & J.R. Turner 1987: *Goal Directed Project Management.* Coopers & Lybrand. London.

66 Randolph, W.A. & B.Z. Bozner 1989: *Effective Project Planning and Management.* Prentice-Hall International Editions, Englewood Cliffs. N.J.

67 Baker, B.N., Fisher, D. & D.C. Murphy 1983: Project Management in the Public Sector: Success and Failure Patterns Compared to Private Sector Projects. In D.I. Cleland & R.W. King (eds.): *Project Management Handbook.* Van Nostrand Reinhold Co. N.Y. 686–699.

68 Burbridge, R.N. 1988: Conception of Projects. *Proceedings of the Ninth World Congress on Project Management 1*, Glasgow. (Unpaged.)

69 Gabriel, L. 1989: Management by Projects – The New Management. In: *Project Management Readings.* Henley The Management College, Project Management Unit. Henley. (Unpaged.)

70 McLennan, R. 1989: *Managing Organizational Change.* Prentice-Hall, Englewood Cliffs. N.J.

71 Yukl, G.A. 1989: *Leadership in Organizations.* (Second edition.) Prentice-Hall, Englewood Cliffs. N.J.

72 Cleland, D.I. & R.W. King 1975: *Systems Analysis and Project Management.* (Second edition.) McGraw-Hill. N.Y.

73 Cummings, T.G. & E.F. Huse 1989: *Organizational Development and Change.* (Fourth edition.) West Publishing, University of Southern California. LA. Ca.

74 Argyris, C. 1964: *Integrating the Individual and the Organization.* John Wiley & Sons. N.Y.

75 Joynt, P. 1979: *Management Concepts and Processes.* Stiftelsen Bedrifts-økonomisk Institutt. Oslo.

76 Likert, R. 1961: *The Patterns of Management.* McGraw-Hill. N.Y.

77 Taylor, F.W. 1911: *The Principles of Scientific Management.* (1967). Norton. N.Y.

78 Koeppel, J. 1968: Motivational Effects of Knowledge of Results: A Goal Setting Phenomenon. *Psychological Bulletin*, December.

79 Latham, G.P. & G.A. Yukl 1975: Review of Research on the Application of Goal Setting in Organizations. *Academy of Management Journal*, December.

80 Becker, L.J. 1978: Joint Effect of Feedback and Goal Setting on Performance: A Field Study of Residential Energy Conservation. *Journal of Applied Psychology*, August.

81 Locke, E.A. 1978: The Ubiquity of the Technique of Goal Setting in Theories of and Approaches to Employee Motivation. *Academy of Management Review*, July.

82 Steers, R.M. & L.W. Porter 1983: *Motivation and Work Behavior.* (Third edition.) McGraw-Hill, N.Y.

83 Powers, R.F. 1971: An Emprical Investigation of Selected Hypoheses Related to the Success of Management Information System Projects. Unpublished doctoral thesis. University of Minesota. Min.

84 Churchman, C.W. 1981: *The Systems Approach.* Dell. N.Y.

85 Merlo, M. 1988: Project Execution. *Proceedings of the Ninth World Congress on Project Management 1.* Glasgow. 791–800.

86 Duncan, R.B. 1972: Characteristics of Organizational Environments and Perceived Environmental Uncertainty. *Administrative Science Quarterly 17*, (September). 313–327.

87 Galbraith, J.R. 1973: *Designing Complex Organizations.* Addison-Wesley, Reading. Mass.

88 Williamson, O.E. 1979: Transaction-Cost Economics: Governance of Contractual Relations. *The Journal of Law and Economics,* October.
89 Davis, K. & W.W. Newstrom 1989: *Human Behavior at Work. Organizational
   Behavior.* (Eighth edition.) McGraw-Hill. N.Y

4   MANAGEMENT AND MOTIVATION IN RELATION TO PROJECT WORK

4.1   General

"All people are motivated; the question is 'Motivated to do what?'"

In this chapter we will discuss, with reference to leading thoughts and literature reviews, the implications a "project management system" may have for the motivation of the project leader. The discussion will begin with a review of leading theories on motivation at work, how such theories have developed, and how they are approved as well as criticized today. A comparison is then made of central elements of such theories to the characteristics of the "project management system" and to behaviour of the project leader, and conclusions drawn on which motivational components in particular may create variations in the motivation and demotivation of the project leader.

The theoretical insight gained is then compared to findings from newer attempts to construct special "project simulation models" in which different leader stimuli are tried out in hypothetical project environments. These findings are finally compared with those from interviews and real-life observations in the field in which both professional and less professional project leaders reveal their feelings and opinions about project work.

4.2   Theories of Management and Motivation

"What's important is not how you make it, but how you take it!"
(Margareth Jessen)

The positive correlation between Man's behaviour and motivation has been confirmed by many.[1, 2, 3, 4, 5] As for motivation itself, the term "motivational research" is defined by Webster[6] as the "systematic and scientific analysis of the forces influencing people so as to control the making of their decisions". It would thus seem reasonable to state that work and motivation are closely connected, and that work has a personal meaning for the individual.

Steers and Porter[6] have in their research defined three phenomena characterizing motivation at work:

(1) What energizes human behaviour
(2) What directs or channels such behaviour
(3) How this behaviour is maintained or sustained

Even long before Steers and Porter first published their comprehensive overview of motivation in work organizations in 1975, interest in motivational problems had attracted a wide and diversified audience. One of the early contributors to theories of motivation was Maslow,[89] arguing that certain needs were basic for the individual and that the needs had to be satisfied in some hierarchical order. McGregor[9] enlarged Maslow's view introducing his two-factor theory, disputing the old theory of Man as unwilling to work and being against assuming responsibility. According to his findings, Man basically wants to both work and take on responsibilities, if conditions are right. Herzberg et al.[3] supported the latter view with their study of factors that particularly enhanced motivation, concluding that favours such as responsibility, acknowledgement, personal growth, interesting work and the possibility to achieve goals are particularly strong motivators. Cyert and March[10] advanced the need for goals and suggested that organizational goals had to be decided by a common change-oriented process between the involved parties. Vroom[11] shifted the view from factors of motivation toward the work process itself as the motivating agent, introducing "valence" (the extent to which a reward is desired), "expectations" (the kind of reward expected) and "instrumentality" (the possibility that a particular effort will result in a desired reward) as crucial parameters in understanding work motivation. Similarly, Madsen and Finger[12] point to the importance of a clear connection between psychological stimuli and responses, and Hackman[13] points to the meaning of work connected to responsibilities and duties as fundamental in today's working environment. Lewin[1] had earlier introduced the need to establish some "psychological contract" between the working parties, in which one must ensure (1) that the expectations of both the individual and the organization correspond, and (2) that there is agreement on what is really going to be exchanged (salary, security, promotion, etc.). Schein[14] too follows these lines, advocating a coherence between the demands of organization and the individual. Campbell and Pritchard[15] argued that motivation has to do "with a set of independent/dependent variable relationships that explain the direction, amplitude, and persistence of an individual's behaviour, holding constant the effects of aptitude, skill and understanding of the task and the constraints operating in the environment".

A Changing Environment

These are but a few of the many research efforts accomplished in order to increase the understanding of human motivation in work settings. Should any conclusion be drawn from these efforts, then it seems to be that Man's own interest in achieving and succeeding as a company or organizational member is a crucial parameter for most of his performance. But what also seems to be clear is that since the business environment itself is continually undergoing change, due to rapid alterations in markets and tools in order to achieve business effectiveness, these changes have also increased the need for a better understanding of human adaptiveness, as well as an increased understanding of how humans respond to responsibility and authority within the organization. The growth in the service industry has also changed the demand patterns and focused in particular on the human behavioural components in business environments. In general these trends have given a deeper respect for the individual, enhancing factors such as security, participation, challenge and meaning of life as crucial parameters at the workplace.

All the three well-established schools of management thought – the "classical school", represented by Follet,[16] Fayol,[17] Urwick[18] and Davis,[19] the "behavioural school", represented by Taylor,[20] Emerson,[21] Gantt,[22] and later von Bertalanffy,[23] Boulding[24] and Katz and Kahn,[25] as well as Ackoff[26] and Kaufmann,[27] and the "behavioural school", represented by Herzberg et al.,[3] Vroom,[11] Schein,[28] Locke[29] and Cummings[30] – have contributed to managers' understanding of organizations and their ability to manage them. Each offers a different perspective to defining management problems and opportunities and to developing new ways of dealing with them. Consequently, they have embodied different views on what energizes and motivates managers.

In their current state of evolution, however, each approach seems to suffer from an inability to deal adequately with all the diverse aspects of modern organizational life.[31] In particular it seems fair to argue that the conclusions on what basically "motivates" people in work settings is today more multifarious and ambiguous than ever.

THE MEASURABILITY OF MOTIVATION

What is important here is that there exists a conviction among researchers and theorists that motivation within organizational structures is highly *recognizable* and that it also appears that this can be *measured* in some way or other. If motivation is to be better understood, one approach may therefore be to look for good measurement criteria, and, if found, to cultivate them for better work performance. The rationale for studying such relationships between management and motivation is perhaps best stated by Steers and Porter:[32] "The topic of motivation at work has received considerable and sustained attention in recent years among both practising managers and organizational researchers. One has only to ask first-level supervisors what their most taxing work problems are for evidence of the importance of the concept to management."

Robbins[33] suggested the following definition of the motivation of managers as being the most adequate in today's business environment: "The willingness to exert high levels of effort toward organizational goals, conditioned by the effort's ability to satisfy some individual need."

This definition, together with the rationale for studying managerial motivation described above, may combine in one argument that fact that the motivation of managers in work settings is conditioned by desire or "will", by ability or "skill" and by characteristics of the work setting itself. These are also central thoughts of the "behavioural school", which assumes motivation to be stimulated by a mix of internal drives and external conditions. Since motivation also has wide decisional impacts, it is therefore appropriate to study its nature from an input–output point of view, and in settings where "input" and "output" are reasonably easy to recognize and possible to measure. These are thoughts which correspond with many of the basic axioms of the "quantitative school". One additional and important issue which has also been directly and indirectly recognized from this is that different work settings may come up with quite different motivational results and new variations peculiar to each situation.[34, 35, 36]

One fact that can be concluded from this is that motivation is a parameter not fully understood and not easy to comprehend in all the work settings modern business comprises. But this also leads us to the assumption that motivation could be better understood if studied in particular, well-defined settings. This is also confirmed by Davis and Newstrom,[37] who claim that different motivation theories may be relatively more important in certain situations, knowing what will be rewarding and when. As will be argued here, the project setting could well be the arena for such a closer study due to its special characteristics and traits, particularly for the project manager.

Projects Enhance Motivational Change

A natural conclusion to draw from the above is that if a project develops "more or less" as intended, it is most probably in itself motivating because it comprises so many of the features that are found to be motivating within organizations. Traditional research and debate also appear to have concentrated on the "motivating" factors in organizational climates, in the sense that factors enhancing positive motivation have been most readily recognized.[7] This is quite natural since goal-directed organizational endeavours are built on the idea of promoting desired changes and achievements for the managers. As also generally supported by Miner,[38] "many jobs, such as those of a managerial, professional, and entrepreneurial nature, frequently appear to engage such high levels of intrinsic motivation that performance is impervious to any negative extrinsic impact".

It can be assumed, however, that for many *projects* such development does not take place; projects *do not* necessarily develop as desired and planned. It seems also, according to first-hand experience, that many projects start out with a more "indifferent" level of motivation,[39] particularly in relation to the project goal, and especially for the leader. This makes it essential to look at demotivation as well when there are project conditions that turn from "positive" to "negative", or from "motivation" to "demotivation". As already clearly noted in the literature, there are many uncertainties in projects, and many problems embodied in the "newness" of the task at hand. The diversified human reactions to not reaching desired goals and to expecting setbacks in personal achievements, and the many overt and covert human reactions to organizational instability and change, all suggest that even if motivation and demotivation are two sides of the same coin, observations which also focus on the *demotivational* effects and implications of project development could bring new insight into the complicated area of project management today. Elster[40] has also brought forward the idea that in many situations it may be more efficient to rely on punishment, which works mainly by deterrence and only secondarily by actual administration. "Punishment is cheaper than reward, because anticipation replaces implementation."[40] Assuming that punishment leads to demotivation, one may well assume demotivation to develop in projects when chances of failure and setbacks increase and a subsequent dissatisfaction among project authorities can be expected.

4.3   Theories of Motivation and Their Relevance to Project Work

"People don't start each day with a desire to lose. Help them win by spreading 'attaboys' around!"

Motivation in projects may be studied from several angles. A study from the psychological angle could for instance provide important information about the participants' understanding of how their identity, self-esteem, and self-realization may develop in a project environment. It could also throw light on the effect of providing the participants with a sense of fulfilment through the way purposes are defined and by clarifying how, through the project work, they may make positive contributions to society. Project work may also be an arena for studying frustration, boredom and a feeling of lack of purpose, dependent on how the characteristics of the individual match the nature of the task. As concluded by Steers and Porter:[7] "People tend to evaluate themselves according to what they have been able to accomplish. If they see their job as hampering the achievement of their full potential, it often becomes difficult for them to maintain a sense of purpose at work. Such feelings can lead to a reduced level of job involvement, decreased job satisfaction, and a lowered desire to perform. Hence, the nature of the job – and the meaning it has for the employee – can have a profound impact on employee attitudes and work behavior."

From the literature it seems generally accepted to define three main groups of theories of motivation:[7] the "content", the "process" and the "reinforcement" theories. All these theories have their particular relevance to project settings and project managerial efforts:

> Content theories are associated with such names as Maslow,[8] McGregor,[9] McClelland[41] and Atkinson,[42] who stress that personal drives or needs are important as motives for the individual's attitudes. In other words, content theories may be said to focus on the "what" of motivation in relation to project work.
> Process theories, or expectancy theories as developed by Lewin,[1] and extended by Vroom,[11] emphasize how and by what goals individuals are motivated. In other words, process theories may be

said to focus on the "how" of motivation in relation to project work.

Reinforcement theories, mostly associated with Skinner,[43] focus on how the consequences of an individual's behaviour in the future. In other words, reinforcement theories may be said to focus on the "way" in which behaviour is learned in project settings.

These theories have developed in close connection with the different management theories as they have appeared. And because management theories have changed to accommodate changes in the nature of managers' jobs, the motivation theories have also changed. Early organizational structures, for example, dealt with the performance of relatively simple management tasks, whereas most of today's organizational systems have to accommodate quite complicated interrelations and processes. There has also been a gradual growth in the understanding of the importance of social processes at the workplace and of effective and ineffective approaches to motivation. Kreitner and Luthans[44] distinguish in this context between the Traditional Motivational Theories focusing on "self-determination", the Organizational Behaviour Modification Theories concentrating on "environmental determinism", and the Social Learning Theories advocating "reciprocal determinism" between Man and environment.

As already contended, it is the theories focusing on understanding of factors within individuals that cause them to act in a certain way which are generally referred to as the *content theories*. Maslow's hierarchy of needs[8] has probably attracted greatest attention among these theories because it not only classified human needs in a convenient way but it also has direct implications for the management of human behaviour in organizations. Despite this fact, the Maslow model has many limitations, and it has been sharply criticized. As a philosophical framework it has also been difficult to study, and it has not been fully verified despite many attempts. Many authors have, however, successfully built on Maslow's "need hierarchy" and enlarged the platform of the understanding of motivational behaviour. Those who have done so include Herzberg,[3] McClelland,[41] Alderfer[45] and, in popularized form, McGregor.[9] The parallels in the need theories can perhaps be demonstrated as shown in figure 4.1.

Murray's "Manifest Needs Theory" is in this respect a particularly relevant variant, because in addition to employing the *individual* human's need as the basic unit of analysis, he viewed personality of the individual as composed of many divergent and often conflicting needs which had the *potential* of motivating human behaviour. Murray[46] defined a need as "a

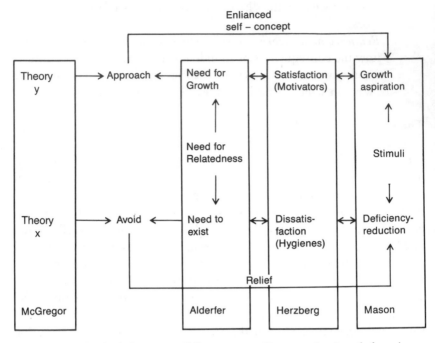

Figure 4.1 The link between different prevailing motivational theories

construct...which stands for a force...in the brain region, a force which organizes perception, apperception, intellection, conation and action in such a way as to transform in a certain direction an existing, unsatisfying situation."

According to Murray, a latent need did not imply that the need was not strong, only that it had been inhibited and had "found no overt form of expression.... Thus, a person may have a high need for achievement but such a need may not be strongly aroused because of impediments in the environment [such as the lack of a challenging task]."[32] Using this approach, Murray was able to construct a long list of needs which he found to be potentially motivating in work settings. Although his list exists in a few variations, and has been criticized for being far too simple since new needs and reactions may easily develop when circumstances and environment change (which is the essence of the "cognitive theories") or have changed (the "drive and reinforcement theories"), his extensive list provides a good basis for a categorization of variations in human motivation in work settings. Murray's list is reproduced in table 4.1.

Table 4.1 Murray's Manifest Needs

NEED	CHARACTERISTICS
Achievement	Aspires to accomplish difficult tasks; maintains high standards and is willing to work toward distant goals; responds positively to competition; willing to put forth effort to attain excellence.
Affiliation	Enjoys being with friends and people in general; accepts people readily; makes efforts to win friendships and maintain associations with people.
Aggression	Enjoys combat and argument; easily annoyed; sometimes willing to hurt people to get his or her way; may seek to "get even" with people perceived as having harmed him or her.
Autonomy	Tries to break away from restraints, confinement, or restrictions of any kind: enjoys being unattached, free, not tied to people, places, or obligations; may be rebellious when faced with restraints.
Endurance	Willing to work long hours; doesn't give up quickly on a problem; persevering, even in the face of great difficulty; patient and unrelenting in his or her work habits.
Exhibition	Wants to be the centre of attention; enjoys having an audience; engages in behaviour which wins the notice of others; may enjoy being dramatic or witty.
Harm avoidance	Does not enjoy exciting activities, especially if danger is involved; avoids risk of bodily harm; seeks to maximize personal safety.
Implusivity	Tends to act on the "spur of the moment" and without deliberation; readily gives vent to feelings and wishes; speaks freely; may be volatile in emotional expression.
Nurturance	Gives sympathy and comfort; assists others whenever possible; interested in caring for children; the disabled or the infirm; offers a "helping hand" to those in need; readily performs favours for others.
Order	Concerned with keeping personal effects and surroundings neat and organized; dislikes clutter, confusion, lack of organization; interested in developing methods for keeping materials methodically organized.
Power	Attempts to control the environment and to influence or direct other people; expresses opinions forcefully; enjoys the role of leader and may assume it spontaneously.
Succourance	Frequently seeks the sympathy, protection, love, advice, and reassurance of other people; may feel insecure or helpless without such support; confides difficulties readily to a receptive person.
Understanding	Wants to understand many areas of knowledge; values synthesis of ideas, verifiable generalization, logical thought, particularly when directed at satisfying intellectual curiosity.

Source: Adapted from D.N. Jackson (1967) *Personality Research Form Manual.* Research Psychologist Press. Goshen, N.Y. Reprinted by permission from Oxford University Press.

He further believed one could only infer needs from observed behaviour, and that a need was composed of two factors; a *qualitative* or directional component, and a *quantitative* or energetic component.

Alderfer[45] introduced important amendments to Maslow's "Need Hierarchy" with his ERG theory, extending Maslow's hierarchy to three levels of needs, i.e. Existence needs, Relatedness needs and Growth needs.

Others have focused on specific needs:

> need for *achievement* (or "n Ach") – (McClelland,[47] Atkinson[42])
> need for *autonomy* (or "n Aut") – (Vroom[11])
> need for *affiliation* (or "n Aff") – (Birch and Veroff[48]), and
> need for *power* (or "n Pow") – (Litwin and Stringer[49])

In addition, the need for *competence* (or to understand), defined as "a drive to do high-quality work",[37] has been stressed as an important need in current organizational life, realizing the necessity to attain high-quality products and services.

It can be summarized from this that one of the clearest signals from the need, or "content", theories is that there may be some basic needs and some less basic needs. The *basic* needs are those of *security, order and system,* which are embodied in human behaviour. The *superior* needs are those connected to being a member of an *organized structure* or participants in an *organizational process,* which seems to be particularly important to the feeling of personal growth and prosperity in work settings.

The specific types of motives assumed in content theories were then incorporated in a new group of theories, which were labelled *process theories.* The basic tenet is that a main determinant of human behaviour is the "belief, expectations, and anticipations individuals have concerning future events".[46] The fundamental view was that of law-of-effect, originally stated by Thorndike[50] as "behavior which seems to lead to reward tends to be repeated, while behavior which seems not to lead to reward or seems to lead to punishment tends not to be repeated". Behaviour is thus regarded as purposeful and goal-oriented, and based on conscious intentions.

EXPECTANCY THEORY

Within the framework of "process theories" one of the most operational theoretical attempts at explaining motivation at work is perhaps done by Vroom,[11] who developed a formal model of work motivation which is variously referred to as "expectancy" theory,[33] "instrumentality" theory, or "VIE" (Valence-Instrumentality-Expectancy) theory.[51] The core of this theory is that motivation is the combined function of the individual's *perception* that effort will lead to performance and of the *perceived desirability* of outcomes that may result from performance. Job performance is thus a multiplicable function of ability and motivation, Vroom[11] described expectancy as a probabilistic notion ranging from 0 to 1, while instrumentality is an outcome–outcome relationship ranging from -1 to +1. Instrumentality he defined as the perceived relationship between performance and other outcomes. Also Nebecker and Mitchell have proposed that a leader's expectancies about the consequences of various behaviour options can be used to explain the leader's choice of behaviour. The extent to which ability in itself is a motivating factor has been questioned,[52] however, while Vroom[11] found it to be a strong motivating factor. The conclusion from other studies[32] is that in general VIE measures have been positively related to performance, satisfaction and effort.

An apparent advantage of the "expectancy theory" is that it was initially formulated, and still seems to work best, as an *individual* motivation model. Because it may be difficult and costly to work at the individual level in large organizations, aggregated models are generally preferred in practical research. The focus on the individual is, however, particularly important when one wants to focus on the motivational reactions of the individual project manager, both as an "individual" and as a "leader".

One of the appealing theories on the processes in organizations that attract and motivate employees is based on a simple typology suggested by Clark and Wilson.[53] They distinguish between three kinds of rewards:

- material rewards
- solidarian rewards, and
- purpose-driven rewards

Organizations which primarily use material rewards are typically "utility" driven; and their leaders will concentrate on the process of submitting enough material resources to maintain their employee's energy. In solidarian organizations leaders support solidarian relationships and processes, and in purpose-driven organizations they focus on the purpose or the goal of the common effort.

Cognitive Theory

The most complicated part of the cognitive theories ("cognitive" because they are based on thinking, feeling or "cognition") is probably the fact that it is difficult for others to observe these needs or measure them precisely. It is important, however, that individuals are regarded as having inner needs which they are motivated to reduce or fulfil through the process in which they are participating. It follows that the cognitive theorists regarded many of the inner needs as dependent on the setting to which people belonged. That the processes existing in organizations have a very pronounced effect on human motivation follows from these theories. It is also important that the different cognitive theories have many common denominators, such as the importance of a goal-orientation and that some reward or outcome is desired and sought.

Drive and Reinforcement Theory

The last group of theories, the "drive and reinforcement theories", stem from "content" and "process" theories, but are generally regarded as belonging to a different class.[37, 38] They are much debated, however, since most of the research in support of these theories is laboratory based. Because of this the complex social processes of real life are ignored.[7] However, one interesting aspect of them is that they state that people generally prefer pleasant outcomes, and are therefore likely to avoid forms of behaviour which lead to unpleasant consequences. This is an easily observable recognition, and one that has also given support to behaviour modification in work organizations, despite having been criticized for not being proven in complex forms of organizations.[54] If we have a clear understanding of the characteristics of the organization within which we intend to apply behavioural modification, however, it may well be applied as a tool for describing human behaviour. Quoting this "historical component",[32] Allport[55] referred to such theories as "hedonism of the past", in the sense that people behave the way they do because, in the past, they learned that certain forms of behaviour were associated with pleasant outcomes and that other forms were associated with unpleasant outcomes. Others had previously used the same concept to formulate laws about past learning and previous stimulus-response connections. These include Thorndike's[56] "law-of-effect" and Woodworth's[57] "drive" philosophy, which both presupposed a logical, predictable connection between human energy and goal-direction.

The Benefits of Process Theory

Arguments have been put forward as to why "process theories" may be considered as more suitable for explaining motivation for work behaviour.[32] The main reason seems to be that compared to the other two classes of theories, they have the least flaws. "Content theories" are explained as doubtful because they in many ways assume motivational drives to be an inherited human quality that is difficult to change, more than a quality which can be cultivated and stimulated in new ways. As for the "reinforcement theories", Steers and Porter[32] have found them generally unsuitable since, although they may be an adequate explanation for subhuman behaviour, they are inadequate and perhaps even incorrect when seeking an explanation for the behaviour of an aware adult. Others have claimed that reinforcement theory is not a theory of motivation because it does not concern itself with what energizes or initiates behaviour.[38]

Though all these theories have been challenged or disputed, they throw light on different aspects of the forces and features that may influence motivation in project work. One preliminary observation is that it seems appropriate to argue that these motivational theories have all evolved in stages from the traditional model, which is initially based on the idea that people are motivated by some necessities, through the human relations model, which emphasizes job satisfaction as a motivator, to the human resource model, which suggests that high performance leads to satisfaction. According to the latter model, people perform best when they can achieve personal as well as organizational goals. That the need for achievement is closely associated with successful performance in the workplace was confirmed by McClelland[41] also.

The conclusion drawn after this is that both the "content theories" and the "process theories" seem to be highly applicable when we want to describe what energizes the motivation of managers and how this motivation is directed in different work settings.

4.3.1 The Motivation of Project Leaders

"Don't spur a willing horse."

When contending that motivation is a very basic force in all human activity, it will be important for project leaders to understand the many aspects of "motivation" in order for them to channel people's efforts toward achieving both personal and project goals. From this it seems obvious to state that the *motivation to manage* must also be a central component in project endeavours.[58] Slevin[59] has stated: "The motivation to manage makes a lot of conceptual sense as a predictive variable in determining whether one is satisfied with the managerial position and successful therein."

This is an important statement because it comprises the fact that managers must understand their own attitude and behaviour; i.e. how to achieve appropriate self-motivation through their own reactions and actions; and how to counteract, neutralize, and mitigate demotivational forces. Miner[38] has referred to this as the "role function" of managers. Steers and Porter[7] have pointed to this as a problem in modern organizations, declaring that:

> Any attempt by managers to improve the motivational levels of their subordinates should be prefaced by a self-examination on the part of the managers themselves. Are they aware of their major strengths and their major limitations? Do they have a clear notion of their wants, desires, and expectations from their jobs? Are their perceptions of themselves consistent with the perceptions others have of them? In short, before management attempt to deal with others, they should have a clear picture of their own role in the organizational milieu.

The importance of managerial self-motivation in project environments is particularly well described by Slevin:[59]

> Many project managers evolve to their positions out of previous scientific, engineering or technical posts, i.e. it is not uncommon to have a highly qualified and very successful engineer move up to the project manager position. The change is dramatic. In his previous role he communicated primarily with things. He now must communicate primarily with people. Previously he could spend long uninterrupted hours reading, reflecting, collecting data and working on technical projects. He now must spend large amounts of time in group meetings, talking on the telephone, being interrupted by subordinates, and the other frenetic activities that encompass a typical manager's day. Before, he could self-actualize by coming up with good technical solutions. Now he must engage in the sometimes unpleasant process of exercising power over others and engaging in competition for key resources. Although

from the standpoint of status and pay the movement into the project manager's position tends to be viewed as a natural incremental progression, for the talented engineer with a low motivation to manage it may be a traumatic metamorphosis indeed. A crucial question that anyone occupying a project manager's position should ask is "Do I have sufficient motivation to manage for satisfaction and success in this position?"

This observation also fits in well with Baker's[62] argument that "project managers who are highly skilled in technical aspects or who have had considerable success in the past must be especially aware that every project represents a potential failure". He also argues that "individual project failures, as well as extensive research, indicate that projects rarely fail for purely technical reasons; failures are most often a consequence of managerial or behavioral factors".

With reference to the earlier range of motivational theories, it seems fair to suggest that there most certainly are particular characteristics of the "project approach" which have both motivating and demotivating effects on the project leaders, depending on the way they are performing their managerial role, but also in terms of the way projects permit motivational stimuli to be activated. Vroom's[11] view, which points specifically to the importance of desire and achievement in human activity, is extended by many others, among them Graen,[61] who made Vroom's basic model considerably larger and more complex. Many of his modifications extended the theory into the leadership realm, adding a dynamic or developmental dimension to it through the use of feedback concepts. In Graen's view, a feedback process is hypothesized in that whenever a role outcome is achieved following the attainment of a work role (effective performance), the level of instrumentality is elevated so that the work role is now seen as more likely to yield that outcome. "Work role" was defined by him as a set of behaviours expected by the organization and considered appropriate of an incumbent within the organization. In this context it seems fair to suggest that the project leader, who has to play a particularly wide range of roles with associated attitudes, may also experience both high motivation or demotivation, depending on the current project situation.

One particular reason for this being so complicated is perhaps the uniqueness of projects, which means that there is no real precedent and therefore a good chance of misjudging the forthcoming need for resources. The risk of not succeeding in fulfilling the desired goal may similarly be high. In addition comes the high probability that external conditions, originally thought to be stable, may change dramatically. All these circumstances may create many demotivational situations. As argued by Miner:[60] "Developing achievement motivation in an individual whose environment does not permit satisfaction of the motive can be self-defeating." And according to Jackson and Shea:[63] "In the past when this has been done [not permitting desired achievement], the people involved have either left the environment...or attempted to change the existing environment through pressure tactics and other conflict-generating efforts."

What is important is to find conditions and features that particularly make the motivation of project leaders vary. From the preceding literature three groups of actors have been found to be central in this endeavour:

> The first is related to the motivational and demotivational effect on the project leader of conditions prevailing in the initial stage, the *desire-to-change* state.

> The second is related to conditions and features operating in the total preparation and executing stage, which comprise all the interactions taking place between the *static* and the *dynamic* forces after the decision to start the project is taken, and before the final goal is reached.

> The third is related to the impact the final project *goal* itself may have on the managerial attitude and behaviour in terms of motivational or demotivational incitements.

The Motivational Implications for the Project Leader of the "Change" Desired by the Project Effort

> "The creative process takes time; so build the time into your projects."

Daft[64] has stated that organizational change requires strong loyalty and an ability to manage and master change. And as many others have argued as well, "change" has strong motivational implications.[1, 36, 65] From the literature we can make the general observation that there is a growing acknowledgement that the need for managerial thinking be directed in particular toward *change*, and become diversified, with its field of application widened.

The subjects of change and leadership have occupied humankind for centuries. Machiavelli[66] wrote over 400 years ago that there was "nothing more difficult to carry out, nor more doubtful of success, nor more dangerous to handle, than to initiate a new order of things."

More recently, Helmer[67] stated that not only is technology and environment undergoing change, but the pace of change affecting the leaders in our time is also accelerating. These statements are only two of the many assertions which confirm change in our societies both to be inevitable and to increasingly influence every managerial effort. Change is obviously one of the most characteristic features of modern management, and one that is the most difficult to handle perfectly. This observation is not revolutionary, as Massie has commented:[68] "Managers of organizations must always face an unfinished world. Rarely do they have all the information to make a perfect decision; rarely do they have full authority to implement the best of one of their solutions; and rarely can they predict specific human responses to events."

The Need for Holism

An early contributor to the psychology and sociology of the management of change was Follet,[16] who interpreted classical management principles in terms of the *human factor*. Central to her thinking was that management must continually adjust to the *total* situation. Her suggested solution was that managers must handle the inevitable conflict in organizational settings by a combination of (1) domination, (2) compromise, and (3) integration. White and Lippitt[69] argued that a group of members work more efficiently under a democratic or socially oriented leader than under an authoritarian leader, which leads to the introduction of various social feedback survey techniques to ascertain employee attitudes to change. In general, motivation in relation to change seems to be understood as closely connected to Man's ability to accept and understand the implications of change. The connection between leadership style, motivation, and subordinates' and superiors' behaviour and action has been studied by many.[30, 70] Joynt[36] makes the innate observation that today's managers will have to understand their role and conduct their responsibilities under conditions of rapid and continuous change, and adjust their way of managing accordingly.

The fact that this component of management responsibility does have a profound impact on the way management research into the impact of change is carried out is clearly stated by Yukl:[71] "Leadership research has been characterized by narrowly focused studies with little integration of findings from different approaches. The research on leader power has not examined leadership behaviour except for explicit influence attempts, and there has been little concern for traits except ones that are a source of leader influence."

Yukl has further classified the necessary research efforts connected to such observations in two major subcategories:

> One line of research must treat leader behaviour as a dependent variable, and research must seek to discover *how the situation influences behaviour.* Role theory may be used to describe the process, with supplementary theories to identify key aspects of the situation that create demands and constraints on a manager. A major question is then the extent to which managerial work is the same or unique across different types of organization and levels of management.

> The other line of research must attempt to identify aspects of *the situation that is "moderated" by the relationship* of the leader traits or behaviour to leadership effectiveness. The assumption is that different behaviour patterns (or trait patterns) will be effective in different situations, and that the same behaviour pattern is not optimal in all situations. This is the approach that is normally called the "contingency" approach because the effects of leader behaviour are contingent on the situation and on the way the leaders perform.

We may from this distinguish between two types of situations: one in which changes are the results of forces outside their control, and the managers must *adjust* to these changes,[36] and the other where changes to some extent have to be promoted and *created* by themselves.[72] Modern societies offer numerous opportunities that require either adjustment to or creation of change or both.

Role Motivation

As already discussed, Miner[38] is one author who has been particularly occupied with *role motivation*. In his view role motivation theory "posits certain generalized role requirements characterizing managerial jobs …[and]…that motives matching these requirements will contribute to managerial success [in both value and reward terms]".[38] In Miner's opinion there are some particular motives that should be toward the top of a manager's preference or valence hierarchy. These motives are:

1. A favourable attitude toward those in positions of authority (especially superiors)
2. A desire to engage in competition (especially with peers)
3. A desire to assert oneself and take charge
4. A desire to exercise power and authority over others (especially subordinates)
5. A desire to behave in a distinctive and different way
6. A sense of responsibility in carrying out the numerous routine duties associated with managerial work

Although Miner admits that he has found the last three roles to be related to success less frequently, especially in professional organizations, he contends that the above motives are consistently associated with managerial success, and that they have been shown to precede and condition success. Other authors[59, 73] have supported Miner's view, contending that role motivation as an achievement-oriented "content" theory may well explain managerial behaviour and attitude at the work place. It may also be noted that although all these motives may be supposed to focus on the manager as a "leader", many of them also strongly stress the impact of the personal, "individual" motives of project leaders.

The Contingency Approach

The other way to regard managerial research in relation to change is to assume that it is the situation to which the manager is exposed and with which he or she interacts that defines his or her behaviour patterns. Many authors have argued that the classical approach of seeking a single universal theory of management and leadership, such as, for instance, "role theory", seems to have been replaced by these new *contingency theories*.[30, 35, 36, 70] These theories also seem to be well suited for explaining leadership responsibility in projects, with its constant need to fit in and react with its environment.

Initially, the contingency approach was developed by managers, management consultants and researchers who tried to apply the concepts of the major management schools to real-life situations. They found that methods highly effective in one situation would often not work in another.

Theories could therefore only be understood in the context of: "Results differ because situations differ." Hersey and Blanchard[35, 65, 74] developed a general leadership theory on the basis of such observations, which they originally called the "life-cycle theory of leadership" and then renamed "situational leadership theory". The theory explains effective leadership in terms of the moderating effect of one situational moderator variable on two broadly defined leader behaviours: *task behaviour*, which they defined as the extent to which a leader organizes and defines the role of followers by (continually) explaining what each person must do; and *relationship behaviour* as the extent to which a leader puts effort in maintaining personal relationships with followers.

A management theory which particularly emphasizes the implications of change and variations to organizations in general is then the already mentioned "contingency approach". By studying the consequences of change and the way change may be controlled in organizations, these theories of management, which are dependent upon the environmental situations in which they are applied, can be particularly rewarding for understanding managerial motivation as well. Darwin too, through his works on population ecology and his suggested "survival of the fittest", or "survival of the fitting" in the more modern expression, emphasizes the need for organisms to use all their resources to adjust to their environment in order to survive. Yukl[71] has described the motivational aspects of this under the common label "situational approach", contending that: "The situational approach emphasizes the importance of situational factors such as the leader's authority and discretion, the nature of the work performed by the leader's unit, subordinate ability and motivation, the nature of the external environment and the role requirements imposed on a manager by subordinates, peers, superiors, and outsiders." For Stoner and Wankel,[31] "the task of the managers is to identify which technique will, in a particular situation, under particular circumstances, and a particular time, best contribute to the attainment of management goals."

In contrast to the structural approach, with its emphasis on the interrelationships between parts of an organization, the contingency approach goes further by focusing on the detailed nature of the relationship between these parts. "It seeks to define those factors that are crucial to a specific task or issue and to clarify the functional interactions between related factors."[31] This "flexible" management approach makes the contingency approach particularly interesting in relation to unstable environments, which after all are one major characteristic of projects, at least in some of their developmental phases. Critics of the contingency approach argue that it does not incorporate all aspects of structural theories, for instance the earlier discussed "Systems Theory".[31] Others argue that it will never develop to a point at which it can be considered a true theory.[75]

The backbone of its approach, "it depends", seems to be highly applicable to the project environment, however, and should thus be a vital element in an analysis of project leaders' behaviour and motivation in projects.

Filley *et al.*[76] suggested four types of leader behaviour in this respect:

> *instrumental leadership* featuring the "planning, organizing, controlling, and coordinating of subordinate activities by leaders", and

> *participative leadership,* defined as the "sharing of information, power, and influence between supervisors and subordinates", and

> *supportive leadership,* defined as "behavior that includes giving consideration to the needs of subordinates, displaying concern for their well-being, status, and comfort, and creating a friendly and pleasant climate", and

> *achievement-oriented leadership* characterized by "leaders who set challenging goals, expect subordinates to perform at their highest level, continuously seek improvement in performance, and show a high degree of confidence that the subordinates will assume responsibility, put effort forth, and accomplish challenging goals".

The Irrationality of Man

However, as argued by Lewin[1] and later Rossvær,[77] there is probably no automatic correlation between human knowledge and human action, and Man is therefore not at all a rational being in all circumstances. And change in itself is not necessarily motivating. Stoner and Wankel[31] have identified three major reasons why organizational members may resist and be demotivated by change:

1. Uncertainty about the causes and effects of change
2. Unwillingness to give up existing benefits
3. Awareness of weaknesses in the change proposed

Carnall[78] has widened this scope by also introducing the effect of different practical techniques for planning, implementing and reviewing major organizational changes and how to cope with the pressure involved if it turns negative. Important for him is that leadership may be developed particularly well by learning from change.

Although the above findings are relevant arguments for both accepting change management to be instituted, and for not doing so, since human nature may be very unpredictable, we may argue that none of these studies have been applied to project settings, thus we can only assume the degree to which projects provide backgrounds for the development of particular managerial styles, or the degree to which managerial styles are congenital. But if such styles also change over the project lifetime, this could serve as a background for measuring the relative impact regarding variations in motivation due to different conditions prevailing in project work.

One important conclusion to draw after this is that managerial motivation in organizational life seems to be strongly connected to how leaders master and react to change. Many authors have also expressed the view that changes brought about by project efforts will particularly influence motivation, due at least to two factors:[73, 79, 80, 81]

a) change due to the *uncertainties* generated by project work
b) change due to the *opportunities* that project work creates

"Uncertainty" can be challenging and *motivating*, if kept at a manageable level, and it can be frustrating and *demotivating* if it creates insecurity and hostile atmospheres. "Opportunity" can be a driving and *motivating* force if success seems achievable, and it can be a distressing and *demotivating* factor if the perceived risks of failure and disgrace are excessive. By persevering with the opportunities, while maintaining understanding and incentives, and by reducing uncertainties, through clarification and conformity with agreed levels of performance, there seems to be general agreement among project experts that project members are able to comply with this by establishing certain "rules of the game", and thus increase their effectiveness and their sense of security despite the change-oriented environment projects create.

To project leaders the challenge of the change itself may therefore have particular motivational implications in relation both to the special way project work is conducted and to the special environment within which project work takes place.

THE MOTIVATIONAL IMPLICATIONS FOR THE PROJECT LEADER OF PROJECT "STRUCTURES"

> "The only purpose for which power can be rightly exercised over any member of a civilized community, against his will, is to prevent harm to others. His own good, either physical or moral, is not a sufficient warrant."
>
> (J.S. Mill, On Liberty, 1859)

To comply with the insecurity and instability prevailing in most efforts, project leaders generally establish different kinds of procedures and conformance rules. In many projects these rules even differ for each of the stages or phases through which their projects pass.[73, 80, 82]

Anderson and Woodhead[83] have suggested that projects may thus be defined by many "management decision processes" which can be gathered in a limited number of project phases, each having "its own specific problems, often calling for the management efforts of different groupings of professional and skilled staff. In addition, these phases are often separated physically and sequentially in time." They also add that "these natural disjointing features, however, are countered by the need for integrating [physical] flows of information and documents, as...[is]...indicated in each...decision process network".

Since projects comprise such a wide variety of methodological efforts, the procedures used are to a greater or lesser extent defined for each individual project, and also the performance levels expected from the participants – the project leader, the project team and other involved project bodies – in a set of specific rules and regulations. This "structure" of rules in use will then most probably have different motivational and demotivational implications for the project enactors, and particularly for the project leader, depending on how these rules match the direct or indirect levels of personal satisfaction and self-fulfilment, both in the short and the long term.

Burbridge[84] has argued that "it is during the conception of a project that the structure and systems are set up which will control [and help or hinder] the development of the project.... If this infra-structure [of the project] is not built on a logical basis from the very start of the project then chaos will ensue and the project will have no chance of success.... It is he [the project leader]...who will provide continuity and ensure that the momentum of the project is not lost." Although Burbridge has based most of these views on experiences from large construction projects in the United Kingdom, his opinions seem valid for many other types of projects as well.

It is also a fact that many of the practical problems related to this "structural" side of project management can be, and are, solved by relevant and continuously improved project planning and execution techniques and procedures. The rapid development of IT (Information Technology) and computer software for project planning and monitoring in these areas (such as PERT and CPM) has furthered the capabilities and opportunities of good project conduct. This field of managerial instruments has been expanded to cover other aspects of managerial work also, today generally referred to as the "use of quantitative techniques"; operations research (OR); or "Management Science". The latter term refers more specifically to the application of quantitative techniques to management problems. The terms tend to be used interchangeably, yet OR is more general and theoretical in its orientation, whilst management science is more application- and problem-oriented. The important issue is that such techniques may also strongly form the way the project leaders do their job.

The Feedback Notion

Porter[85] has stated: "what an organism senses affects what it does, and what it does affects what it senses". Forrester[86] developed a theory of "system dynamics" around this, which Cannon[86] many years earlier had introduced as the concept of "homeostasis", his definition being that "'homeostasis' [is] a state of disequilibrium within an organism which existed whenever internal conditions deviated from their normal state. When such disequilibrium occurred...the organism was motivated by internal drives to reduce the disequilibrium and return to its normal state. Inherent...was the idea that organisms exist in a dynamic environment and that the determining motives for behavior constantly change, depending upon where the disequilibrium exists within the system."

If such a dynamic interplay exists, interpreted in figure 4.2 as a feedback system between project structure and project managerial attitudes, and which becomes effective from the very beginning of the project process, then the project approach would increasingly cause certain attitudes to become typical for project leaders.

"Attitudes" are defined here as "the feelings and beliefs that largely determine how [people] will perceive their environment".[37] The willingness to match such characteristics is thus not only a function of managerial likes or dislikes, but also part of a self-regulating system that is hard to escape when adopted. The implications of the feedback system are that

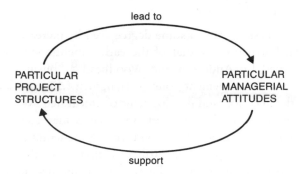

Figure 4.2 The feedback system between project structure and project managerial attitudes

should the feedback start to become negative, this could be an unfortunate and inescapable executing style for any project leader. As suggested by Elster,[40] "when change is the rule, norms emerge that regulate people's attitudes towards change". And as he also states, "people are [generally] more likely to be swayed by social norms than by means–ends considerations, simply because less is known about means–ends considerations". Since uncertainty about the goal attainment success is one of the "trademarks" of project work, this may well be an incitement for keeping to norms and rules rather than pursuing the project goal.

Bounded Rationality

Many authors have been occupied with this phenomenon, referring to it as cognitive "traps", and suggested ways of reaping the benefits of the *concentration,* and then simultaneously trying to maintain the necessary degree of *flexibility* that is normally required as well. Simon[88, 89] argued that concentration is a major reason why projects should be managed under some form of structure or organization. He used the expression *bounded rationality* to explain how the concentration of efforts within defined limits has obvious benefits. This can be applied to projects, and as such it will serve as one major reason why a deliberately organized project structure is the best strategy for motivating people. This is so because a concentrated project structure can limit both the burden of managerial strain and enhance the opportunities of reward by fully putting into effect the benefit of concentration on the "once-only" task normally existent in projects.

Integrative Efforts

The flexibility necessary can to some degree even be increased despite a bounded formal structure by that of the earlier mentioned *integrative* efforts. As argued by Anderson and Woodhead,[83] "business-oriented concerns and many management policies strengthen…linkages and focus attention on the need for, and development of, integrated systems". The need for integrative behavioural efforts in projects may stem from the *decoupling principle* introduced by Thompson.[90] Stinchcombe and Heimer[91] have developed this principle further, stating that "the more two activities are independent in detail, the more the combined authority for making adjustments in both activities will save time, cost and administrative headaches". Also Kolltveit[82] reaches the same conclusion in his study of large Norwegian offshore projects. This is also why managers have traditionally divided work into specialized functions or departments, increasing both their own and other's productivity and efficiency within organizations. The subsequent *coordination* is then the process of integrating the objectives and activities of the separate units in a systematic and orderly way in order to achieve the organizational aims efficiently. As stated by Stoner and Wankel,[31] "without such coordination, both individuals and groups will lose sight of their roles within the organization".

These principles of concentration and integration also coincide with the newer findings on what develops and nurtures motivation in organizations.[92] In a search for possible links between motivation and "structural" project efforts, it is therefore worthwhile to study which factors in particular enhance concentration and integration in project settings, and which factors do not.

The natural conclusion to draw from this seems to be that the literature clearly shows that structures of projects can create effects that make the *motivation* of project leaders increase. It is important, however, that this structure can also produce many *demotivational* stimuli if the feedback process between structure and attitude turns negative. This may end up both as short-term and long-term negative effects. It seems a reasonable concluding suggestion, therefore, that in order to administer a project properly it is necessary for effective project management to have both an understanding of which *structural* features support the managerial role at different steps in the development process of a project and an understanding of which *conditions* make motivation vary most significantly.

THE MOTIVATIONAL IMPLICATIONS FOR THE PROJECT LEADER OF "PROCESSES" PRESENT IN PROJECT WORK

"No good idea ever entered the head through an open mouth."

Menkus[93] suggested that, in addition to the project decision to change something, which according to him focuses mostly on personal desires based on impatience or need, and to structure the project environment properly, in order to seek stability and order, at least six other important aspects of running projects should be considered:

(1) competence and attitude of staff
(2) organizational relationships
(3) accuracy in defining project process and evaluating anticipated pro-product benefits
(4) accuracy in predicting time and cost
(5) quality of documentation, and
(6) follow-up evaluation of process effectiveness and factual product benefits

These aspects may well be said to be closely connected to the "processes" already observed from the literature as taking place in project development. Tichy and Devanna[94] found that in order to master the ongoing processes in complex organizations, there was a need for *transformational leaders* who had the following attributes:

(1) They saw themselves as change agents
(2) They were prudent risk takers
(3) They believed in people and were sensitive to their needs
(4) They were able to articulate a set of core values which guided their behaviour
(5) They were flexible and open to learning from experience
(6) They had cognitive skills and believed in disciplined thinking and the need for careful analysis of problems; and
(7) They were visionaries who trusted their intuition

These are aspects which may also be said to conform very well with the role expectations of project leaders. If project managers, or leaders, are to act and perform as "agents of change", as already discussed in the preceding chapter, or as transformation leaders as described above, they have to be given the opportunity to obtain the necessary self-motivation in order to take on the required leadership responsibilities. To accomplish this, however, demands a thorough understanding of what is particularly motivating and demotivating in such processes. This is a topic studied by Mintzberg.[95] Besides his conclusion that managers more often than not act irrationally and unsystematically, due to a constantly, often unpredictably, changing environment, he also found that he could classify external influences on organizations according to certain norms. According to him environmental factors imposed different and contradictory norms and goals on the organizational leaders. Such factors had a particularly destabilizing effect on managerial activities, and could not be overlooked if a fuller understanding of managerial actions and motivational reactions was needed.

The implications of this for project leaders are that both project external and project internal processes may be equally important for their motivation, and since projects tend to develop through phases that contain different issues which may be differently affected by the project environment, the implications of different management styles in different project phases must be essential.

It may be concluded after this that many fragments of organizational systems and structure affect the "process" responsibilities of today's project leader, and certain basic concepts for "process" management seem therefore particularly important. Much of this has to do with the human side of organizing, and includes keywords such as authority, influence, power, identification, loyalties and responsibility. As suggested by Massie,[68] earlier assumptions by economists about "economic man" have definitely evolved into a behavioural style commonly referred to as the "administrative man". This is a role function which focuses in particular on the need for satisfactory integration, system and structure, and demands organizational designs suited to management and administration of both "hard" structure and "soft" human preferences. According to Massie, one of the most important and controversial contributions of modern organizational theory involves this new concept of authority. The modern "administrators" of projects must establish managerial structures that ensure that they have an authority which is large enough to be self-motivated to formulate desirable and obtainable "technical" goals, whilst at the same time having a dynamic setting which gives them the possibility to motivate other people to accept and achieve these same goals. In this respect authority and leadership through some kind of established "process" functions seem necessary already at the very early stages of the project life-cycle development.

THE IMPORTANCE OF DECISIONS

"When all men speak, no one hears."

One topic which has gained increased attention in this respect is the development of different kinds of *decision-support* systems for managers. Originally such systems were mainly connected to technical issues, but this has become an area where advanced computer-oriented software has been increasingly user friendly. This growth in applications both in daily, operational, as well as more strategic, project work is impressive. For the management of projects, it brings in many new emphases, in the sense that whereas the earlier, typical tools for computer-aided project management concentrated on the straightforward planning and control of projects, the new tools also cover knowledge-bases, expert-systems, dynamic feedback systems, AI-systems ("artificial intelligence" systems) and interactive computer simulation systems which often perform advanced types of consequence analyses, interactively operating with the human mind. This has extensively broadened the scope of what can be measured and systematized in projects, and has also considerably widened the scope regarding the "interactive" tools that may exist or be applicable in the mastering of project "processes".

However, while these techniques have improved the project leader's ability to master many processes, there are still many areas of project work which have to rely solely on human judgment, where there are fewer tools available, as in fields where the qualitative aspects of the human factor dominate, such as creativity, human productivity, and knowledge-building. Here the judgment of the person in charge, the project leader, is crucial in terms of whether the performance will be successful or unsuccessful. This is particularly important because these seem to be the areas where there is perhaps the greatest possibility for variations in managerial motivation and demotivation.

Anderson and Woodhead[83] have identified twelve project management decision processes and their "decision process interfaces" concerned with manpower only, where the human mind is particularly effective in intuitively "understanding" process consequences. These also comprise factors that significantly impact on and change work effort and its effectiveness, and which therefore are a management responsibility to master. The factors may be classified into three main groups:[83]

1. Those intuitively affecting the physical environment in which the project work is to be performed.
2. Those which establish the best management environment under which constraints project work is to be performed.
3. Those which affect the mental hygiene and aspiration that basically form the individual's attitude and drive to work.

In order to accomplish this, Anderson and Woodhead have recommended a strong focus on "the changing requirements on a Management Information System through the different life phases of a project, together with the integrating Management Information System pressures that endure over the project's duration. In this way both the formal and informal aspects of the project manpower management process can be understood."

From the above it seems natural to draw the conclusion that the magnitude and practical application of different kinds of decision aids in project management efforts is an important issue to study, also in relation to possible motivational implications.

THE IMPORTANCE OF THE PROJECT SETTING

"The best way to make good friends is to be a good friend yourself!"

Once it was realized how important it was that the organizational setting was as flexible and "process"-oriented as possible, many scholars have produced different kinds of "guides" for making the organizational setting favourable for process management. The one thing which they all seem to have in common is that all managers have to understand and in some way make a controllable setting for the human resource component for benefits to be reaped and frustration and despair avoided. As McGregor[9] has argued, successful management depends significantly upon the ability to predict and control human behaviour. And as Morton[96] also claims, "the Project Manager must manipulate the technical elements through the human elements to obtain his project objectives".

Conflicting Interests

There are also, however, theorists who have come to less favourable conclusions about the potentially positive effect of planned organizational settings, even if the organizational climate is well cultivated. Reve and

Levitt[97] have, for instance, argued the possible development of special *conflicting psychological interests* between the parties involved in a project. Because a project is a special kind of common endeavour, as soon as the project is started the project leader and his or her environment may develop what they call *idiosyncratic relations*. The definition of such relations is that after a project has run for a while, it becomes more and more difficult for the client to change its enactors, especially the project leader. Similarly, the project leader is "locked" into the specific relationship of the project setting to a high degree. An idiosyncratic situation like this, if combined with opportunism, may create a "hold-up" situation where information can be strategically utilized to work against the interests of the parties involved.[97, 98] The parties are totally dependent on each other, but they may pursue their own interests to get as much as possible out of the contract or the project. In many cases, lack of trust is counteracted by the use of advanced scheduling, cost control and quality assurance systems.[97] The occurrence of this has been observed particularly well in large-scale projects.[99] Although such studies have not been applied to other types of projects, it is thought that the same relationships may well apply to projects in general. This is one of the reasons why the integration efforts in projects are often more complicated than integrative endeavours at similar hierarchical levels in the traditional line-organizational systems. This may well be situations creating demotivational attitudes and behaviour amongst project leaders.

THE IMPORTANCE OF THE PROJECT LEADER'S PERSONAL MOTIVES

"There is nothing so unequal as the equal treatment of unequals."

Since projects are organizations containing both well-identified "structural" components and well-known organizational "processes", this must have clear implications for the project leader's personal motives in projects. When the need hierarchy concept is applied to work organizations, the implications for managerial motivation become even more obvious. In addition to having responsibility, managers also have to create a "proper climate"[32] in which they can develop their fullest potential.

Hyman and Singer[100] stated that when the individual (such as a manager) takes his employing organization as a reference, and thus incorporates the operative goals of the company in his own, often self-established, role prescriptions, motivation will be enhanced. McGregor[9] too emphasized the importance of both the leader and the subordinates guiding and being guided by personal motives. The correlation between motivation and leader-member relations (together with task structure) were also central issues for Fiedler[101] and Hersey and Blanchard.[65] The work of Herzberg *et al.*[3] on employee motivation is also fundamental in this respect, due to the fact that the strongest criticism of their work has been that it mainly refers to managerial, professional, and upper-level white-collar employees. We may therefore assume that their findings on high "negative feelings" and high "positive feelings", referring to factors such as "maintenance" or "hygiene", and "motivational" factors, respectively, may be highly applicable to managers of projects. Nonetheless, it is worthwhile bearing in mind that their method of research has also been criticized for its lack of full "objectivity".[36]

What is particularly important, however, in the opinion of Steers[102] too, is that managers who have a high need for achievement, also tend *themselves* to be better performers. In general, there is evidence in the literature of a strong link between managerial motivation and managerial effectiveness[103] in many settings. Atkinson and Birch[104] and others also hold the view that healthy adults have a reservoir of potential energy which they make rational use of when desirable goals are attainable. This is carried further by Porter and Miles,[105] who have suggested that a systems perspective on motivation will be most useful to managers because it enhances effectiveness.

Morton[106] has argued that "attitudes will develop in any event. It would be beneficial if the environmental stimulant situation to be managed is done in such a way that a favourable attitude towards work, colleagues, and self would be formed."

Since this book focuses on the role of management and the motivation of project leaders, it seems appropriate to make reference to such theories which state that the "higher" needs for achievement, recognition and self-actualization may be expected to be activated when people have satisfied "lower" needs. Since managers generally are in positions where basic organizational backing can be assumed, or perceived, they also seem to have the good fortune of having the opportunity to fulfil higher needs.

THE IMPORTANCE OF POWER FOR THE PROJECT LEADER

> "Loose goat don't know how tie'goat feel, but tie'goat know how loose goat feel!"

Another specific aspect to be considered is the importance of *power* as a motivating force in project relations. "Power" is in this context defined as having "great influence, force, or authority".[6] The study of power motives in organizations can be dated back to the early works of Adler.[107] He believed that power was the major goal of human activity, and that a person's ultimate satisfaction comes with his or her ability to have influence over the environment. As already discussed, the need for power ("n Pow") is assumed to be one of the specific forces in the content theories.[41, 46, 49] Power and structure are strongly linked, as are power and motivation. The concept of power should be related to the concept of the legitimacy of power wielded:[108]

> Power is legitimate to the degree that, by virtue of the doctrines and norms by which it is instituted, the power holder can call upon sufficient other centres of power, as reserves in case of needs, to make the power effective.

In general, managers are often in a position to make changes because they are permitted a particular power base within their culture, and the discretion to make such changes as will serve the greater good of the society.[109] But Thomason[110] has also stated that, "their [the managers] remit...tends to run in respect of individual practices within the industrial organizations themselves". Yukl[71] states that "research on the use of different forms of power by leaders suggests that effective leaders rely more on personal power than on position power". But, as he contends, "position power is still important, and it interacts in complex ways with personal power...". Simon[88] proposed an "acceptance theory of authority", and stated the view that a communication carries authority only if the receiver accepts it. Thomason[110] states that "managers are often suspicious of...delegation [or participation] because of lack of trust and confidence in the wills and abilities of subordinates", and claims this to be one major reason why managers maintain personal power as most important for their managerial conduct.

Through their research, Steers and Braunstein[111] demonstrated that individuals with a high need for power or dominance tend to be better performers and tend to feel comfortable in supervisory positions. Power-oriented individuals were also rated by others as having good leadership abilities. One major reason for this is probably Davis and Newstrom's[37] claim that "power is the ability to influence other people and events", and that "power is earned and gained by leaders on the basis of their personality, activities, and the situations in which they operate".

They have also categorized power in four major types:

1. "Personal power", as the ability of leaders to develop followers from the strength of their own personalities. "They have a personal magnetism, and air of confidence, and a belief in objectives that attracts and holds followers."
2. "Expert power", also known as the authority of knowledge, and comes from specialized learning. "It depends on education, training, and experience, so it is an important type of power in our modern technological society."
3. "Legitimate power", also known as position power and official power, and which comes from higher authority. "It arises from the culture of society by which power is delegated legitimately from higher established authorities to others. It gives leaders the power to control resources and to reward and punish others."
4. "Political power", which comes from the support of a group. "It arises from a leader's ability to work with people and social systems to gain their allegiance and support."

From this one can clearly recognize that the two first issues of power are "individually" oriented, and the last two issues are related to a positional situation, such as that of being a project "manager".

Power and Performance

There are, however, many questions regarding the way power affects performance. The general agreement seems to be that while it is important to have a certain number of high achievers in managerial positions, an organization will not function effectively if it is staffed exclusively by those for whom achievement is the dominant motive. But, as generally contended, successful organization needs its share of take-charge types, people who are willing to specify organizational goals, and influence others to achieve them. This may be a paradox in today's organizational cultures, where wide participation in organizational decision making and extensive distribution of power are seen as mandatory for successful organizational performance. As Hunsaker and Cook[112] have observed: "Unfortunately, our society has backed away from acknowledging the legitimate value of power as a dominant personal motive. The stereotypical image of a power-motivated person is that of a cruel and self-serving tyrant, who uses tactics of force and coercion to manipulate others. Of course it's true that power can be wielded negatively. But there is an equally strong positive kind of power that is used by successful managers in whom the power motive has developed as a socialized need."

What seems obvious is that project leaders are in positions where the way they handle their power may be of great importance for the project work. Harrison[113] has suggested that power in projects should be measured as an "authority gap", and is crucial both in the project leader's overall effectiveness and as a means of dealing with conflict. In his opinion the project leader's limited authority, and his or her attempt to overcome it, are probably the biggest sources of conflict in project management. The reason for this is that both the client organization and the project leader's own organization generally have legitimate power within the project structure. The basis for the project leader's organizational power is the "ownership" of the project, and that for the client that they "own" the "need" and thus the rationale for the execution of the project. In effect, in many projects the project leader lacks sufficient formal authority and has to exert his or her leadership solely through *influence*. Morton[106] has stated that by recognizing the dynamic aspect of the project, the concept of centralization and power gains "special significance". In his view the project leader "is one of the few people to see the project from beginning to end, [and therefore] moves steadily to a more central and influential position [in the project]". This view is, however, disputed by Kerzner,[114] who argues that the amount of authority should vary with the amount of risk that the project leader must take; "formal authority is not a very effective means of motivating and controlling employees".

Despite the many aspects of power and authority in projects, it is a parameter which must play an important role in project management. The interrelationship between different kinds of "ownership" in project settings also strongly supports the notion that power is a very important element at different stages of a project's life, and must be reflected in the way the project "process" is planned to run. Most certainly, therefore, the presence and non-presence of power may cause variation in the motivation and demotivation of the project leaders.

THE MOTIVATIONAL IMPLICATIONS FOR THE PROJECT LEADERS OF PROJECT GOALS

There seems to be general agreement among practitioners and theorists alike that a desired change means that it should be possible to identify a *goal* to strive for, an *achievement* to work for and, more often than not, a *reward* to be expected when the task is completed. In addition, such aspects will by nature have special *motivational* implications for the people involved.[8, 9, 11, 41, 42, 45, 46, 51, 60, 102, 115, 116] Goal attainment is also the backbone of the "process" theories. Perhaps the best suggestion of the interactive importance of goals is that of Steers and Porter,[7] who claimed the following four factors to be mandatory for proper managerial conduct:

(1) needs or expectations
(2) behaviour
(3) goals, and
(4) some form of feedback

Purpose and goal, therefore, need to be objectively determined for any given behavioural situation, in terms of the objective situation corresponding to the hypothetical perception. This also corresponds with Steers and Porter's[7] argument for using goal-setting as one of the direct motivational approaches in a managerial context. Among other things, they state that "goals are the most immediate regulators of human action and are more easily modified than values of sub-conscious premises".

The Importance of Managerial Goals

The realization of the importance of managerial goals, i.e. the idea that managers need to have defined the specific aim of the effort, or the objective or deadline to meet in order to achieve more and increase their efficiency, is not new. The individual goal concept was the cornerstone of Scientific Management, founded by Frederick W. Taylor more than seventy-five years ago. About thirty-five years ago the idea of goal setting reappeared under a new name, management by objectives, or MBO,[117, 118] this time as a technique designed for managers. Later research[119] has also supported the contention that management generally reacts very positively to a goal-directed atmosphere.

Other researchers have revealed, however, that there are specific factors that interfere with the goal-directed efforts by managers, amongst them the influence of external constraints, and that goals set by superior management may contradict or conflict with the goals aimed at by managers and employees at lower levels. Culbert and McDonough[120] have discussed how individuals' self-interest and personal goals may affect organizational behaviour, and Lindblom[121] has used the term "preseptoric system" to describe situations where organizational culture has had a negative controlling ("indoctrinating") effect and restrained organization-al efficiency, because personal goals were not achieved. Joynt[36] has argued that new concepts of innovation and job satisfaction are in the process of replacing the older concepts of effectiveness and efficiency, and conse-quently the goal definition process may need to be changed too.

Changing Goals

The observation that goals within organizations may easily change is not new. Barnard[122] suggested early on that "once established, organizations change their unifying purpose. They tend to perpetuate themselves; and in the effort to survive may change the reason for existence."

Assuming that organizations and individuals pursue goals that are behaviourally connected, a focus on the organizational forces in goal-directed environments could yield valuable insight into motivational variations too. A considerable amount of research has in this respect been carried out that supports a link between goal-setting and action.[51] Researchers have also found that goal-setting not only affects performance levels but also affects satisfaction directly. Moreover, according to Ilgen and Hamstra,[123] when a situation is perceived as yielding less than what is expected, the individual will be less satisfied than when it is perceived as yielding the same as expected. When the situation is perceived as yielding more than expected, the individual will be more satisfied than when it is perceived as yielding the same as what is expected.

Goal-setting Theory

One particular theory, the "goal-setting" theory, developed around these thoughts. The theory has its basis in the "content" theories, or more specifically in the "expectancy" theories. Locke,[51] who is one of the early advocates of the goal-setting theory, even claimed the expectancy theories were too limited, since they are nothing more than a cognitive hedonist theory where the individual cognitively selects the course of action which he or she believes will lead to the greatest degree of pleasure and involve the least degree of pain. Latham and Locke[119] stated that goals for individual tasks help promote better individual responsibility and make it easier to appraise individual performance. The degree of task interdependence involved is one factor that should be taken into account. Others, such as Likert[124] and other human relations experts, have argued that the setting of group goals is beneficial because it promotes cooperation and team spirit.

To begin with therefore, management should not decide on their own goals, but should first collect adequate information about the desires and capabilities of lower levels, and then formulate final goals in a combined effort with their subordinates. This is also the essence of the MBO process. But the extent to which the final goal will conform well enough with the initial individual goals, has become a problematic issue, and many have therefore disputed the effectiveness of the MBO technique.

The conclusion after this is that at present opinions amongst researchers and practitioners seem to vary about how proper goal definitions should be made in order to appeal to managers. What is important, however, is that goals and goal attainment appear to be a very central issue in managerial efforts.

In goal-setting theory there are two cognitive determinants of behaviour: *values* and; intentions or *goals*. Thus the goal-setting model of motivation has five elements:

VALUES – which lead to – DESIRES – which lead to – GOALS – which lead to – PERFORMANCE – which lead to – CONSEQUENCES

Motivational Cause-and-effect Notions in Projects

The logical cause-and-effect notion above may be directly transferable to the project situation. Assuming that the project goal is a desired goal defined through values agreed on at the project selection, and that project selection is linked to the strategic objectives and plans of the organization that brings it forth, the project goal must be defined with care and its consequences continually reviewed by appropriate means in order to ensure lasting value over the project period leading to the desired final goal attainment. Further, as argued by Liberatore,[125] "projects may be required to maintain a threshold of competence in technologies of strategic importance, or to boost the morale of scientists". This focuses on the need for the project leaders to have a personal motivation associated with the project goal.

The Formulation of Project Goals

However, although the achievement of goals is one of the basic features of projects, and project work by definition implies a greater opportunity for the creation of strong goal direction, especially by the project leader, it does not necessarily follow that a project goal influences motivation by itself. A characteristic of the project goal is that whilst it is often very precisely tailored to the task at hand, it is in many instances also the case that it is formulated neither by the project team nor by the individual project leader. Far more frequently it is "handed over" to the project by somebody else, by some superior body, for instance the project client, and then expected to be fully understood, adopted and striven for by the project leader and his or her team, both undisputed and unchanged. According to Andersen et al.,[126] the latter may not happen; instead the outcome of a project goal procedure may equally well be that several, conflicting goals appear simultaneously. Even if this is not patently obvious "out in the open", such conflicting goals may well exist. Andersen et al. distinguish in this respect between "overt" and "covert" project goals, "overt" goals being the (official) statements of desired change, and "covert" goals being the undisclosed (private) objectives held by people who are involved in the project. Depending on the type of project and on the project environment, project leaders and project teams may then end up pursuing goals that contradict the desired main company goal for the project at hand.

The recommendation given by Anderson et al. is that "a project should [therefore] not just have technical goals. It must also have goals to change the culture of a company, to develop the people, systems and organization...." Although their primary statement is that "the main criterion for the success of a project is that it meets its objectives", this makes little allowance for the above description of their recommended, very diversified project goals. However, the need for clear, operational and mutually accepted goals, even in a "multiple goal" environment, is also advocated by various authoritative authors, such as McGregor,[9] Cummings,[30] and Mintzberg.[127]

Motivational Behaviour and Organizational Models

Joynt[36] found four different models of organization with different goals (i.e. effectiveness, efficiency, innovation and satisfaction). He interpreted this in the light of contingency theory and found that the managers showed different motivational behaviour according to the type of organizational model to which they belonged. Other researchers have found similar variations between stages of the progress of the project and its goal.[80, 128] Other theorists again have looked at other aspects of "goal-directed" behaviour. These include Festinger's Social Comparison Theory,[129] which advocates that goals have to be measured in relation to other goals put up by socially comparable individuals, or Attribution Theories where Fishbein's conceptual model of job attitudes[130] is central. However, these ideas have only widened the goal perspective and have not rejected goal-setting as an important motivational force.

Since so little disagreement with the goal-setting theory could be found in the prevailing literature on organizational behaviour, it seems logical to conclude that goals are important determinants of performance. It also seems reasonable therefore to consider project *goal* formulation and the subsequent attitude to the process of project goal fulfilment as a very important aspect that deserves further study in order to clarify some of the motivational and demotivational aspects of project management.

One of the most important conclusions to be drawn is that goal-setting theory suggests that the origin of behaviour, and of motivation, is to be found in the "mind" of Man. Despite the fact that this may mean that we are unable to "even see the goal toward which a purpose is guiding behavior until behavior does finally reach the goal state",[131] it will be argued here, as several of the above researchers have also confirmed, that goals and goal attainment should be possible to operationalize and study in the project context.

4.3.2   Findings from Recent Research

THE MOTIVATIONAL IMPLICATIONS FOR THE PROJECT LEADER OF THE PROJECT LIFE-CYCLE DEVELOPMENT

> "Conflicts mean people care! Conflict is a process to be managed, not eliminated."

The notion that project life-cycle development in itself has motivational implications was already contended in chapter 2.[80, 83, 133, 134] The theory set forth was that for the project leader the level of motivation varies both within each project phase and between subsequent project phases. The second suggestion was that there are important "whats" of motivation. These "whats" refer to the extent to which there are certain needs or causes, or *contents,* embodied in the "project approach" which affect the motivation and the demotivation of project leaders and make it vary from one project phase to the next in a specific, recognizable way. The third suggestion dealt with the "hows" of motivation, referring to the extent to which the project *process* itself generates stimuli to the project leader's motivation, which vary from one project phase compared to the next project phase.

From the above it may be assumed that motivational "needs" among project leaders are, on the one hand, "caused" and that these "causes" can be found and studied and, on the other hand, that the same "needs" can be expressed by certain "stimuli" which can also be found, particularly in project settings. A typical example of such logical connections existing is the allegation that when a project is on or ahead of schedule, this will generally be seen as positive project "progress" which "causes" "motivation" to develop. The motivational "need" particularly "stimulated" by this is "n Ach", or the "need for achievement". Contrarily, when behind schedule "demotivation" may well develop, and the "n Ach" is "not stimulated". Similar logic can be used for the fact that a project (generally) breaks new ground, and "causes" "motivation" to develop because this enhances the project leader's "capability" and competence. This should stimulate his or her "need for understanding" ("n Und").

Conditions for Causality

According to the positivist tradition,[135] there are three conditions for inferring causality:

(a) continuity between the presumed cause and effect,
(b) temporal precedence, in that the causes have to precede the effects in time, and
(c) constant conjunction, in that the cause has to be present whenever the effect is obtained.

In the very complex environment in which a project normally operates, the way to comply with these conditions would perhaps be to observe a limited set of factors where deductions of this kind can be obtained by studying either the cause or the effect aspect of the relationship. This is in line with the view of Baker,[61] who states that "failure [in project work] is often attributable to combinations of factors, but one or two factors are [often] predominant in causing the failures". This does not necessarily mean that causal patterns in projects are simple, which is why it is preferable that probabilistic causal models be used. Within projects it often happens that many causes create effects which are in turn causes giving rise to new effects. A change in a client's behaviour may, for instance, *cause* a change in the project leader's productivity, which again could *cause* reduced fulfilment of the project leader's desire to obtain personal prestige, which in turn *causes* a decrease in his or her motivation. To avoid such "multiple internal validity threats",[135] it is advisable that we look for only *two particular effects*, namely *first "level" motivational* effects and *first "level" demotivational* effects, both related to recognizable causes which may occur during the project process. This would exclude any possible feedback effects from "higher" or "lower" motivation or demotivation as causes in themselves of new effects on the project leader's behavioural patterns. Although this deterministic perspective contrasts with the freewill image of human behaviour, in which social phenomena are the product of personal decisions, it can be argued that the project approach restricts the full freedom of choice of the project manager to an extent which justifies a deterministic approach.

The Creation of Dynamic Processes

One approach settled for by this author was to assume that, by their nature, projects create *many* dynamic processes, and many of those are new to humankind and to managers because projects so often are unique, break new ground, and challenge established systems and structures. The project leader's responsibility is not to inhibit these processes, but to master them and make them challenging and to provide incentives. Many theorists have studied the effect *stimuli* generated by such change processes may have on human behaviour. The general conclusion seems to be that the processes following change need to be related to their consequences if behaviour shall be properly understood. Motivation therefore does not come mechanically; it has to be nourished and prepared for. This is also the essence of one of the leading organizational socio-techniques of today, that of "Organizational Development" (OD), which focuses on the need for full human participation in the change processes in an organization, of which the project effort must be the expression of a typical change effort.

Many modern developments in management thought have been aimed specifically at the problems of handling uncertainty and turmoil by means of relevant decision support. These are central issues in quantitative analyses, generally referred to as "operations research" (OR), when used as a management tool.

In a study carried out by this author,[39] a triangular approach was selected in order to study the phenomenon of motivational variations in time in project developments, with particular focus on the project leader. By using questionnaires, interviews and computer simulation modelling, it was possible to observe and study patterns of motivational reactions. Of particular explanatory value was the simulation model which was based on the principle of System Dynamics. The model challenged the traditional view of sequential developments in projects. This "Project Dynamic

Model" represented by its *basic feedback loop* in figure 4.3 describes projects as goal-directed, feedback-oriented, cause-effect structures.

The elements are also closely connected to the "elements of a project management system" discussed earlier, in the sense that the "project goal" equals the "purpose", the "discrepancy" complies well with the "strategy" notion, and the "achieving effort" is the "process" component. It is important that this feedback loop questions the notion of simple, linear, left-right causalities in nature. More often the right question to ask is of the type: "Does the population cause births, or do births cause population?",[136] with the answer being that birth and population may well be regarded as *one* phenomenon, which can be treated as only *one* factor to study. The basic project structure thus treats projects as goal-seeking efforts, but also as feedback-oriented endeavours. This stems from studies of literature on the subject of managerial goals,[117, 119, 124] and on the principle of "homeostasis" suggested by Cannon[87] and later formalized under the name of "cybernetics",[137] and converted to master industrial and social relationships by Forrester.[86]

The project loop starts out with a "project goal" affecting a "discrepancy" function, which reports back that there is a difference between the final desired outcome of the process and the existing status. This information causes the "discrepancy" function to send signals to the "effort to achieve goal fulfilment" function that more effort is needed. The plus sign indicates that the greater the discrepancy, the more effort is demanded. The "effort" function again affects the "discrepancy" function, which calculates a new difference between the desired goal achievement, the "project goal", and the present achievement. The minus sign indicates that the greater the effort the smaller the discrepancy. The "discrepancy" function in turn affects the "effort" function again, and this process continues until the "discrepancy" equals zero, or the "project goal" is fulfilled.

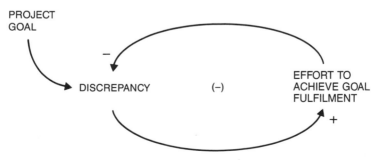

Figure 4.3 The basic project feedback loop

The total loop is "negative", or "goal seeking", implying that the process automatically terminates to zero activity when the desired goal is reached.

In System Dynamics this loop belongs to the class of loops that reach a certain level and then stop. Other loops are "positive", in the sense that they continue indefinitely if isolated or undisturbed by other forces, e.g. the loop for "birth" and "population" in which the two components keep on interacting positively with each other and forever growing if nothing intervenes to stop the process, such as for instance famine, birth control or other human interference. Loops can also have only negative interactions, such as, for instance, a loop combining "motivation" and "productivity". A decrease in "motivation" would presumably negatively affect "productivity", which in turn may negatively affect "motivation" and so on. Such processes will eventually stop, either because of no "motivation" or no "productivity", or both. Such loops are, naturally, closely related to the former goal-seeking loops, in the sense that by changing "motivation" to the opposite, "demotivation", the loop actually becomes a negative loop and will in the end terminate if nothing else intervenes to affect the two components or variables.

A total project dynamic model[39] with more than one hundred interconnecting elements of the above type produced a motivational variation over the lifetime of a general project as shown in figure 4.4. The most important conclusion drawn from this is that many motivational components have a discouraging development during many of the project phases, leaving the project with many types of social behavioural difficulties for quite a long time. This is particularly well demonstrated in

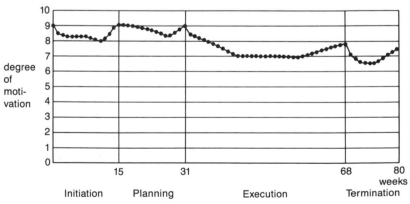

Figure 4.4 "Weekly" representation of the project manager's motivational level as obtained by model simulation

figure 4.4 in which the basic pattern is that there is a relatively high resultant managerial motivation early on in the project, slowly entering a more demotivating development situation and passing through a minimum during the execution phase, followed by a certain increase in total motivation when the project nears its end. A "hammock-shaped" development in each phase is also clearly demonstrated. Since each component behind this motivational development are known in the model, this also implies that those parts of the model which describe causal relationships and indirectly portray motivational stimuli to a high degree may *reflect the most important components of the motivation and demotivation of project leaders.* From this the "forces" that appeared to dominate were found to be the following:

1. The desire to "progress" and "achieve".
2. The desire to be more "capable" in doing the requested work.
3. The desire to "avoid rework".
4. The desire to be "trusted" by one's own superiors.
5. The desire to attend to "new" things and to maintain a sense of curiosity.
6. The desire to achieve "milestones" along the way toward the final goal.
7. The desire to avoid too much "mending" of earlier mistakes.
8. The desire to be self-"confident".

Factors Causing Managerial Motivation in Projects

In the following paragraphs each of the above "forces" are identified more closely, and this identification is also supported by first-hand knowledge of practical project management and research findings[39, 138] in the sense that the motivation or "will" related to project "progress", own "capability" ("skill development"), and "trust" ("superior's role") is directly mentioned as causes of motivational change, while motivation related to the discovery of "rework", to own "confidence", to reaching "milestones", to "mending" incomplete performance, and to experiencing "newness" and innovation may well be said to be indirectly observed.

For the purpose of differentiation, these eight motivational sub-factors or special causes of motivation were divided into two groups:

1. Predominantly *long-term* motivational causes, and
2. Predominantly *short-term* motivational causes.

The four in the first group are:

Progress-will, which was defined as a sub-component directly connected to the general achievement over the whole project period. This was mainly based on the research of McClelland *et al.*[139] on the need for achievement, or "n Ach", in organizations. In their opinion, which is typical of the Need Theories of Motivation, the high need for achievement is characterized by:

(1) A strong desire to assume personal responsibility for finding solutions to problems,
(2) A tendency to set moderately difficult achievement goals and take calculated risks,
(3) A strong desire for concrete feedback on task performance, and
(4) A single-minded preoccupation with task and task accomplishment.

Usually, the project leaders seek to obtain a continuous picture and feedback about the project's development. The nature of projects and the system of rewards for achievement make project progress toward its final goal an item that orients the leader toward achievement. The model outputs confirmed that "progress" is an important motivating factor for project leaders. There seems undoubtedly to be a positive relationship between project progress as it is perceived and the project leader's motivation.

Capability-will, which in the model was the direct consequence of learning. Its root is mainly in the Reinforcement Theories of Motivation. Social scientists suggest that learning can be defined as "a relatively permanent change in behavior that results from reinforced practice or experience".[140] It is assumed that projects are endeavours where productivity rates usually improve with practice, in which case – according to Starr[141] – the equation for the learning curve is:

$$T(n) = kn^{(1-\beta)}$$
where
$T(n)$ = cumulative time to make n consecutive units
k = time required to make the first unit = 1
n = the number of units made
β = the learning coefficient, $0<\beta<1$

Such a curve approaches the typical "plateau of productivity" at which the learning process eventually levels off. Although several authors[141, 142, 143] take the view that learning models suffer from many flaws, is important that Starr[141] concludes that "in project planning, the learning model has introduced predictive ability." He further maintains that the learning function should match the specific situation. The general "learning curve" approach was adopted for the simulation model, and the database material provided the input parameter that allowed the learning curve to represent the "capability-will", thus assuming a positive relationship between actual project progress, which is the real basis for learning, and project leader's motivation.

Rework-will, which here was taken to be a function of "aversive stimuli". In contrast to the use of positive reinforcement, aversive stimuli are the means by which organizations motivate individuals to stop a particular type of behaviour that is not desired by the organization and turn to the more desired type of behaviour. Research in this area is often referred to as "Attribution Theory".[144] Attribution theory, which is part of the Cognitive Theories, attempts to explain:

(1) how people make inferences about causes of their own and other people's behaviour, and
(2) how they act upon those inferences.

Although the theory was developed mainly for the performance of subordinates,[145] it was thought that it could be applied to leaders who, through their own observations (and also through indications by their own superiors, such as the client), adopt attributional remedies when they notice that they commit errors in their task performance. Leaders are also likely to attribute the causes of failure to inadequate internal motivational factors.[146]

The simulation model assumed such a link, and the "rework-will" was taken to be a limited function of the "amount of the accumulated rework discovery". "Limited" function means that if rework becomes extensive, project leaders might take a more indifferent attitude to it and thus respond with less attributional eagerness. The main cause-effect relationship adopted for the model was, however, that there is a positive relationship between the total rework discovery, and the project leader's demotivation, i.e. more rework leads to reduced motivation.

Trust-will, by which was meant the client's or the superior's confidence in the project leader's ability to deliver the desired output. It was thought that the need for affiliation ("n Aff"), the need for autonomy ("n Aut"), and the need for power ("n Pow"), are all affected by this function. They all come under the "Need Theories" of motivation, which assume that individuals are "wanting" creatures, motivated by a desire to satisfy certain specific types of needs.[8, 9, 19, 45, 46]

In the model the project leaders' need for approval and reassurance, "n Aff", their need for controlling their own pace, "n Aut", and their need to influence others and control their environment, "n Pow", have been combined into one parameter, in the sense that if "trust" declines, the reallocation of needed resources to the project become hampered, and thus all the above desires would be adversely affected. In the model it was assumed therefore that there is a positive relationship between parameters that express superiors' trust in the project leader and the project leader's motivation, i.e. more trust leads to higher motivation.

The four in the second group are:

Newness-will, which is a sub-component that was not only closely connected to achievement, but also to curiosity, creativity and similar attitudes. Steers and Porter[32] suggest that achievement and entrepreneurial success are often closely associated. Characteristic of such behaviour is a high effort toward personal accomplishment and improvement. The task accomplishment was also tied to short-term feedback on performance. This is also the essence of Expectancy Theory, where motivation, or the force to perform, is a function of:

(1) the perceived probability (expectancy) that a particular effort will lead to the achievement of a certain performance level, and
(2) the valence of this performance level.

The Valence–Instrumentality–Expectancy, or "VIE",[11] states that motivation is a combined function of the individual's perception of the desirability of outcomes that may result from performance. Expectancy can then be described as a probabilistic notion ranging from 0 to 1. It is important also to note that Vroom has defined valence as "perceived desirability".

The simulations showed that there was a strong tendency to indicate high motivation at the beginning of each project phase. This may well be rooted in a desire to accomplish new things, and thus to coincide with a special "will" in leaders to solve the new and challenging problems that usually prevail in projects. We may therefore assume a positive relationship between the newness-effect in projects, and the project leader's motivation, i.e. the more innovation the higher the motivation.

Milestone-will, which was a sub-component closely connected to goals and goal setting. "Goal-Setting Theory" is a special branch of the Cognitive Theories of Motivation, which in contrast to Expectancy Theory advocates that harder to achieve goals (with lower expectancies) lead to higher performance than easier goals (with high expectancy). Two cognitive determinants of behaviour are identified in goal-setting theory: values and intentions (goals). According to Locke,[51] the most fundamental effects of goals on mental and/or physical action are of a directive nature. Goals guide people's thoughts and overt acts to one end rather than another in a sequence which briefly goes through the identification of values, emotions and desires, intentions (goals), responses and performance, and consequences, feedback, or reinforcement.[32, 116]

The model simulation showed that project leaders tend not only to indicate high motivation at the beginning of each project phase, but also toward the end of each phase. This can be taken as a reflection of a goal-attainment interest, and was used to construct the "milestone-will" parameter in the model. This assumed that there is a positive relationship between the achievement of intermediate goals in projects and the project leader's motivation.

Mending-will, which was defined for the model as a motivational sub-component directly connected to the amount of rework discovered. In addition to the long term effect of discovered rework described under "rework-will", it was also thought that rework discovery has a short-term effect. This effect was more dependent on the relative change in the amount of rework per time unit, in the sense that by looking back to see what happened before, project leaders get a basis for judging the present achievement. Theories which have such "historical" components generally belong to the "Drive Theories". Drive theories assume that decisions concerning present behaviour are based in large measure on evaluation of the outcome of past behaviour. This position was first elaborated by Thorndike[56] in his "law of effect", while the term "drive" was first introduced by Woodworth.[57]

To some extent the "Social Comparison Theory" could also be used in this context. Although this theory is mainly used to evaluate individuals' perception of inequality with other individuals,[129] the concept is based on a general equality formulation in which it is desirable to mend undesired inequality.

Since rework is a factor than can be observed and compared over time, and rework presumably is an undesired situation which ought to be mended, it became logical that the "mending-will" was a factor for inclusion in the model. It was thus assumed that there is a negative relationship between relative rework discovery over time and the project leader's motivation, i.e. the more immediate rework discovered, the lower the immediate motivation.

Confidence-will, which was a sub-component connected to the self-perception of performance. Many writers have argued that employee perceptions of their own competence and self-esteem play a crucial role in motivation and work performance.[147, 148, 149] "Employees with a high degree of self-confidence and self-esteem are more likely to internalize high performance standards, have greater expectations about their own performance and show greater willingness to put forth effort on challenging tasks."[46] This behaviour is described in Steers and Mowday's article, "The Motivational Properties of Tasks",[150] where the basic sequence is that the individual attempts to identify a cause or causes consistent with the event itself. This involves reasoning backwards from the observation of the event to a cause or set of causes that led to the event. While the cognitive processes that are involved in forming attributions flow from an event to an inferred cause, the process of forming beliefs resulting from the attribution flows in the opposite direction, from inferred cause to the event.

It was thought likely that such attitudes could well develop in projects, where events and causes related to perceived progress compared to planned progress are easy to observe. It was therefore assumed that there is a positive relationship between the "perceived-on-planned" progress and project leaders' motivation, i.e. the more the project progress is perceived to be equal to or ahead of the planned progress, the greater the motivation.

The output of the model simulation was not limited to presenting only the above combined level of motivation. Figure 4.5 presents separate curves for the level of motivation for the two groups (1) "predominantly long term motivational sub-components", and (2) "predominantly short-term motivational sub-components". Together with the total, or combined motivational level (since the "motivation" in the model is a multiplicative function), this gives a development as shown in figure 4.5.

The figure clearly reveals that the two groups of motivation have quite different development patterns. The "long-term" motivation shows a steady decline from the start of the project Planning phase (at around Time = 3) and until the last part of the project Execution phase (at around Time = 14). From there on the motivation "oscillates" to some degree, maintaining the relatively low value it has reached at this point in time in the project effort. On the basis of this we may suggest that from a "leader" viewpoint the project effort does not necessarily end up as a motivational instrument, in the sense that as a leader the "long-term" implications tend to be more important than the "short-term" developments. The short-term motivation is also more varied, maintaining a good and high level throughout the project lifetime, with occasional high peaks at the start and end of each project phase.

Simulated Managerial Response to Motivational and Demotivational Forces

We may conclude from this that it is the personal, individual, "short-term" motivation that really encourages the project manager and which gives him or her the real stamina to continue with the project effort despite the setbacks experienced by the increasing rework discovery and faltering trust.

Expressed in very general terms, the project process seems to *demotivate* the project manager as a "leader", but to *motivate* him or her as an "individual".

This is a very important observation, which gives a very special

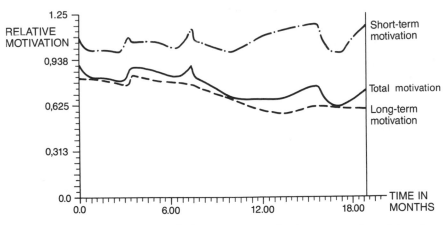

Figure 4.5 Long-term and short-term motivation as produced by the model simulation

This is a very important observation, which gives a very special characteristic of project work and its managerial implications. The main conclusion is that the motivation of the project leader varies in different ways and for different reasons in the different phases of a project's development. From this it seems natural to identify specific causes of motivation, together with possible motivational stimuli prevailing among project leaders in project settings. It is clear that this simulation model is built on a cause-effect notion, it is predominantly motivational *causes* that we are able to identify directly. Indirectly, however, these causes lead to motivational stimuli, as already suggested when defining them. For instance; "progress-will" may well be connected to "achievement" ("n Ach"), "capacity-will" to learning or a desire to understand ("n Und"), "trust-will" to a desire to maintain good relationships with authorities and other influential people ("n Aff"), and so on. A confirmation of a hypothesis about "causes" for the motivation of the project leaders also indirectly points to the fact that particular motivational "effects" prevail in project settings. By preparing projects so that important causes for motivation are present, one should be able to produce better settings for successful project performance at the managerial level.

That this is a practical possibility can also be confirmed by integrating some of the existing theoretical views on the motivational forces within the "whole person". A simplified drawing of such relationships is shown in figure 4.6.

The conclusion we may draw from this is that project leaders show behaviour which can be directly led from the particulars of the project setting, and that these particular reactions comply well with prevailing motivational theories.

Applying an operationalized, algebraic expression for testing such hypotheses based on the model findings, using a conservative rule of a 5 per cent absolute difference in degree of influence of the same motivating cause as a prerequisite for declaring that a significant difference exists, the results displayed in table 4.2 were obtained.

The general conclusions drawn from this were that when one motivational or demotivational cause has one particular degree of influence in one project phase, the same motivational or demotivational cause has a different degree of influence in the succeeding project phase. This statement clearly points to the possibility that individual project work and project management are better understood when such frequency and magnitude of realizing the variations in causes in the general project context.

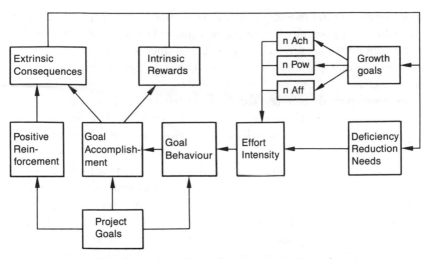

Figure 4.6 Suggested combination of some motivation theories

PROJECT INITI- ATION	PROJECT PLANNING	PROJECT EXECUTION	PROJECT TERMINA- TION
Newness		Newness	
		Newness	
	Milestone	Milestone	Milestone
	Confidence		
		Progress	Progress
	Rework		
	Capability		
Trust	Trust	Trust	

Table 4.2 The motivational causes from the model simulation that most significantly dominate and vary from one project phase to the next

Conveyed Managerial Response to Motivational and Demotivational Forces

An additional source of information is to interview project leaders about their motivational reactions at different stages of a project's development. According to Boyd et al.,[151] "knowledge, opinions, motivations, and intentions are usually not open to [simple] observations as for instance in questionnaires (and models)", in the sense that (1) the interview offers a much better opportunity for sample control, and (2) an interview offers far better opportunities for including in-depth and complex questions and answers. Strong proponents for the "interview approach" are, among others, Glaser and Strauss,[152] and Rose.[153]

In this respect an interview sequence covering thirty Norwegian project leaders was performed by this author in 1988– 1989,[39] and the material gave many confirmable clues as to which motivational reactions seem to prevail in project settings.

One first vital observation from this material was that the majority of the interviewees revealed very high levels of enthusiasm about the project they described, which resulted in a form of presentation that encouraged very sensitive information to be conveyed both about other people and themselves, and only occasionally did they warn that what they were telling should not go any further. In the case of some project leaders one could observe that this high enthusiasm could in fact have been a drawback for the project effort, in the sense that by pursuing very *"personal"* *preferences,* they indirectly ruined good plans and complicated the project execution. A conclusion that may easily be drawn from this is that when we take on a project duty, we tend to live out our real feelings and personality, and that the way the project leader conducts his or her job is a very subjective matter. For the purpose of investigation this was very fortunate, in the sense that true information on motivational issues was really brought out into the open.

Another important observation was that the project leaders were also very eager to inform about how important they were *personally* for the success of the project. Even in projects where the number of participants was quite sizeable, they generally referred to "me" and "I" far more often than "we" when successful decisions were drawn or important activities were performed. Often they gave special mention to their success as diplomats, while this indirectly described themselves as very cunning manipulators. If setbacks occurred, however, they almost without exception blamed someone else. It is also interesting to note that many mentioned which "important" people they communicated with while performing their job, as a means of enhancing their own status. This "networking" also seemed to have lasting effects long after they had terminated their projects, and thereby gave an important and deliberate "value-added" aspect to the assignment.

A general feature was that of high creativity when problems arose, not only in the early stages of the project work, but also when new and critical problem solving was demanded during later project stages. Many project leaders saw this as basic to their personal development and to strengthening their self-esteem. Quite a few of them actually saw the freedom to take risky decisions as a personal right embodied in the assignment. We may therefore assume that the project challenge, although in different forms, is always a central issue for their motivational reactions.

What was perhaps more surprising was that many of the highly experienced project leaders had simplified and often unclear ideas as to how they would define the project concept and its formal procedures at a level that would be satisfactory for other participants. When they themselves had got the project idea "under their skin", they felt content, and used most of their energy in conveying to the rest of their staff the aim of the effort and its importance. For this reason many problems in the detailed work of their projects were forgotten but arose at a later stage and caused unnecessary problems which they themselves took little blame for. We can most probably regard this concentration on "strategy" matters as a strong need to "simplify" the project effort for their own benefit, but which thereby results in a failure to keep track of the important detailed "process" work which is also of crucial importance for successful project execution.

Another interesting topic was that of the external environment. The majority of the project leaders expressed an "aggressive" attitude toward the project environment, regarding it with a certain suspicion and anticipating it to be "hostile". This attitude seemed to help them to fight their projects through, to protect themselves and to use "questionable" methods in certain circumstances. This they defended as a prerequisite for project success.

Although only ten per cent of the interview base were women, it is noteworthy that female project leaders were more cautious about describing incapabilities among their co-workers, and instead blamed setbacks on the "system" or themselves. They, however, were equally eager to achieve success, though with a tendency to "give up", take "sick leave", etc. if they had to fight too hard to get their way.

As with the simulation model approach, diagrams comprising the different motivational reactions for the interviewed project leaders was constructed.

The four diagrams (figures 4.7–4.11) are typical for the findings. In each diagram, the frequency of different kinds of "needs" is represented relative to the total number of statements mentioning stimuli which are thought to support the prevailing need, as extracted from each interview for each project phase. (Example: If 100 "stimuli" are recorded and found to relate to one particular project phase, and 60 of these can be classified as affecting the need for achievement, or the "n Ach", the result is a 60 per cent representation of the "need to Achieve". One statement can contain stimuli supporting more than one class. Each diagram expresses the average figure for all interviews.)

The two shades in the diagrams express the extent to which a need is classified by the project manager as satisfied or not, i.e. whether it stimulates the motivation (no shadow) or is felt to be demotivating ("black" shadow). The sum of motivational and demotivational influences gives the total curve, or the total motivational influence. In the diagrams the profile of the needs that according to the interviews are best stimulated in each phase is shown, grouped in "personal"-oriented needs and "leader"-oriented needs. Figure 4.7 shows how this is divided in the project initiation phase.

The Project Initiation Phase

The most outstanding feature of this diagram for the first project phase, the initiation phase, is the dominance of the "personal" motives stimulated in this phase, particularly the "n Und" (the need to understand), the "n Ach"(the need to achieve), and the "n Exh"(the need to "exhibit" oneself). According to the diagram, the majority of the project managers seem to find few reasons to be stimulated as a typical leader in this phase but are

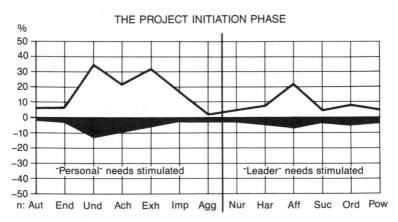

Figure 4.7 Frequency distribution of needs influenced during project initiation using Murray's classification

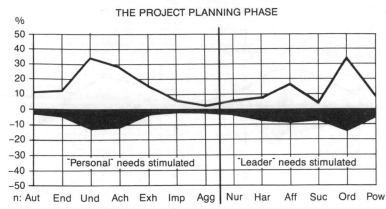

Figure 4.8 Frequency distribution of needs influenced during project planning using Murray's classification

instead very occupied with personal achievement, understanding (the project or the problem), and enjoy being at the centre of attention. We also can see that except for the fact that some felt lack of problem understanding, few demotivating stimuli are mentioned.

Compared to this, the profile of the needs that are most influenced during the project planning phase is shown in figure 4.8.

The Project Planning Phase

Compared to the profile describing the project initiation phase, changes have taken place. Although "n Und", "n Ach" and "n Aff" (the need to affiliate) still show high relative importance (by adding the positive "motivational" impact and the negative "demotivational" impact), "n Ord" and to some extent also "n Pow" are now the strong representatives of stimuli. These are needs which are thought of as being more "leader"-oriented. The natural interpretation of this is that a shift towards control and decisiveness and creating or maintaining an organized environment are important needs for many project managers, and are those which mostly stimulate their leadership attitude. Noticeable, too, are the black shadows in "n Und", "n Ach", "n Aff", and "n Ord", implying that these needs are not necessarily felt to be satisfied, so that they should also have demotivational impacts on the performance of the project manager.

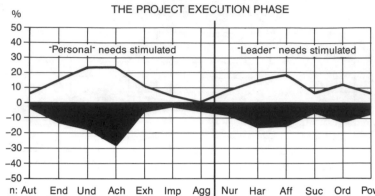

Figure 4.9 Frequency distribution of needs influenced during project execution using Murray's classification.

The Project Execution Phase

In the project execution phase a slightly different picture emerges, as shown in figure 4.9.

In this phase the profile is more "balanced", in the sense that, for the majority of project managers, both "personal" and "leader"-oriented needs seem to be influenced. The increasing presence of black shadows for many needs clearly points to the fact that those needs are now not satisfied, implying that demotivation is developing. As for particular needs, the "n Ach" and also "n Und" dominate among the "personal" needs, while "n Har" (the need for harmony) and "n Aff" seem most frequently mentioned as "leader"-oriented needs necessary to satisfy. From this pattern several interpretations can be given:

- One is that the characteristics of this project phase seem to resemble those of the project initiation phase, in the sense that "personal" motives start to regain their importance, and the "leader"-oriented preferences which were central in the project planning phase are now less predominant.
- Another interpretation is that the project execution phase seems to stand out as a "trouble" zone for many project managers, with many needs dissatisfied, and thus enhanced demotivation. This is an interpretation which coincides well with other findings related to research literature in general on this topic.
- A third possible interpretation is that many project managers in

this project phase are in a confusing situation where the "leader" demands are to keep order, system, harmony, team collaboration, and risk minimalization, while personal preferences are to be active and willing to take risks in order to be an achiever (which in projects may be obtained by good project progress through the accomplishment of generally difficult tasks), to endure and to make strong effort to understand the problem, or the problems, surfacing when executing the project work ("n Und"). These different types of needs may well contradict each other, and create stress, confusion and demotivation.

The Project Termination Phase

Finally, the project termination phase shows these variations.

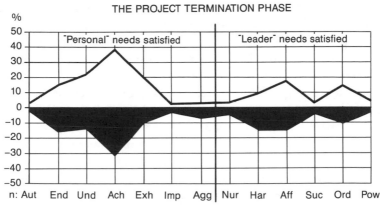

Figure 4.10 Frequency distribution of needs influenced during project termination using Murray's classification

In diagram 4.10 we find to some extent the same need patterns as in the project execution phase, perhaps with relatively more weight on "personal" needs similar to the project initiation phase but with a relatively more pronounced lack of need satisfaction. The same interpretations as earlier may therefore be used, and with the conclusion that frustration and demotivation among most project managers is high. We may notice that besides the managerial need for affiliation, "n Aff", "n Ord" and "n Har" are increasing their relative importance as was typical for the project planning phase, which should imply a desire towards a more "leader"-oriented behaviour towards project termination, although the signals indicating this are not unanimous. Among "personal" needs the stronger representation of "n End" is of importance, perhaps indicating a tendency to keep on with the work, or prolong the project, in this phase.

The complete findings from this analysis[1] revealed that there are many stimuli affecting the project manager's motivation, and these seem to vary between the project phases. It appears, too, that demotivation is an issue that must be handled carefully in the management of projects. For example, the need for an organized environment is clearly a project planning issue, and when moving into project execution it is "affiliation", "nurturance" and "harm avoidance" which are comparably the more dominating leader-oriented stimuli. Comparably, the "need for achievement" through "endurance" is the most important as regards personal stimuli. This may imply that a "soft" or influencing approach to problem solving is more typical for the majority of the project leaders (of today), and that rigorous monitoring and the use of power as a means of obtaining project success are less used, or felt to be less applicable* at this stage.

Instead the achievement of personal development and excellence scores high, implying that we tend to avoid personal misfortune through the project assignment and seek stimuli which promote personal success. One important observation is that the need for exhibition, or the desire to be recognized and to get attention, seems highly pronounced in the project initiation phase. From this we may draw the conclusion that it is the "personal" need for being identified with the possible project success that dominates early and late in the project effort. This predominance of "personal" stimuli also in the project termination phase points to the importance of nurturing personal preferences in the project completion stages.

It is, however, worthwhile mentioning that the findings clearly show that the project execution phase seems to have comparatively fewer stimulating effects than the other project phases. This is important, because although this phase generally dominates in size and resource expenditure, it may be that the real challenge, the inspiration and motivation to manage and lead projects come from the other project phases.

Conclusively, we may say that:

---

* This is an argument closely related to "western" cultures, where "team performances" have been a central issue since Simon (1957), Herzberg et al. (1959), Thorsrud (1983) and many others began to research and develop theories around it. The author's own experience from projects in other cultures, for instance in developing countries, shows less evident team-dependent behaviour for projects. Even very "Theory-X"-related project management styles (McGregor 1960) were reported by some of the interviewed project managers to produce quite successful performances in certain cultural environments.

During project *initiation*, the majority of the project managers are predominantly occupied with strategic choices. They are also particularly eager to *achieve*, to *understand*, to *affiliate*, and to *exhibit* or present themselves to others. This appears to be a consequence of the self-attention they experience when they are assigned, or "promoted", to be the responsible person for the project. A high need for achievement, or "n Ach"-value, already at this stage pointed to the tendency for project managers in general to be typical "achievers", and the fact that there is a link between the project manager's promotion and the acknowledgement of or belief the superiors have in his or her ability to do the assigned tasks successfully. Of particular interest should be the high need to "understand" and to be "impulsive", in this phase supporting the notion that project managers should be subjected to their project responsibility as early as possible in order to enhance their creativity and to get their projects "under their skin".[20, 82] The most prominent "leadership" features in this phase are accordingly their need to be *distinctive* and to *compete* for their project.

During project *planning*, most project managers seem to be concerned as to how they should manipulate and control people and the environment. They seek *order* and organized structures around themselves. Their need for "taking charge", to "achieve", to "endure", and for "autonomy" all point to a desire to "do it their way". This may well be a consequence of the way that project planning is typically promoted, with specific rules and regulations for the planning process, often enforced by very strict planning techniques. These techniques demand very orderly environments and attitudes, which is probably the reason why the need for autonomy, the need to express power and to take charge score high compared to other need factors.

During the project *execution*, a mixture of personal preferences and leadership-oriented preferences characterized the picture, with the "own-behaviour"-factor, "n Ach", dominating to some extent. But also the need for and the occupation with *endurance*, "n End", and *understanding*, "n Und", score high. Of the factors that describe "leader" attitude, *harm avoidance*, *affiliation*, and *nurturance* show high values together with a high desire for *succourance* compared to the project termination phase. This may be a consequence of the way projects are normally executed, with a generally sharp focus on the person in charge, the project manager, and a strong need for him or her to make the team function and contribute. The high pressure on the individual makes the project managers very occupied with their personal responsibility, which may also be the reason for the high values observed for the need to "understand" and to "take charge" compared to these needs in the last project phase.

The findings also reveal an increasing concentration on needs that are negatively affected, in particular the project manager's need for achievement, harmony, affiliation and understanding. But also "n End", "n Nur" and "n Ord" are negatively affected. This is likely to be an expression of increasing dissatisfaction with forces or "causes" which the project leader feels he or she cannot escape, and which are hindrances to better *achievement* imposed by somebody else (the client or other stakeholders), or in some cases revealed by the project leaders themselves through their own lack of skill or ability to do the job. It is also important that in general they feel they have less collaboration than desired ("n Nur" and "n Suc"), that they have less ability to *understand* things which affect the project without being an intrinsic part of it, that they experience conflicts and *harmony disturbances*, lack desired *order*, and lack the possibility to exercise the *power* necessary to make the project proceed satisfactorily. Together this forms a picture of the project execution phase as having many motivating potentials, but also as a phase resulting in many demotivational outcomes.

During the project *termination* phase some factors similar to those in project execution seem to prevail. The difference is a slightly smaller representation of the needs which are classified as "leadership"-oriented. Affiliation scores high again, but so does many project leaders' need for *order*, "n Ord" and *harmony*, "n Har". Among factors characterizing the "personal" side, *achievement* is increasingly high, with the project manager's need for personal *exhibition*, to *understand*, and to support *endurance* also high. Many of these factors have a negative side to them. This is perhaps a consequence of generally observed problems in projects related to time and cost overruns, distrust from their own superiors concerning the way they are conducting the project, problems with their own subordinates, and a general lack of possibility to impose their own views and actions on the project. The findings can easily be judged to disclose such relationships, particularly regarding the desire for many project leaders to expose themselves, to have harmonious surroundings, to excel, to order, to affiliate and, what they probably most of all want, to really achieve something and satisfy their own "ego" with their particular project.

The complete findings from the model simulation and the interviews are summarized in figure 4.11.

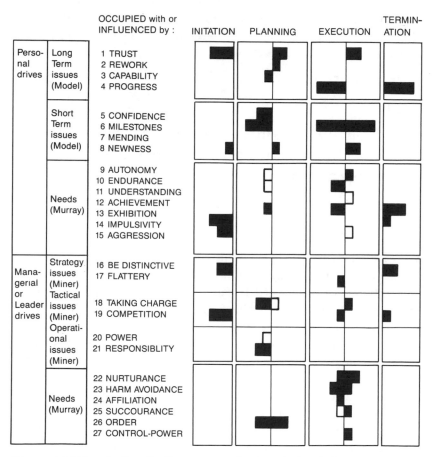

Figure 4.11 Concluding findings on motivational stimuli from interviews. (Arranged alphabetically within each sub-category)

The figure may be used as a two-dimensional description of the motivational reactions by the person in charge of the project effort. The upper part focuses on the project leader as an individual, with the individual, "personal" needs which are more or less supported by the stimuli described within each phase. The last four blocks present stimuli from a "leadership" point of view, in which stimuli felt to be more "strategy"-oriented are gathered in one block, stimuli with a more typical "tactically"-oriented direction are gathered in the next block, and stimuli with a typical "operational" content in the next bloc, with "general" stimuli extracted from Murray's[5] classification system gathered in the last block.

No doubt project managers do reveal different motivational stimuli as important in the different project phases. Their reactions also clearly demonstrate the varied ways of motivating and demotivating project managers during project development.

4.4   Conclusions on the Theoretical Foundation for Understanding the Behaviour of Project Leaders

"We need a concept of productivity that considers together all the efforts that go into output and express them in relation to their results."
(Drucker)

Many authors and researchers have discussed the implications of change in human behaviour in organizational settings. Leavitt[154] states that an organization can be changed by altering its structure, its technology, and/or its people. Changing the organization's structure involves re-arranging its internal systems, such as its lines of communication, its work flow or its managerial hierarchy. Changing the organization's technology means altering its equipment, engineering processes, its research tech-niques or its production methods. Changing the organization's people involves changing the selection, the training, the relationships, the attitudes or the role of organization members.

One conclusion which is easy to draw from the large amount of management literature available today, and from the newer research that is referred to in the preceding paragraph, is that change is natural and inescapable in modern organizations, and that a leader who desires to do a change effort must proceed cautiously, realizing that behavioural change is more difficult to conduct than change in the systems or of the technology. Modern managerial approaches such as the "contingency approach", "behaviour modification" theories, and Management By Objectives (MBO) have been tried in an effort to solve the many conflicts embodied in change procedures. Joynt,[36] for example, found that managers expressed different motivational behaviour dependent on the type of organizational model they belonged to. Scofield et al.[103] characterized the major aspects of behaviour which are the most influential in the management process as: (1) learning, (2) perception, (3) motivation, (4) communication, and (5) attitude formation and change. Fiedler[155] stated, however, that: "Both the directive managing, task-oriented leaders and the nondirective, human relations-oriented leaders are successful under some conditions. Which leadership style is the best depends on the favourableness of the particular situation and the leader. In very favourable or in very unfavourable situations for getting a task accomplished by group effort, the autocratic, task-controlling, leadership works best. In situations intermediate in difficulty, the non-directive, permissive leader is more successful."

Many other modern authors and researchers have similarly pointed to the problem of defining proper leadership under changing conditions. These reasons have lead to a general interest in the particular concept embodied in the "project approach" and "project leadership", which is created to facilitate *change,* by an end result which is something "new" and different, and which alters existing patterns of producing or doing things, and is used as a means of enhancing the change process itself. By inspecting the prevailing literature in this area, we find that since the "project approach" was first launched as a special management technique some thirty years ago, it has grown at a rate similar to the speed of change observed in society in general. To master it, "projects" have been subjected to a process of "definition", in a search for the most clear and distinct way of explaining the process, and for a way of "isolating" the concept from other ongoing endeavours in an organization.

The Human Behavioural Patterns in Project Work

As for the human behavioural patterns within the different phases projects run through, Morris[156] found that "large projects require a decentralized organization during production with centralization before and after", and that "the project organization must change according to the needs of the project size, speed and complexity".

In a historic perspective, managerial traits and skills have attracted considerable attention. The kind of traits studied most often in early leadership research included physical characteristics (height, appearance, etc.), personality (self-esteem, dominance, emotional stability, etc.) and ability (general intelligence, verbal fluency, creativity, social insight). Stogdill[157] examined the results of hundreds of trait studies and suggested that the following trait profile is characteristic of successful leaders:

> The leader is characterized by a strong drive for responsibility and task completion, vigour and persistence in pursuit of goals, venturesomeness and originality in problem solving, drive to exercise initiative in social situations, self-confidence and sense of personal identity, willingness to accept consequences of decision and action, readiness to absorb interpersonal stress, willingness to tolerate frustration and delay, ability to influence other persons' behaviour, and capacity to structure social interaction systems to the purpose at hand.

Later the "Assessment Centre" approach developed a standardized set of procedures to identify managerial potential. Although many programs are referred to as assessment centre methodology, they all utilize multiple methods of assessing traits and skills, including projective tests and situational tests in addition to traditional methods such as interviews and written tests. Dunnette[158] reviewed a limited number of assessment studies and found six traits related to managerial success:

(1) energy level,
(2) organizing and planning skills,
(3) interpersonal skills,
(4) cognitive skills,
(5) work-oriented motivation, and
(6) personal control of feelings and resistance to stress.

Bennis and Nanus[159] collected data with the former used unstructured or "open" interviews of 90 corporate leaders, and found that despite a great amount of diversity among them, they seemed to have three common themes in the way they adapted to environmental changes, which had a close resemblance with the traits of the "transformational" leader (see chapter 4.3). These were:

- developing a *vision,*
- developing commitment and *trust,* and
- facilitating organizational *learning.*

Yukl[71] argues that "much of the management literature has described decisions as discrete events made by a single manager or group in an orderly, rational manner". He further argues that "this picture is sharply contradicted by the descriptive research on managerial work and related research on managerial decision ... Instead of careful analysis of likely outcomes in relation to predetermined objectives, information is often distorted or suppressed to serve preconditions about the best course of action or a self-serving interest in a particular choice".

A Taxonomy of Managerial Roles and Managerial Instruction

Mintzberg[95] was one of the first authors to develop a taxonomy of managerial roles to use for coding the content of managerial activities. In his opinion, each managerial activity can be explained in terms of at least one role, although many activities involve more than one role. Three roles deal with the interpersonal behaviour of managers (leader, liaison, figurehead), three roles deal with information-processing behaviour (monitor, disseminator and spokesman), and four roles deal with decision-making behaviour (entrepreneur, disturbance handler, resource allocator, negotiator). All of the managerial roles apply to any manager or administrator, but according to him their relative importance may vary from one kind of manager to another. He also argues that "a manager's roles are largely predetermined by the nature of the managerial position, but managers have some flexibility in the way each role is interpreted and enacted".

Slevin[59] used Miner's original findings to construct an action plan for "motivation to manage". His conclusion was that "if you can better understand where you are concerning your motivation to manage, you will be in a better position to perform your job at peak efficiency". Hill[160] investigated a group of high and low producing project managers, and concluded that typical for high producing managers was their "encouragement of openness and emotional expression" and their "counselling or exhorting parties to behave differently". The same factors were also recorded as problems for low producing project managers. Morton[96] expresses the view that "during the complete life cycle [of projects] he [the project manager] may find his reporting levels, his authority and his legitimate power varying. He must, therefore, be aware of the ramifications of the different types of management leadership styles which are available to him and the expected results that each could produce for him."

Dealing specifically with each project phase, many authors have more indirectly discussed the difference in needs prevailing in different project phases. McDonough and The Leifer[161] found that the project manager uses a "bounded delegation style" of leadership at the early stages of the project process in order to interpret the business strategy behind the project and define task boundaries. Lord and Birchall[162] supported this, and added that "the project manager's key role during project initiation, is to ensure that the needs of the project are identified, its significance to the various participants is recognized and their active participation, if not total co-operation, is encouraged".

Ashley[163] suggested that "resource" availability and "motivation" were necessary to focus on during project conception and initiation, that "endeavour" was required at project execution, and that "quality" performance was central during the project completion stage. Stuck-enbruck[79] recommended "interface management" in projects, saying that the multidisciplinary approach to project demands makes it necessary to manage diverse interfaces within the diverse project functions such as "planning, organizing, staffing, directing and controlling". Lord and Birchall[162] have also used the term "interface management" in their explanation of why "project managers must take steps during project initiation to ensure that where formal procedures are inadequate, they [must be] either rewritten or superseded by informal agreements [during project development]". Similarly, Birchall and Dingle[164] have argued that "the root cause of project failure is often said to be poor project definition, so that any means of defining projects better would reduce the likelihood of project failure". Turner[165] also pointed out that "the most innocent enquiries by the client may lead to unforeseen complications in the "logic" and implementation" of project endeavours". Beck[166] suggested "mid-course corrections" be instituted in projects, pointing to projects as endeavours having to adjust their code of conduct when forces such as the external market, top management redirection, resource constraints, and project management's own course directions successively affected their progression. Cleland and King[80] used the term "Life Cycle Management" stating that "life cycle reflects very different managements' requirements at its [the project's] various stages." Adams and Barndt[128] supported this view and identified four project phases, each with five–six different task accomplishment characteristics. They also ranked "conflict sources" and

"conflict resolution modes" within each phase, finding that "confronta-
tion" dominated all phases, whilst "smoothing" was required more often
than "forcing" in the Conceptual and the Termination phases, and
"compromising" more often than "withdrawal" during the Planning and
Execution phases. They also recorded that "general satisfaction", which
comes fairly close to "motivation", declined from Initiation through
Planning, to Execution. Their main conclusion was that:

> major changes may occur in the organizational and behavioural
> environments of the single project as it progresses through the
> phases of its life cycle. Such changes could have numerous
> implications for managers of project managers and for project
> managers themselves.... Project organizations tend to be more
> mechanistic in nature and exhibit less favourable organizational
> climate in their mid phases than in either the early or late phases of
> the life cycle. The most favourable organizational climate and the
> most organic type of organization is found in the initial phase of
> the project life cycle. This may be related to the size of the work
> groups found in the individual phases and to the resulting
> differences in organization structure.

The Managerial Need for Structure, Flexibility and Self-motivation

The main conclusion we arrive at after all these views combined with the
research findings is that the managerial need for applying a combination of
structure and flexibility in an integrative manner in project efforts is
apparent, and so is the need for a self-motivating climate during the project
process. Some of the views above may have less obvious support, for
instance Adams and Barndt's views on the relationship between project
size and managerial motivation. In the simulation modelling study referred
to earlier,[39] the conclusion drawn was that project size had no effect on the
project leader's motivation, while interviews produced indications that
size in some settings was an important factor in the way leaders felt and
performed in terms of motivation. Adams and Barndt also observed that
"the smaller the project, the more closely it reflects the characteristics
classically recognized as representing project teams – participative,
dynamic, and collegial efforts. Larger efforts clearly display the characteristics of more bureaucratic organizations" (in the sense that projects might

be so small that it becomes difficult to distinguish phase differences).

This observation seems to be reasonably correct, even if it is more appropriate to say that if the *relative* incidence of certain project characteristics decreases, then project leaders tend to find the factors related to project dimensions of importance to their motivation. Spirer,[167] when observing leader behaviour during project Termination, mentions factors such as "fear of no future work" and "loss of interest in tasks remaining" as important demotivational factors.*

These factors did not surface in the responses to a questionnaire research conducted by this author.[39] In fact, there appeared to be no evidence of leader demotivation toward the end of a project's lifetime. Instead it was found that project leaders on the whole tended to increase their motivation the closer the project came to its finalization. The model simulation, however, indicated some demotivation when the project termination phase became considerably extended, with little perceived progress per unit time. Conclusions are therefore not unanimous at this point.

Factors affecting project success related to distinct project phases are also discussed by Baker *et al.*[168] in a very illuminating manner. Although they only distinguish between two main project phases, "before the invitation to bid" or "the conceptual phase", and "after contract award or go-ahead" or "the implementation phase", they comment on the managerial attitudes needed in these phases for them to be successful. In particular, their main claim is that project managers must "be given sufficient authority", "develop commitment and "enhance the project image", as prerequisites to success in the early stages. During the following steps, project managers should "develop back-up strategies for potential problems", "develop an appropriate project organization structure", and "maintain influence over people and key decisions even though their formal authority may not be sufficient". During the end phase the "importance of meeting cost, schedule and technical performance goals" and "orderly phase-out of the project" are mentioned as important items.

---

* Miner[38] has, with reference to Atkinson and Raynor,[169] brought in the concept of "future goals". Performance of a task could thus be viewed as being a means to an end rather than an end in itself. "Considerations such as the motivation to achieve career success and to avoid the shame of career failure, along with expectations and incentive values related to career considerations, became part of the calculation used to explain present achievement behavior." As he suggests, considerations of this type have "important implications for the understanding of entrepreneurial behavior" – and it could be added, influence the managerial motivation in special task efforts such as projects.

A Shift in System and Attitude as Projects Proceed

The findings of Baker *et al.*[168] support those from research done by this author,[39] advocating a shift in the organizational "system" dependent on which stage the project has reached. Many of their keywords also agree with the observation of behavioural attitudes referred to in this book.

We may conclude from this that although research clearly supports a theory of motivational variation among the project leaders in project developments, and the fact that particular causes and stimuli to motivation are discernible, findings so far are not necessarily unambiguous in supporting every conclusions for every project.

It must be borne in mind that we can always find projects which portray "special cases" and where general observations are contradicted. Such project cases, although less usual, should not alter the main conclusions arrived at about motivational variations. We can also compare such findings with those of Scott and others, where the general opinion is that the management approaches in modern time have developed through different stages of "open", "closed", "rational", and "natural" systems thinking. By applying two of these descriptions to the project approach, using keywords particularly relevant to "rational" and "natural" systems, the following structure may be constructed as illustrated in table 4.12.

The table shows, in the first place, what is already contended, that different motivational attitudes seem to dominate each of the project phases. What is particularly interesting is that a shift between a "natural" and a "rational" type of system may well be said to take place during the project development. An obvious conclusion from this then is that project leaders become both motivated and demotivated in their project efforts because of the many stimulating and destimulating factors created during project development. But it is also clear that such factors will vary and

	INITIA-TION	PLANNING	EXECU-TION	TERMINA-TION
Key words for managerial profile	Self-profiling and Curious	Self-confident and Systematic	Affiliating and Decisive	Self-profiling and Decisive
Predominant system profile	NATURAL SYSTEM	RATIONAL SYSTEM	NATURAL SYSTEM	RATIONAL SYSTEM

Table 4.12 A summary of the project manager's behavioural preference in each project phase

operate with varying frequency from one project phase to another, and that the general theories of "rational" and "natural" systems have a special applicational value for project development. By changing the leader's role accordingly, and giving project leaders the opportunity to manage so that such issues can be properly and adequately dealt with, more effective and efficient project leadership may well develop.

Conclusions on the Managerial Component in Project Work

The first general conclusion to be drawn after this is that the managerial component is a very important factor in project efforts. There is also reason to believe that this component can be studied as a system of its own, or as a "project management system". There are further two main effects to consider if the project leader's motivation shall be understood: one is connected to the "horizontal" process in projects going from the "change desire" to the "goal attainment", while the other is the "vertical" process between the "static" elements of structure and system and the "dynamic" process components of interaction and interplay during the life-cycle development of the project effort. Based on these thoughts several more particular conclusions can be drawn.

The first special conclusion is that it seems fair to suggest that there are two approaches which perhaps offer the best insight to the practising managers. They are the *systems approach*, based on systems and structure as the main components for proper managerial effort, and the *contingency approach*, based on a belief in flexible management. Both these views seem to point to the following important observation; namely that management behaviour is both a function of or a reactional attitude *to* the environmental conditions present, and imposes special conditions *on* the environment. The balance between these two "directions" will vary from one organizational setting to another. What seems basic is that project leaders must learn when to *adjust* to and when to try to *direct* their operational environment. The balance is not only vital to the task at hand, but also for the motivational climate they create – for themselves and for others.

The second conclusion is that the role of managers in projects seems to be both of a "leadership" character and of an individual, "personal" character, in the sense that project management is, as also suggested by McGregor,[9] both doing "the right things", which is to define the project properly and initiate the right "change" and by this stimulating one's own opinion of *what* should be done, and then doing "things right", which encompasses motivating and guiding the common effort adequately and efficiently towards the project goal and by this stimulating the impression of *how* things should be done.

The third conclusion drawn is that individual motivation at the project leader's level rests on a number of heuristic distinctions, the most prominent one being that we may distinguish between *rationality* and social *norms* as motives. As also contended by Elster,[40] to explain individual motivation in collective action, the "rational" directed motivation is probably the most easy to observe, and thus forms the best avenue for a methodological research effort. To make such an effort more explicit, we may subdivide it into rational, (selfish), *outcome-oriented* behaviour, and rational, (selfish), *process-oriented* behaviour. These two directions may be explained through the two particular conditions prevailing in project work, namely that of *stability*, of structural features, and of product orientation, and that of *dynamism*, processes, and feedback. It can be concluded from the literature that structure and its built-in stability seem to have special effects on the attitude and behaviour of the participants in the project, and thus must also create strong motivational and demotivational reactions in the project leaders. There is also positive confirmation in the literature that a considerable amount of effort is applied to structuring projects so as to promote obvious motivational effects within project work. This is in contrast, however, to the little effort devoted to avoid or limit demotivational effects, apparently with the notion that projects need few stimuli in this area due to their built-in incentives.

Finally, it may be sufficient to point out that *projects* represent the intended changes and *initiate* such changes, and that these changes activate internal and external forces which may have a profound effect on the project leaders' motivation. If we therefore seek to identify these forces, and thus provide an understanding of why and how they influence the motivation in projects, we must give high priority to research centred on the *causes* of change and on the *effects* of such changes on the different project participants. It is likely to be especially rewarding, therefore, to look for the results and developments of change brought about by projects, and which affect the project leaders.

The Variations in the Project Leaders' Motivation

One of the main issues seems to be that there obviously are *variations in the project leaders' motivation* throughout the lifetime of their projects. However, care has been taken when making suggestions and drawing conclusions, in the full awareness of the nature of "project management" as a discipline which is subject to constant change due to its need to match the ever-changing environment within which it is operating. Since so much work needs to be done in this field of management research, we should probably not aim at firm conclusions, but it should be practicable to point to feasible ways of achieving improvements, and to elaborate on possible new areas of study.

A specific observation is that project *conception* and project *goals* seem to have particular effects on the project leader's motivation, since this has been increasingly noticed in current management literature. It is also clear that change in modern societies is inevitable. The expectancy that the individuals have in respect of these changes and the goals they strive for are important. If goals are realistic, achievable and rewarding, there seems to be general agreement that the goals will have clear, positive effects on managerial performance. But goals can also be complicated, difficult to achieve, and create frustration and reduced confidence. In the frequently turbulent environment of projects, goals can easily be changed to become unachievable or unclear. Flawed project goals may therefore be the main cause of managerial demotivation.

The following two issues deserve particular attention:

- The fact that the field of management and leadership theory seems at present to be in a state which should perhaps be labelled "ferment" or "confusion".[71] Many of the widely known theories have increasingly been proven to have conceptual weaknesses, and they lack sufficient empirical support.[7] For half a century or more, empirical studies have been conducted on leader traits, behaviour, power, and situational variables as predictors of leadership effectiveness, but many of the results have contradictory implications and are not conclusive. Miner[132] concluded that "the concept of leadership has outlived its usefulness", and he suggested a moratorium on traditional leadership research. According to Yukl[71] the leadership literature currently includes over ten thousand studies, and the number continues to increase by several hundreds each year. He, however, concludes positively by stating that no research "supports the conclusion that leadership is unimportant or that leaders are unnecessary".

- The fact that the term "project" remains a relatively "open" definition of the many different efforts aimed at reaching purposely set goals and objectives. Perhaps we should therefore concentrate on endeavours associated with the more precisely defined characteristics of projects, i.e. that they may be seen as deliberate, goal-directed activities within delimited resources. This tend, however, to exclude some of the more recent studies of "project work" covering predominantly process-oriented aspects, such as initiating new organizational cultures, creating environmental opinions or stimulating other behavioural changes. Since it cannot be ignored that these "quasi-projects" in many ways resemble the more strictly defined projects, and with very small adjustments many of these endeavours fit in well with the present definition of "projects", they should therefore also be considered as "projects".

4.6   References

1 Lewin, K. 1951: *Field Theory in Social Science: Selected Theoretical Papers.* Harper & Brothers. N.Y.
2 Morse, N. & R. Weiss 1955: The Function and Meaning of Work and the Job. *American Sociological Review.*
3 Herzberg, F., Mausner, B. & B.B. Snyderman 1959: *The Motivation to Work.* John Wiley & Sons. N.Y.
4 Katz, D. & R.L. Kahn 1978: *The Social Psychology of Organizations.* John Wiley & Sons. N.Y.
5 Handy, C.B. 1987: *Understanding Organizations.* (Third edition.) Penguin Books. Hammersworth.
6 Webster, N. 1983: *Webster's New Universal Unabridged Dictionary.* (Second edition.) Dorset & Baber. N.Y.
7 Steers, R.M. & L.W. Porter 1987: *Motivation and Work Behavior.* (Fourth edition.) McGraw-Hill. N.Y.
8 Maslow, A.H. 1943: A Theory of Human Motivation. *Psychology Review 50,* 370–396.
9 McGregor, D. 1960: *The Human Side of Enterprise.* McGraw-Hill. N.Y.
10 Cyert, R.M. & J.G. March 1963: *A Behavior Theory of the Firm.* Prentice Hall. Englewood Cliffs. N.J.
11 Vroom, V.H. 1964: *Work and Motivation.* John Wiley & Sons. N.Y.
12 Madsen, D.B. & J.R. Finger 1978: Comparison of a Written Feedback Procedure. Group Brainstorming Individual Brainstorming. *Journal of Applied Psychology 63.*
13 Hackman, J.R. 1976: Group Influences on Individuals. In M. Dunnette (ed.): *Handbook of Industrial and Organizational Psychology.* Rand McNally. Chicago.
14 Schein, E. 1980: *Organizational Psychology.* Prentice Hall, Englewood Cliffs. N.J.

15 Campbell, J.P. & R.D. Pritchard 1976: Motivation Theory in Industrial and Organizational Psychology. In *Handbook of Industrial and Organizational Psychology.* Rand McNally. Chicago.

16 Follet, M.P. 1918: *The New State.* Peter Smith. Gloucester. Mass.

17 Fayol, F.W. 1919: *Scientific Management.* Harper & Brothers. N.Y.

18 Urwick, L. 1956: The Manager's Span of Control. *Harvard Business Review 34,* 3,

19 Davis, M.W. 1985: Anatomy of Decision Support. *Datamation 15.* (June).

20 Taylor, F.W. 1911: *The Principles of Scientific Management.* (1967.) Norton. N.Y.

21 Emerson, H. 1913: *The Twelve Principles of Efficiency.* N.Y.

22 Gantt, H. 1919: As referred to in J.A.F. Stoner & C. Wankel (eds.): *Management.* Prentice-Hall International Editions. N.J. 186–187.

23 Bertalanffy, L. von 1951: General Systems Theory: A New Approach to the Unity of Science. *Human Biology* (December), 302–312.

24 Boulding, K. 1956: General Systems Theory: The Skeleton of Science. *General Systems. Yearbook of the Society for the Advancement of General Systems Theory 1,* 11–17.

25 Katz, D. & R.L. Kahn 1966: *The Social Psychology of Organizations.* John Wiley & Sons. N.Y.

26 Ackoff, R.L. 1967: Management Misinformation Systems. *Management Science* (December).

27 Kaufmann, H. 1971: *The Limits of Organizational Change.* University of Alabama Press. Ala.

28 Schein, E. 1968: Organizational Socialization and the Profession of Management. *Industrial Management Review 9,* 2.

29 Locke, E.A. 1969: What is Job Satisfaction? *Organizational Behavior and Human Performance 4.*

30 Cummings, L.L. 1977: Emergence of the Instrumental Organization. In P.S. Goodman & J.M. Pennings (eds.): *New Perspectives on Organizational Effectiveness.* Jossey-Bass. San Francisco. Cal.

31 Stoner, J.A.F. & C. Wankel 1986: *Management.* (Third edition.) Prentice-Hall International. N.Y.

32 Steers, R.M. & L.W. Porter 1983: *Motivation and Work Behavior.* (Third edition.) McGraw-Hill. N.Y.

33 Robbins, S.P. 1983: *Organization Theory. The Structure and Design of Organizations.* Prentice-Hall. Englewood Cliffs. N.J.

34 Lawrence, P.R. & J.W. Lorsch 1967: *Organization and Environment: Managing Differentiation and Integration.* Graduate School of Business Administration. Harvard University. Boston. Mass.

35 Hersey, P. & K.H. Blanchard 1984: *Management of Organizational Behavior.* (Fourth edition.) Prentice-Hall. Englewood Cliffs. N.J.

36 Joynt, P. 1979: *Management Concepts and Processes.* Stiftelsen Bedriftsøkonomisk Institutt. Oslo.

37 Davis, K. & J.W. Newstrom 1989: *Human Behavior at Work. Organizational Behavior.* (Eighth edition.) McGraw-Hill. N.Y.

38 Miner, J.B. 1980: *Theories of Organizational Behavior.* The Dryden Press. Hinsdale. Ill.

39 Jessen, S.A. 1990: The Motivation of Project Managers. A Study of Variation in Norwegian Project Managers' Motivation and Demotivation by Triangulation of Methods. Thesis submitted for the Degree of Doctor of Philosophy at Henley, The Management College, and Brunel University. August 1990.

40 Elster, J. 1989: *The Cement of Society. A Study of Social order.* Cambridge University Press. Cambridge. Mass.

41 McClelland, D.C. 1971: *Assessing Human Motivation.* General Learning Press. N.Y.

42 Atkinson, J.W. 1977: Motivation for Achievement. In T. Blass (ed.): *Personality Variables in Social Psychology.* Erlbaum Associates. N.J. 22–108.

43 Skinner, B. 1953: *Science and Human Behavior.* Free Press. N.Y.

44 Kreitner, R. & F. Luthans 1986: *High Involvement Management: Participative Strategies for Improving Organizational Performance.* Jossey-Bass. San Francisco. Cal.

45 Alderfer, C.P. 1969: A New Theory of Human Needs. *Organizational Behavior and Human Performance 4,* 142–175.

46 Murray, H.A. 1938: *Explorations in Personality.* Oxford University Press. N.Y.

47 McClelland, D.C. 1961: *The Achieving Society.* Van Nostrand. N.J.

48 Birch, D. & J. Veroff 1966: *Motivation: A Study of Action.* Brooks/Cole, Monterey. Ca.

49 Litwin, G.H. & R.H. Stringer Jr. 1968: *Motivation and Organizational Climate.* Division of Research, Graduate School of Business Administration, Harvard University. Boston. Mass.

50 Haire, M. 1964: *Psychology in Management.* (Second edition.) McGraw-Hill. N.Y.

51 Locke, E.A. 1968: Toward a Theory of Task Motivation and Incentives. *Organization Behavior and Human Performance* (May).

52 Porter, L.W., Lawler, E.E. & J.R. Hackman 1975: *Behavior in Organizations.* McGraw-Hill. N.Y.

53 Clark, P.M. Q. Wilson 1961: Incentive Systems: A Theory of Organizations. *Administrative Science Quarterly 6* (September)

54 Whyte, W.F. 1972: Skinnerian Theory in Organizations. *Psychology Today* (April).

55 Allport, G.W. 1954: The Historical Background of Modern Social Psychology. In G. Lindzey (ed.): *Handbook of Social Psychology.* Addison-Wesley Cambridge. Mass.

56 Thorndike, E.L. 1911: *Animal intelligence: Experimental studies.* Macmillan. N.Y.

57 Woodworth, R.S. 1918: *Dynamic Psychology.* Columbia University Press. N.Y.

58 Butler, A.G. Jr. 1983: Project Management – Its Functions and Dysfunctions. In D.I. Cleland & R.W. King (eds.): *Project Management Handbook.* Van Nostrand Reinhold Company. N.Y.

59 Slevin, D.P. 1983: Motivation and the Project Manager. In D.I. Cleland & W.R. King (eds.): *Project Management Handbook.* Van Nostrand Reinhold Co. N.Y. 552–566.

60 Miner, J.B. 1973: *The Management Process. Theory, Research, and Practice.* The Macmillan Company. N.Y.
61 Baker, B.N. 1988: Lessons Learned from a Variety of Project Failures. *Proceedings of the Ninth World Congress on Project Management 1.* Glasgow. 113–118.
62 Graen, G. 1969: Instrumentality Theory of Work Motivation: Some Experimental Results and Suggested Modifications. *Journal of Applied Psychology Monograph 53,* 2.
63 Jackson, K.W. & D.J. Shea 1972: Motivation Training in Perspective. In W. Nord (ed): *Concepts and Controversy in Organizational Behavior.* Goodyear. Pacific Palisades. Cal. 100–118.
64 Daft, R.L. 1989: *Organization Theory and Design.* (Third edition.) West Publishing Company. St.Paul. Min.
65 Hersey, P. & K.H. Blanchard 1977: *Management of Organizational Behavior.* (Third edition.) Prentice Hall. Englewood Cliffs. N.J.
66 Machiavelli, N. 1532: *Il Principle.* Translated by P. Lorange in 1967 (*Fyrsten*). Dreyer. Oslo.
67 Helmer, O. 1983: *Looking Forward. A guide to future research.* Sage Publications Inc. Beverly Hills. Cal.
68 Massie, J.L. 1987: *Essentials of Management.* (Fourth edition.) Prentice-Hall International Editions. Englewood Cliffs. N.J.
69 White, R. & R. Lippit 1953: Leader Behavior and Member Reaction in Three Social Climates. In Cartwright & Zande (eds.): *Group Dynamics.* Row Peterson. Evanston. Ill. 586– 611.
70 Adices, I. 1979: Organizational Passages – Diagnosing and Treating Life-cycle Problems of Organizations. *Organizational Dynamics* (Summer), 3–25.
71 Yukl, G.A. 1989: *Leadership in Organizations.* (Second edition.) Prentice-Hall. Englewood Cliffs. N.J.
72 Quinn, R.E. & K. Cameron 1983: Organizational Life Cycles and Shifting Criteria of Effectiveness: Some Preliminary Evidence. *Management Science 29,* 1.
73 Meredith, J.R. & S.J. Mantel Jr. 1989: *Project Management. A Managerial Approach.* (Second edition.) John Wiley & Sons. N.Y.
74 Hersey, P. & K.H. Blanchard 1969: Life-Cycle Theory of Leadership. *Training and Development Journal 23,* 2, 26–34.
75 Longenecker, J.G. & C.D. Pringle 1978: The Illusion of Contingency Theory as a General Theory. *Academy of Management Review 3,* 3.
76 Filley, A.C., House, J.H. & S. Kerr 1970: *Managerial Process and Organizational Behavior.* Scott & Foresman. Glenview. Ill.
77 Rossvær, T. 1987: *Organisasjonsteorier i sosiologisk belysning.* TANO. Oslo.
78 Carnall, C. 1990: *Managing Change.* Prentice Hall. Herefordshire. UK
79 Stuckenbruck, L.C. 1981: *The Implementation of Project Management: The Professional's Handbook.* Addison-Wesley Inc. Mass.
80 Cleland D.I. & R.W. King 1983: Life Cycle Management. In D.I. Cleland & R.W. King (eds.): *Project Management Handbook.* Van Nostrand Reinhold Co. N.Y. 209–221.
81 Augustine, N.R. (ed.) 1989: *Managing Projects and Programs.* Harvard Business Review. Mass.

82 Kolltveit, B.J. 1988: *The Technical Concept and Organizational Effectiveness of Offshore Projects.* Henley The Management College, March. Henley.

83 Anderson, S.D. & R.W. Woodhead 1987: *Project Manpower Management. Decision-making Processes in Construction Practice.* Wiley-Interscience Publication. John Wiley & Sons. N.Y.

84 Burbridge, R.N. 1988: Conception of Projects. *Proceedings of the Ninth World Congress on Project Management 1.* Glasgow. (Unpaged.)

85 Porter, M.E. 1973: *The Rise of Big Business 1860–1910.* Harlan Davidson. Arlington Heights.

86 Forrester, J.W. 1961: *Industrial Dynamics.* M.I.T. Press. Cambridge. Mass.

87 Cannon, W.B. 1939: *The Wisdom of the Body.* Norton. N.Y.

88 Simon, H.A. 1957: *Administrative Behavior.* MacMillan. N.Y.

89 Simon, H.A. 1966: *The New Science of Management Decision.* Harper & Row. N.Y.

90 Thompson, J.D. 1967: *Organizations in Actions. Social Science based on Administrative theory.* McGraw-Hill. N.Y.

91 Stinchcombe, A.L. & C.A. Heimer 1985: *Organization Theory and Project Management, Administrative Uncertainty in Norwegian Offshore Oil.* Norwegian University Press. Oslo.

92 Peters, T.J. & R.H. Waterman 1982: *In Search of Excellence.* Harper & Row. N.Y.

93 Menkus, B. 1980: Systems Projects: Process and Product. *Journal of Systems Management 31.*

94 Tichy, N.M. & M.A. Devanna 1986: *The Transformational Leader.* John Wiley & Sons. N.Y.

95 Mintzberg, H. 1983: *Structure in Fives. Designing Effective Organizations.* Prentice–Hall. Englewood Cliffs. N.J.

96 Morton, G.H.A. 1983: Project Manager, Catalyst to Constant Change. A Behavioral Analysis. In D.I. Cleland & R.W. King (eds.): *Project Management Handbook.* Van Nostrand Reinhold Co. N.Y. 533–551.

97 Reve, J. & T.Levitt 1984: Organization and Governance in Construction. *Project Management 2, 1.*

98 Kreiner, K. 1976: *The Site Organization: A Study of Social Relationships on Construction Sites.* Danmarks Tekniske Højskole. København.

99 Williamson, O.E. 1979. Transaction Cost Economics; Governance of Contractual Relations. *The Journal of Law and Economics* (Oct).

100 Hyman, L. & L. Singer 1968: *Readings in Reference Group Theory and Research.* The Free Press. N.Y.

101 Fiedler, F.E. 1967: *A Theory of Leadership Effectiveness.* McGraw-Hill. N.Y.

102 Steers, R.M. 1977: Antecedents and Outcomes of Organizational Commitment. *Administrative Science Quarterly 22,* 46–56.

103 Scofield, R.W., Bogart, D.H. & D.R. Domm 1968: Human Behavior and Administration (Pre-publication edition.) University of Houston, Houston. Texas.

104 Atkinson, J.W. & Birch, D. 1978: *An Introduction to Motivation.* (Revised edition.) Van Nostrand Reinhold. N.Y. 346–348.

105 Porter, L.W. & R.E. Miles 1974: Motivation and Management. In McGuire (ed.): *Contemporary Management: Issues and Viewpoints.* Prentice-Hall. Englewood Cliffs. N.J. 546–550.

106 Morton, G.H.A. 1983: Human Dynamics in Project Planning. In D.I. Cleland & R.W. King (eds.): *Project Management Handbook*. Van Nostrand Reinhold Co. N.Y. 265–282.

107 Adler, A. 1930: Individual Psychology. Translated by Langer. In Murchinson (ed.): *Psychologies of 1930*. Clark University Press. Worchester. Mass.

108 Stinchcombe, A.L. 1968: *Constructing Social Theory*. Brace & World Inc. N.Y.

109 McClelland, D.C. & D.H. Burnham 1976: Power is the Great Motivator. *Harvard Business Review 54*, March–April.

110 Thomason, G.F. 1988: *A Textbook of Human Resource Management*. Institute of Personnel Management. Wimbledon. London.

111 Steers, R.M. & D.N. Braunstein 1976: A Behavioral Based Measure of Manifest Needs in Work Settings. *Journal of Vocational Behavior 9*, 251–266.

112 Hunsaker, P.L. & W.C. Cook 1986: *Managing Organizational Behavior*. Addison-Wesley Publishing Company. Boston. Mass.

113 Harrison, F.L. 1988: Conflict, Power and Politics in Project Management. *Proceedings of the Ninth World Congress on Project Management 1*. Glasgow. 513–520.

114 Kertzner, H. 1983: Evaluating the Performance of Project Personnel. In D.I. Cleland & R.W. King (eds.): *Project Management Handbook*. Van Nostrand Reinhold Co, N.Y. 482–494.

115 Porter, L.W. 1961: A study of the perceived need for satisfaction in bottom and middle management jobs. *Journal of Applied Psychology 45*, 1–10.

116 Lawler, E.E. 1967: The multitrait multirater approach to measuring managerial job performance. *Journal of Applied Psychology 51*.

117 Drucker, P. 1954: *The Practice of Management*. Harper & Brothers. N.Y.

118 Humble, J. 1976: *Målrettet ledelse*. Hjemmets Forlag. Oslo.

119 Latham, G.P. & E.A. Locke 1979: Organizational Dynamics. *AMACOM 8*, 2, 68–80.

120 Culbert, S. & J.J. McDonough 1980: *The Invisible War. Pursuing Self-Interest at Work*. John Wiley & Sons. N.Y.

121 Lindblom, L.E. 1959: The Science of Muddling Through. *Public Administration Review 19*, 79–88.

122 Barnard, C.I. 1938: *The Functions of the Executive*. Harvard University Press. Cambridge. Mass.

123 Ilgen, D.R. & G. Hamstra 1974: Realistic Expectations as an Aid in Reducing Voluntary Resignations. *Journal of Applied Psychology 59*, 452–455.

124 Likert, R. 1961: *New Patterns of Management*. McGraw-Hill. N.Y.

125 Liberatore, M.J. 1987: An Extension of the Analytic Hierarchy Process for Industrial R&D Project Selection and Resource Allocation. *IEEE Transactions on Engineering Management* Vol. EM–34, No. 1, Feb.

126 Andersen, E.S., Grude, K., Haug, T. & J.R. Turner 1987: *Goal Directed Project Management*. Coopers & Lybrand. London.

127 Mintzberg, H. 1979: *The Structuring of Organizations*. Prentice-Hall. Englewood Cliffs. N.Y.

128 Adams, J.R. & S.E. Barndt 1983: Behavioral Implications of the Project Life Cycle. In D.I. Cleland & R.W. King (eds.): *Project Management Handbook*. Van Nostrand Reinhold Co. N.Y. 222–244.

129 Festinger, L. 1954: A Theory of Social Comparison Processes. *Human Relations 7*, 117–140.

130 Fishbein, M. (ed.) 1967: *Readings in Attitude Theory and Measurement.* John Wiley & Sons. N.Y.

131 Powers, R.F. 1971: An Empirical Investigation of Selected Hypotheses Related to the Success of Management Information System Projects. Unpublished doctoral thesis. University of Minnesota. Min.

132 Miner, J.B. 1975: The Uncertain Future of the Leadership Concept: An Overview. In Hunt & Larson (eds.): *Leadership Frontiers.* Kent State University Press. Oh.

133 Cox, B. & M.W. Dale 1987: The Management of Finance. In H. Darnell (ed.): *Total Project Management.* Book 2. The Asset Management Group of the British Institute of Management.

134 Stephanou, S.E. & C. Obradowich 1985: *Project Management. System Development and Productivity.* Daniel Spencer Publishers. Malibu. Ca.

135 Cook, T. & D. Campbell 1979: *Quasi-Experimentation. Design & Analysis Issues of Field Settings.* Houghton Mifflin Company. Boston. Mass.

136 Richardson, G.P. & A.L. Pugh III 1981: *Introduction to System Dynamics Modelling With DYNAMO.* M.I.T. Press. Cambridge. Mass.

137 Weiner, N. 1948: *Cybernetics.* John Wiley & Sons. N.Y.

138 Jessen, S.A. 1986: *Prosjektadministrative metoder.* Universitetsforlaget. Oslo.

139 McClelland, D.C., Atkinson, J.W., Clark, R.A. & E.L. Cowell 1953: *The Achievement Motive.* Appleton-Century-Crofts. N.Y.

140 Hammer, W.C. & H.L. Tosi 1974: *Organizational behavior and management: A contingency approach.* St. Clair Press. John Wiley & Sons. Chicago. Ill.

141 Starr, K.M. 1989: Organizational Growth and Development. In J. March (ed.) *Handbook of Organizations.* Rand McNally. N.Y.

142 Baloff, N. 1967: Estimating the Parameters of the Startup Model – An Empirical Approach. *The Journal of Industrial Engineering 18*, 4, 248–253.

143 Pegels, C.C. 1961: The Analysis of Goals in Complex Organizations. *American Sociological Review 26.*

144 Shaver, K.G. 1975: *An introduction to attribution processes.* Winthrop. Cambridge. Mass.

145 Kelley, H.H. 1971: *The Limits of Organizational Change.* University of Alabama Press. Ala.

146 Mitchell, T.R. & S.G. Green 1978: Leadership and Poor Performance: An Attributional Analysis. Paper presented at the Eighty-sixth Annual Convention of the American Psychological Association. Toronto.

147 Korman, A.K. 1974: *The Psychology of Motivation.* Prentice-Hall, Englewood Cliffs. N.J.

148 Weiner, B. 1974: *Cognitive Views of Human Motivation.* Arcade Press. N.Y.

149 Hall, D.T. 1976: *Careers in Organizations.* Goodyear. Pacific Palisades. Cal.

150 Steers, R.M. & Mowday 1977: The Motivational Properties of Tasks. *Academy of Management Review 2*, 645–658.

151 Boyd, H.W., Westafal, R. & S.F. Stasch 1981: *Marketing Research.* (Fifth Edition.) Irwin, Homewood. Ill.

152 Glaser, B.G. & A.L. Strauss 1967: *Discovery of Grounded Theory: Strategies for Qualitative Research.* Aldine de Gruyter. Na.

153 Rose, G. 1982: *Deciphering Sociological Research*. MacMillan Education. London.

154 Leavitt, H.J. 1964: Applied Organization Change in Industry: Structural, Technical and Human Approaches. In Cooper, Leavitt & Shelly (eds.): *New Perspectives in Organizational Research*. John Wiley & Sons. N.Y. 55–71.

155 Fiedler, F.E. 1964: A Contingency Model of Leadership Effectiveness. In Berkowitz (ed.): *Advances in Experimental Social Psychology*. Academic Press. N.Y.

156 Morris, P.W.G. 1988: Initiating Major Projects – The Unperceived Role of Project Management. *Proceedings of the Ninth World Congress on Project Management 1*. Glasgow. 801– 813.

157 Stogdill, R.M. 1974: *Handbook of Leadership: A Survey of the Literature*. Free Press. N.Y.

158 Dunnette, M.D. 1971: Multiple Assessment Procedures in Identifying and Developing Managerial Talent. In McReynolds (ed.): *Advances in Psychological Assessment*. Science and Behavior Books. Vol. 12, Palo Alto. Ca. 30–37.

159 Bennis, W.G. & B. Nanus 1985: *Leaders: The Strategies for Talking Charge*. Harper & Row. N.Y.

160 Hill, C.W.L. 1983: Conglomerate Performance over the Economic Cycle. *Journal of Industrial Economics 32*, (UK), 197–211.

161 McDonough, D.C. & R.P. The Leifer 1985: Effective Control of New Product Projects: Interaction of Organization Culture and Project Leadership. *Journal of Production Innovation Management 3*, 3, 149–157.

162 Lord, A.M. & D. Birchall 1988: The Choice of Management Structure and Staffing the Team during Project Initiation. *INTERNET Proceedings*, 189–196.

163 Ashley, G. 1988: The Art of Management of Human Resources Generation and Implementation of Human Capital. *Proceedings of the Ninth World Congress on Project Management 1*, Glasgow. 87–95.

164 Birchall, D. & J. Dingle 1988: A Fresh Look at Project Preparation. *Proceedings of the Ninth World Congress on Project Management 1*, Glasgow. 329–336.

165 Turner, E.K. 1988: Scope Definition for Bidding Project-Control Services. *International Journal on Project Management 6*, 1, 39–44.

166 Beck, D.R. 1983: Implementing Top Management Plans through Project Management. In D.I. Cleland & R.W. King (eds.): *Project Management Handbook*. Van Nostrand Co. N.Y. 166–184.

167 Spirer, H.F. 1983: Phasing Out the Project. In D.I. Cleland & R.W. King (eds.): *Project Management Handbook*. Van Nostrand Co. N.Y. 245–264.

168 Baker, B.N., Fisher, D. & D.C. Murphy 1983: Project Management in the Public Sector: Success and Failure Patterns Compared to Private Sector Projects. In D.I. Cleland & R.W. King (eds.): *Project Management Handbook*. Van Nostrand Co. N.Y. 686–699.

169 Atkinson, J.W. & J.O. Raynor 1974: *Motivation and Achievement*. Winston. Washington D.C

5 PRACTICAL CONSEQUENCES OF THE THEORETICAL ASPECTS OF PROJECT LEADERSHIP

"Love me most when I deserve it least, 'cause that's when I need it most"

5.1 General

As is the case with many other new and developing disciplines, the gap between the theoretical insight gained and the real-life, practical application of theory has also been widening in the field of project management. For project work this is quite natural, since it by its very nature contains so many unique circumstances that general theoretical applications rarely fit each particular situation. This should not, however, prevent each and every project leader from considering the theoretical wisdom that is actually available, and from thus taking steps to include the best theories in an effort to improve his or her own leadership style and performance.

This is also the rationale for this chapter, in which a discussion and demonstration of a set of five possible project management steps or stages are suggested, each with two sub-headings highlighting the issues apparently most essential to successful modern project leadership.

5.2 Practical Consequences of the Project Concept

As already contended, project work is today recognized by a set of key characteristics typical for its applicational strength. They are:[1]

1. A project is always *problem-oriented*, i.e. the effort is not haphazard but the result of a qualified desire, an identified problem or a recognized need.
2. The project effort is a *goal-seeking* endeavour, i.e. its main objective is clearly definable and practically attainable.

3. Project work is *resource-constrained*, i.e. it has to be executed within well-defined limits in terms of time, personnel and capital outlay. A further restriction is that the period of time spent on the project must fall within a particular *starting and finishing date*, the monetary resources requested should cover both *direct and indirect expenditures* and the human resource component must be defined in terms of the *quantity and quality* required to fulfil the chosen objective.

4. Project work is by nature *unique*, i.e. it has few, or at least more than just, routine components and the work therefore has to break new ground or provide new insight for enactors and stakeholders. In doing so, the project effort introduces both a certain level of *risk* and a certain degree of *challenge* for the involved parties.

5. Project work is *recognizable and visible*, i.e. it always relates to an actual situation, a "base" organization, a specific enterprise or a specific endeavour which then becomes the reference condition for its contemporary existence.

These characteristics must be seen as the most prototypical for projects of today. The important observation is then that on the basis of these characteristics we can identify a specific set of *consequences* which then also become typical of project work. As will be suggested here, no project leader should accept that any project for which he or she is responsible commences without ensuring that those involved are aware of these consequences and are capable of, or are given the opportunity of, acting accordingly. The connection between the above key characteristics and the recognizable consequences is illustrated in figure 5.1.

It must at this stage be stated that projects may have additional characteristics which must also be considered when managing them. Many projects have for instance a *cross-disciplinary* relationship amongst those engaged. But since we may well have projects where all participants are specialists within only one field of professionality, for instance in a conventional data-processing project or in a pure construction-oriented project, the presence of cross-disciplination should not be seen as an unalterable project condition.

Another often mentioned condition is that of *interdependencies*. Many projects often interact with other projects being carried out simultaneously by their parent organization, and projects always interact with the parent's standard, ongoing operations. Although the functional departments of an organization (marketing, finance, manufacturing, and the like) interact with one another in regular, patterned ways, the patterns of interaction between projects and these departments tend to change. The project leader should be aware that in many projects it is imperative to keep all such interactions clear and maintain appropriate interrelationships with all external groups. Still, interdependence will here be regarded as not being a *general* precondition for successful project performance.

A third factor is that of *conflict*.[2] It is a fact that most project leaders live

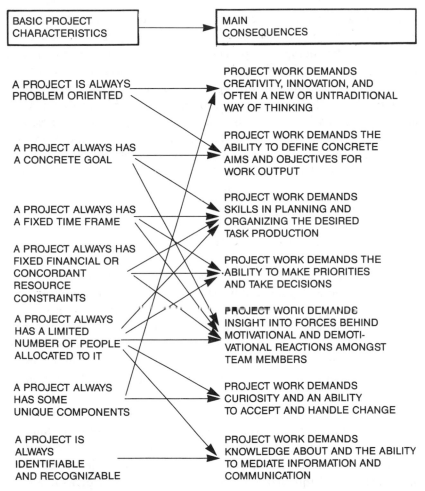

Figure 5.1 The link between the basic project characteristics and their consequences

in a world of conflict. Projects compete with functional departments for resources and personnel. The members of the project team are often in conflict over the project's resources and over leadership roles in solving project problems. Individuals working on projects are often responsible to more than one boss at the same time, bosses with different priorities and objectives. To deem every project a battle-ground is, however, to stretch this issue too far. In the interview survey with professional project leaders of today described earlier[1] the conclusion drawn was that to turn emerging conflicts into challenges and opportunities is quite often possible if handled with care and control.

A last issue often used as a recognizable character of project work is that of *life-cycle development*.[2, 3] Like organic entities, projects have life cycles. From a slow beginning they progress and increase in size, then peak, decline, and must finally be terminated. This was a trend easily recognizable when project work mainly took place in the construction industry. Today when the project approach is used so widely, we find that some projects may have quite different life-cycle patterns and still remain "projects" according to the former basic project characteristics. A project may for example start out fast and place great demands on resources from the first day and then gradually terminate until only a few people are involved at the "wrapping-up" stage. Typical examples of such projects are emergency-projects and ad-hoc assistance projects. Other projects may start slow but end in a comprehensive collaborative effort by all involved parties at the same time. Many R&D projects or "term-paper" oriented projects will automatically proceed like this due to the "dynamic" nature of the research process itself, enhanced by the accelerating knowledge normally gained and the possibly narrow time limit for the effort. We should therefore, perhaps, not declare one particular life-cycle process as prototypical for how project work should best be executed today, but rather allow for many individual approaches to be accepted by the project leaders. This may collide with the former theoretical observations (chapter 3) on project life-cycle structures, but seems to be a valid observation in practical project work today.

Despite the fact that the characteristics mentioned in figure 5.1 may not after this be sufficient to provide a complete description of every kind of project work, the referred characteristics seem to be so common today that we may well use them as a sound prerequisite for active project work. And in the next round this makes the work process itself recognizable in a particular way for those who shall lead the project work, and as will be demonstrated in the following, makes it a very challenging but also a very demanding endeavour at the same time. In this respect the project goal definition, the project plan, the project organization, and the way the project is executed, is of fundamental importance, basically because any project relates to a parent organization who uses its own rules and regulations in its problem-solving efforts. Regardless of which organizational form used though, it seems correct to conclude that any project must have a special form of project "leadership" in order to fulfil all the desired obligations. These conditions may be visualized by sorting the above consequences according to a few main keywords which, both historically and according to modern research, seem to prevail in project settings.[1, 2, 4] These keywords are shown in figure 5.2.

It is relatively easy to see that the keywords italicized in the right column correspond well with the earlier research suggestions on motivational *stimuli*, particularly those of Miner[4] and Murray[5] in their lists of needs

TYPICAL PROJECT CONSEQUENCES	RECOGNIZABLE NEEDS FOR PROPER PROJECT LEADERSHIP
Project work demands creativity, innovation, and often an untraditional way of thinking	The need to CREATE
Project work demands desire and ability to define concrete aims and objectives for work output	The need to understand and define PURPOSE
Project work demands skills in planning and coordinating task production	The need for systematization and ORDER
Project work demands ability to make priorities and take decisions	The need to take charge and DECIDE
Project work demands insight in forces behind motivational and demotivational reactions amongst team members	The need to understand and respond to human attitude and BEHAVIOUR
Project work demands curiosity towards and ability to accept and handle change	The need to initiate and accept CHANGE
Project work demands knowledge about and ability to handle information and to communicate	The need to INTERACT
Project work demands acceptance of hardship and willingness to compete	The need to PROGRESS and use one's capability

Figure 5.2 Project consequences and their related needs

prevailing in organizational settings. The need to "create" covers both the "n Imp" (the need for "impulsivity") and the "n Aut" (the need for having "autonomy", to break away from constraints, and to be "free"). The need to have a "purpose" is found both in the "n Ach" (the need to "achieve" and to work towards preset goals) and the "n Und" (the need to "understand"). The need for "order" covers the "n Ord" (the need for "order", for organized environment, and for logical progress) and a sense of responsibility in carrying out necessary routine duties. The need to "decide" corresponds to "n Pow" (the need for "power" and influence), "n Exh" (the need to "exhibit" oneself, to be the centre of attention), to some extent the "n Agg" (the need for "aggression", to combat for one's sake) and the desire to assert oneself and take charge as well as the desire to exercise power and authority over others. The need to understand human "behaviour" is found both in the "n Aff" (the need for "affiliation"), the "n Har" (the need for "harm avoidance"), the "n Nur" (the need to "nurture"), the "n Suc" (the need for "succourance"), as well as maintaining a favourable attitude toward those in positions of authority. The need for "change" must be said to be embodied both in the "n Ach", the "n Imp" and perhaps the "n Pow", in the sense that the latter need is defined as a desire to influence and direct environment and people. At the personal level this need can also be defined as a need to behave in a distinctive and different way. The need for "interaction" can be found both in the "n Aff", the "n Exh", the "n Nur" and the "n Suc". And the need to "progress" corresponds well with the "n Ach", the "n End", (the need to "endure", or the willingness to work long hours and be patient and unrelenting in work habits) and perhaps the "n Agg". Also the willingness to engage in competition and to be responsible seem well covered.

Also the particular *causes* of motivation prevailing for project leaders derived from laboratory research and interview findings done by this author[1] correspond well; the "newness-will" comes close to the need to "create", the "milestone-will" is also the need to define and engage in goal-directed efforts, the "rework-will" and the "mending-will" enhance the need for order and progress, the "progress-will" naturally coincides with the need to progress, to achieve and to succeed. The "trust-will" can only be obtained by understanding human behaviour and reactions. The "confidence-will" is a necessity if we are to have the courage to initiate and tolerate change. And the "capability-will" is a natural precondition for understanding, for interaction and for success in own work progress.

Comparisons with other findings and observations may also be performed,[6-28] but the general conclusion we can draw is that the needs above seem very typical for the driving forces behind proper project leadership today. Naturally, most of these conditions also prevail in ordinary organizational work and in social interaction in general. What makes the project setting so special is that all these conditions are present at the same time! We cannot, for instance, define an effort as a project even if all the above characteristics are present but there is no clear project goal and a conveyed purpose of the effort. And the reason is that project work has to be *goal-directed*. Similarly, we cannot let go the precondition of a time limit, since project work is to complete something *within a given time*, etc. The challenge for the project leader is henceforth to cater for *all* the needs and desires above in the right sequence, in the right manner, and with the right kind of devotion.

5.3   The Conceptualization of a Specific Project Procedure for Improved Project Leadership

In relation to the characteristics and parameters contained in the project concept as defined here, project success must firstly depend on the initial *project selection*, or simply "Do we have the right project?" This is not an easy question to answer at an early stage, especially not before we have begun to formulate the project's goal. But we must naturally as early as possible try to avoid the wasting of resources on wrong or, perhaps in the end event, undesired efforts. As suggested by many authors,[42] therefore, project work should always be preceded by some kind of "deliberate" creativity, followed by a "first screening" of ideas before the desired goal-directed project effort is commenced. Creativity is in this respect the attribute of bringing into existence a unique concept that would not have occurred or evolved naturally. Creative persons in this way become able to "combine, mix, and expand past experience so that new, non-obvious concepts, variations, or extensions of knowledge are generated".[1]

The Problem of Innovation Intolerance

One problem is, however, that most organizations, even forward-looking ones, often have a limited tolerance for innovation. Managers are more engaged in avoiding disturbances of organizational balance, or they squelch creative suggestions because they are afraid these will threaten their positions.[43] Another kind of reinforcement is due to the fact that innovation is risky. And modern managers are taught to be risk avoiders. Risk avoidance, and hence avoidance of creativity, is also manifested in another way, fear of the future. Many organizations insist on very short payback periods by citing the high cost of capital. Part of this can be justified when the environment is turbulent, as most of the 1990s look likely to be, but part of it may also be explained by the fact that executives see little personal advantage in long-run projects. When rewards are tied to the present, it seems irrational to reduce present profits by investing in an uncertain future.[9] If failure in risky projects is also punished, sensible people will avoid such projects. And if the only reward available lies in the administrative ladder, successful creativeness manifests itself in higher administrative positions. Scientists and inventors often accept these moves because of the higher salary and prestige usually associated with the "promotion".[44]

The Problem of Short-sighted Project Selection Models

The above constraints to a more "unconditional" creativity in the majority of our organizations have in time led to increased emphasis on project evaluation and selection models. The following brief categorization of models and techniques used for project selection[9] gives an idea of how different issues have been focused on throughout the years:

TIME PERIOD	PREDOMINANT PROJECT SELECTION TECHNIQUES
1945–1955	Simple payback calculations, or the related "average annual rate of return". Useful when the uncertainties surrounding project selection are so great that a higher level of sophistication is unwarranted. Many models, for instance of the so-called Operations Research (OR) type, were introduced as interesting but not really reliable tools for interpreting future returns.
1955–1965	The introduction and growth of formal models, particularly strictly profit–profitability models. More information was included in the model trials, but the models also tended to shorten the time horizon of project investment decisions.[45]
1965–1975	The introduction of investment–calculation models, including calculations of a variety of ROI-factors (Return On Investments) and the IRR (Internal Rate of Return). These models were particularly useful when the rate of return on interest was high, and one tended to rely more on the model outputs than on the old "business feeling". In this decennium economists and others with high formal education with a basis in economy (such as MBA's) became the very dominant decision makers.

1975–1985	Still sharp growth in the use of formal models with great emphasis on profitability. But also a growing interest in models that use multiple criteria for decision making. Also a development of interactive decision systems that allowed users to examine the effects of different mixes of possible projects was observed.[46, 47] Such models brought new insight into the decision process per se, in the sense that one realized that "many decision criteria are not easily quantified, and the typical approaches to quantifying subjective preferences are far from satisfactory".[46]
1985–1990	The area of sophisticated scoring and simulation models. Because it is easy to enter all the parts (the data-base, the decision model, and the list of potential projects) into a computer, it is also easy to simulate many solutions to the project selection problem.[9] The decision makers can also investigate the sensitivity of decisions, and this has manifested itself in so-called Decision Support Systems (DSS), Expert Systems (ES) and Artificial Intelligence Systems (AIS). Of particular value are computerized project simulation models allowing for "real-time" feedback on project decisions. What these systems have clearly revealed is that profitability alone is not a sufficient test for the quality of an investment.
1990–	An increased awareness of the merits of interactive computer simulation models, where "cultural" components such as motivation, recentness, personal likes and dislikes, etc. are combined with the traditional structural components such as budget deviations, product quality and use of time. Typical examples of such models are the strategic simulation models developed by the SMG group and the project simulation models used by QMT – Qualitation Management Training[77] – in Norway.

The conclusion we can draw from this is that an increasing interest during the last 40–50 years has taken place in respect of better project selection. According to Porter[48] and Suresh and Meredith,[49] in the future the firm's portfolio of (potential) projects will be the key element in its competitive strategy.

Recommendable Project Steps

When turning to the practical project work after the preliminary project selection is done, we can clearly see that the issues and parameters listed above under project "characteristics", the main project "consequences" related to these characteristics and the project "needs" of today deduced from these consequences support a creative attitude in project developments but also try and avoid a too haphazard and too risky project execution. This is suggested taken care of by sorting the above list of needs in a sequence of occurrence in which the practical project work follows a well planned and thought out procedure. This is concretized in 5 points for proper project conduct as shown in figure 5.3.

The use of concentric squares for each project "step" attempts to describe the operational inter-linkages between the successive actions a professional project leader should attend to. The procedure suggests that the "project definition" comes first, describing the project's goal and objective as well as the constraints necessary to impose on the project effort due to special obligations or limitations in the project environment. Once the project goal and its constraints are set, the next natural step is to plan for goal fulfilment. Important elements of such a plan[20] are a well thought of milestone structure so that achievement and progress can be readily

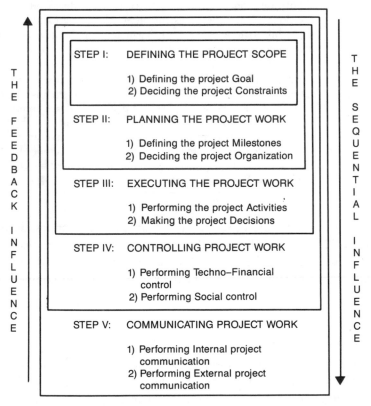

Figure 5.3 Suggested steps in professional project leadership

attended to, and that the project organization which in the best way can comply with the plan and fulfil its purpose is constructed. Once the plan and its proper organization are found and decided, the next step is the project execution itself. This execution will contain two important tasks: (1) to perform the necessary activities, and (2) to make the necessary decisions in order to go ahead with new activities.

In an ideal project development process these first three steps should be enough to complete a project. Since, however, project work is also new and (mandatorily) unique, and the tasks in hand often difficult and even unpredictable, both the project's objective and its initial constraints may change in time for reasons unknown at project start-up. A natural next step is therefore to introduce some kind of project monitoring and control system to the process. One class of elements in such a process is that which concentrates on technical and economical issues, another is the procedure imposed in order to ensure that the project staff are motivated, diligent and capable of performing the project work. This "control" should also be enacted on the project leader him- or herself. The last "step" is then to attach a well-performing information and communication system to the effort, ensuring that the internal flow of decisions and task performances are conveyed in a proper way, as well as informing the project environment about project progress and problems in such a manner that allows important adjustments based on real-life observations to be introduced and executed.

In the following paragraphs each of the key elements under each main step of the project procedure above is described in an operational context. The description concentrates in particular on the obligations tied to the role of the project leader, and will also be suggested as the best way for the project managers of today and tomorrow to attend to project work.

5.3.1 The Project Goal

As already contended from the theoretical section in this book, purpose and goal are important for much of human activity,[29] and the goal-directed notion is one of the earliest observations of characteristics fundamental to project work.[10] As already debated in chapter 2, the theory has its base in the "content" theories, and a considerable amount of research has been carried ut which supports a link between goal-setting and action.[30] Locke, for instance, suggested that the common element in most theories of motivation is goal striving.[32] Davis and Newstrom have further defined leadership as "the process of encouraging and helping others to work enthusiastically toward objectives",[34] and Tannenbaum and Massaryck suggested "interpersonal influence, exercised in situations and directed through the communication process toward the attainment of a specific goal or goals" as a good definition of leadership.[41] This logical cause-and-effect notion which is the fundamental aspect of goal-setting theory[31] is directly transferable to the project concept of today. What is important is that the final goal comes as close as possible to that suggested by Hunsaker and Cook,[33] namely that "highly energetic goal-seeking behavior is more likely if there are reasonably clear, specific, and challenging objectives".

The Problem of Multiple Goals

However, one should be aware that goal definition is not an easy matter. As thoroughly examined by Wenstøp *et al.*,[57] both organizations and individuals tend to have "multiple goals", i.e. they do not have only *one* goal but *several goals at the same time*. Even then it would not have mattered so much, if the situation had not been that many such goals often are in strong conflict with each other.

A typical example is that two of the most frequently mentioned requirements for a well-performing decision-process within our western organizations are:

1. That the decision process is highly *democratic*
2. That the decision process is *fast and simple*

It should be no surprise to observe that these two desires easily end up in strong conflict with each other. If democracy is to be attained satisfactorily, everyone affected by a particular decision should be given both the right and the opportunity to participate to a personally satisfactory extent. But since decisions in a complex society are difficult and affect many, this immediately implies that many issues must be discussed in their full length, that many referendums have to be written, that hearings have to be held, that new amendments may have to be included, new revisions undertaken, etc. This is a process which becomes both time-consuming and, often, very sluggish.

The problem is that if we try to satisfy both these goals at the same time – to chose an "in-between" solution between democracy and rapidity – we end up perhaps even more frustrated because then nobody is satisfied! The process is easily doomed both to be too undemocratic and too slow. A perfect solution to this dilemma is not easy to find. But as will be suggested here, in project work we should perhaps allow for some kind of "goal discrimination" in this respect depending on the individual project situation. In some phases or stages of a project development cycle fast and "effective" decisions should be given priority, while in others a highly democratic process should be chosen, being fully aware that the latter consumes time and perhaps leads to a more "ineffective" progress in the short run. This is also the backbone of the "contingency theories" (chapter 3) for leadership,[35, 36, 37] and which this author has christened a "discontinuous management" style recommendable for project work demanding swift changes in roles and attitudes as the project develops (chapter 2).

The Problem of Goal Sanction

Another problem of goal-setting is related to who sets the goal? Frequently project managers complain that upper management is far more willing to state what they *do not* want than what they *do* want.[38] But the lack of a clear goal definition in the project initiating stage is often quite understandable. If the problem was so clear, the project was perhaps not worth doing since a perfectly described goal often comes very close to the full solution of a problem! (Except for purely technical and financial project investments.) Goal clarification should therefore be regarded more as the result of the *process* of goal-setting. One way of capturing good project goals is to state them in user terms. Good questions are: "How will we know we are finished?" "What will the end result look like?", etc.

Often the value of goal-planning lies in getting started[39] and allowing the final goal description be a dynamic outcome of the project development process itself. We must in this respect, however, ensure that the other item in this project step, that of project *constraints*, is not altered too much. This will be discussed in the following paragraph. The important issue is that goal-setting has a central role in the path–goal process, and it tends to be the establishment of sound targets and objectives that makes successful performance.[34]

The Problem of Goal Preferences

A third important issue is that of goal preferences. Those who define the project goal may have hidden motives embodied in the goal description.

A good example comes from the Norwegian medical care industry. After a year-long dispute a few years ago over which projects to choose in the Norwegian State Hospital, the following two objectives for their project work in general were launched:

1. Every disease shall be cured
2. Every patient shall be cured

The two objectives may look the same, but this is not necessarily true. By inspecting several on-going projects, one found that some projects promoted the first objective, others promoted the last one. This manifested itself in the fact that if every disease is to be cured, even the rarest and most unusual diseases naturally have the right to be treated with every kind of attention and financial outlay. But with the financial constraints under which the medical sector has to live in Norway, there is not enough money available to fully cover both objectives. In this situation the first objective obviously is given the highest priority. The result is that there are a growing number of patients today not treated because their illness is "too common". Examples are patients suffering from stress-sicknesses such as devastating migraine attacks, troublesome back-pain, heart-trouble, etc. And this latter group is consequently the one filling the waiting-lines for medical treatment.

The reason for this priority lies most certainly in biases in the minds of the decision makers. It is a well-known fact that to be allowed to enter medical school in Norway today one must do pretty well in the mark hunting process at college level. The result is that only those with very high marks, and therefore those with a particularly good "academic" aptitude become doctors of medicine in Norway. (Today many doctors receive their education abroad and this has to some extent begun to "level out" this unbalanced trend.) Due to their academic talent, they naturally find more excitement in a "new" disease than in curing an "everyday" one. Rumour has it, in fact, that recently a Norwegian doctor discovered a new disease which nobody has ever had! And doctors themselves claim that in Norway today there are a hundred times more people *living* from AIDS than *suffering* from AIDS. A similar observation has been made in the UK,[40] and such biases are obviously connected to the popularity of the metier. If one gets good school marks, one tends to choose a particular academic profession, perhaps dictated by the expectation that this leads to higher prestige in the future. The same trend is found among economists and MBA's at some of the prestigious schools in Norway today, producing candidates who prefer "marketing research" instead of "selling the product".

A similar kind of problem is found in foreign aid projects, where one can wonder if the real goal of certain projects is to support the aid organization, to really help the target-groups in the recipient country or to protect oneself from being accused of using the income-tax money on unsuccessful projects.

Problems like these are not easy to master. In any company or organization one must realize that top management as well as other stakeholders also have their own personal fortune in mind when selecting projects and deciding project goals.

Goals and Objectives

For project work this brings in the important difference between *goals* and *objectives*. It is not always easy to distinguish between the two, but there is a general tendency to categorize "objectives" as something broader, more loosely defined than "goals" which are supposed to be more precise, more exactly measurable. Perhaps a better way of separating the two is to see them as part of the hierarchy within an organization, with the organizations' purpose or "mission" at the highest level. The resulting interconnection is illustrated in figure 5.4.

The meaning of the hierarchical structure is that any organization, be it large or small, should have an overall purpose for its existence. A commercial enterprise aims probably at earning so much money that it can

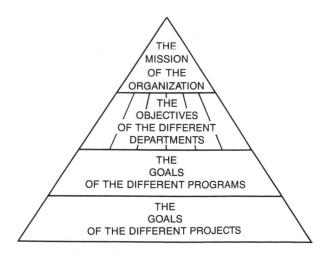

Figure 5.4 A hierarchy for goals, objectives and mission in an organization

be financially stronger (thereby preventing itself from bankruptcy and elimination), a public institution may aim at providing a fast and effective service for its clients or serve its public impartially and equitably. These are typical descriptions of "missions". And, as demonstrated, "missions" should be possible to define both for public and private institutions or business ventures. If, for instance, the "mission" is simply to survive, then the "objective" for each and every department must be to support this. The sales department must see to it that they sell enough goods to survive, the productions department that enough relevant goods are produced, the personnel department that enough skilled workers are available today and in the future, and so on. At the next level we must then see to it that all the different "programmes" in turn have "goals" that support these objectives. The sales programmes must have sales targets that match the sales objectives, the training programmes must have contents that match the need for qualified people, etc. Projects can then be developed as smaller or separate portions of programmes. While programmes may cover a relatively large set of activities, each project has a limited scope and a distinct number of directives concerning assignments and time. And accordingly, each "project" must both be part of well-defined programmes as well as support its own clear goal. The development of a new prototype must comply with a recognized need for such a new product in order to fulfil the mission to survive. A project that investigates the possibilities for developing a new training module must support a particular need for training in the relevant business area, which in turn must, for instance, be part of a recognized survival-mission.

The different levels above are normally linked together by different sets of policies, procedures, and plans. A "policy" is a general guideline for decision making. It sets up boundaries around decisions, including those that can be made and shutting out those that cannot. In this way it channels the thinking of organization members so that it is consistent with the mission and the objectives. Policies are usually established deliberately and formally by top managers, but may also emerge informally and at lower levels in the organization from a seemingly consistent set of decisions on the same subject made over a period of time.

"Procedures" provide normally a more detailed set of instructions for performing a sequence of actions that occurs often or regularly. Such detailed instructions guide the employees who perform project tasks and help insure a consistent approach to specific situations.

Project "plans" are then developed to achieve the specific project goal in the most appropriate way. They describe down to the necessary detail how each step of the procedure from start to finish most preferably shall be performed. The specific features of good project plans are described in section 5.3.3.

Naturally, the rigidity in the project goal and the procedure behind its formulation will depend on the status in which the business is at present. If there is no immediate pressure for surviving only, projects may fulfil objectives and missions such as better market profiling, the investigation of new and interesting business ventures or the use of business margins to improve the standard of physical facilities or social collaboration amongst employees. The initiative may also then come from many different layers in the organization, and we may chose to have a high degree of freedom in terms of who should be allowed to start new project ventures.

Contrarily, if budgets are tight and time is pressed, every effort should be made to run the project almost like a "military manoeuvre", towards its defined goal.

It should be mentioned that the same "private business" way of thinking with regard to goals and procedures will today apply well for public organizations and institutions as well. If the mission is to render a better service to certain groups of people in a society, then an objective perhaps is to do this as equitably and effectively as possible, and the projects initiated should accordingly have goals that measurably respond to this objective.

The Concrete Goal Description

Once agreed on, the next step should be to describe each project goal in a manner that is operationally good enough. Many attempts have been made to make project goals better for those involved. One frequently recurring problem is that new goals automatically imply change, and change means uncertainty, risk and perhaps unpleasantness. To suggest change is also a hidden criticism of the established system. As someone represents it, accordingly they will feel they are blamed. There is also the fear that the change may lead to our established competence or qualifications vanishing or becoming worth far less, or that the new situation the project creates may demand far more effort and far more personal contribution than we have been accustomed to regard as one's "normal" output. Kolb, Rubin and McIntyre[64] have suggested five main reason why managers may hesitate in setting proper goals:

1. Unwillingness to give up alternative goals
2. Fear of failure

3. Lack of organizational knowledge
4. Lack of knowledge of the environment
5. Lack of confidence

If we should extend these elaborations to the world of goal-setting techniques, perhaps the so-called MBO,[56, 58] or Management by Objectives technique, comes closest to one that links the whole spectra from missions to concrete plans together in an operational way. The technique has experienced both enthusiastic applause and strong negative reactions since it was first launched as a new management tool in the early 1960s. Many similar programmes have been developed, including "Goal Management",[18] "Management by Results",[59] "Work Planning and Review",[59] "Goals and Controls Systems"[59] and others. Not only for use in business, they are found in typical non-business environments also, such as educational, health, religious and government organizations.[60]

MBO refers to a formal, or moderately formal, set of procedures that begins with goal-setting and continues through performance review. The key to MBO is that it is a participative process, actively involving managers and staff members at every organizational level. The starting point for MBO is a very positive philosophy about people and what makes them want to work. If objectives are right, it should be possible to define each person's major areas of responsibility in terms of expected, measurable results. These objectives are then used by subordinates in planning their work and by both subordinates and their superiors for monitoring progress. Performance appraisals are conducted jointly on a continuing basis, with provisions for regular periodic reviews.

Early it was recognized that the MBO technique was particularly well-suited for project management.[61] The most apparent advantages are those observed by Tosi and Carroll:[62]

1. It lets individuals know what is expected of them.
2. It aids in planning by making managers establish goals and target dates.
3. It provides communication between managers and subordinates.
4. It makes individuals more aware of the organization's goals.
5. It makes the evaluation process more equitable by focusing on specific accomplishments. It also lets subordinates know how well they are doing in relation to the organization's goals.

However, it has also become quite clear that MBO has weaknesses as well. Especially because appraisals of subordinates involve status, salaries, and promotions. Even in the best MBO programme, the review process might well cause tension and resentment.[59] Nor can all accomplishments be quantified or measured. There are also weaknesses that theoretically should not exist but that frequently seem to develop in even properly implemented MBO programmes such as:[59, 63]

1. Lack of managerial support or a management style which does not encourage MBO.
2. A general resentment to adaptation and change.
3. Managerial lack of skill in interpersonal relations.
4. Difficulties in making proper job descriptions.
5. Difficulties in setting and coordinating objectives.
6. Difficulties in control of goal achievement methods.
7. Conflict between creativity and MBO.

For these reasons we should perhaps have a careful view of MBO if we decide to try implementing it today. But the technique has so many advantages that at least part of it is indeed very applicable. And seen from the angle of project leadership, it will here be contended that one module, that of *goal description*, is particularly well-suited for defining project goals. In that case, the conditions outlined in figure 5.5 should be present.[20]

The first prerequisite points to the fact that if people are not sure whether the project goal is reached or not, they may easily become frustrated and even demotivated.

The second points to the importance of giving focus to the individual.

A GOOD PROJECT GOAL	
should be:	should not be:
1. Quantitative or Measurable	1. Qualitative or Unmeasurable
2. Recognized at the Individual level	2. Without Individual Connection
3. Realistic	3. Minimum- or Maximum-oriented
4. Simple	4. Complicated
5. Result-oriented	5. Cost-oriented
6. Motivating	6. Uninteresting

Figure 5.5 Suggested prerequisites for effective project goals

Even if this may glorify the "ego", we should bear in mind that if things go wrong it is often too easy to find someone else to blame if it was a group effort. If we are the single responsible person, we must also accept single personal responsibility. And similarly, if things go well we get the deserved credit.

The third point focuses on the need for individuals to set their own goals. If higher management do so they may easily set them too high and unattainable or too low and unchallenging.

The fourth point stresses the need for the project goal to be understandable and conveyable to all involved. Unfortunately, it seems far easier to make a complicated goal than a simple one, particularly for the more research-oriented projects where academicians formulate the goals.

The next point focuses on the tendency to orient a task towards cost and cost reduction instead of concentrating on improving the result of an effort or investment. We should be mindful that it is the gap between expenses and income which makes the living. One way of broadening the gap is to keep the income at the same level and reduce the costs, another is to *increase* the costs providing the income increases correspondingly! In the long run we should be aware that the first approach always has a limit – we can only reduce to a certain minimum – while increasing both parameters produces almost unlimited possibilities!

The last issue, that of motivation, is of course one of the most interesting factors, since there seems to be almost "no limits" to the productivity human beings can attain when properly motivated. A demotivated person is likewise a considerable threat to the project effort and the goal fulfilment.

The above list of project goal recommendations is not necessarily exhaustive. But it gives a good approach in making a project goal operational and challenging. It is also useful both as a monitoring instrument to project execution and as a clarifying mental process at the individual level in the project initiation stage so as to find out the real objective of the desired project effort.

5.3.2   The Project Constraints

The project constraints are often treated in a surprisingly haphazard manner in many projects. There seems to be a general belief that the constraints to the effort are well known to all involved, whereas it often becomes deplorably clear at later stages that fundamental issues initially were not taken care of, that project superiors, for instance the client, wrongly thought that absolute limits were well understood by project executors, and that changes in goals and directions were not thought by the project leader to be his or her responsibility, even when circumstances clearly pointed to this to be evidently so.

One way of evaluating the project's constraints is to identify its most apparent "success factors".[53] These are normally factors which are defined as those most critical to project success and may be identified both individually and in combination. Normally they are decided by the project authorities (such as the client, the top management or similar bodies who bear the responsibility of defining the mission of the project effort).

The "Terms of Reference" (T.O.R.) for Projects

Such guidelines are often referred to as the "Terms of Reference" (T.O.R.) for the project. Normally the T.O.R. consists of an integrated three-part package:[54]

1. A project formulation framework intended as a tool to help project formulators in systematically analyzing key issues and agreeing on basic content and structure of a project before allowing the project execution to take place or the project documents to be written.
2. An annotated project format to guide the actual project execution or the production of the project documents.
3. A check-list intended as a project appraisal tool to use after the project work is terminated or the final project document is presented.

The three parts complement each other and are intended to form an integrated whole. Important is that though the purpose of the T.O.R. is to provide guidance for the systematic and logical examination of those interrelated elements which constitute a well-formulated project, it can be changed if circumstances prove this to be necessary. Its use is intended to stimulate the articulation, in succinct outline form, of the major elements of the project. The process described above may therefore be a successive refinement of the T.O.R. until it provides the basis for agreement on the major elements of logic of the project. In complicated project efforts one first approach for the project executors could after this well be to interpret and debate the proper meaning of the T.O.R. formulations, including the proposal of reformulations if necessary. Once such a T.O.R. is agreed upon, it will provide a ready basis for the subsequent planning of the fully-fledged project document.

If properly developed, the T.O.R. can be used throughout the full life of the project as a background document for its monitoring and evaluation. A copy of the T.O.R. in the form agreed to by the parties involved in the formulation of the project should therefore be maintained in the active project file at the unit directly responsible for the project. The T.O.R. will then become the basis for preliminary screening, support and feedback by the different bodies involved in the project effort.

A Framework for Project Reference Factors

A useful framework for implementing key reference factors is done by a study of over 400 projects by Slevin and Pinto[55] and elaborated by Graham.[83] This is shown in figure 5.6.[55]

As the framework is intended to demonstrate, ten factors were identified as critical to project success, and there was a relationship among them. Conceptually the factors are sequenced logically rather than randomly. For example, it is important to set goals or define mission and benefits of the programme before seeking top management support. Similarly, unless consultations with client occur early in the process, the chances of subsequent client acceptance may be reduced. In the figure three additional factors are hypothesized to play a more overriding role in the

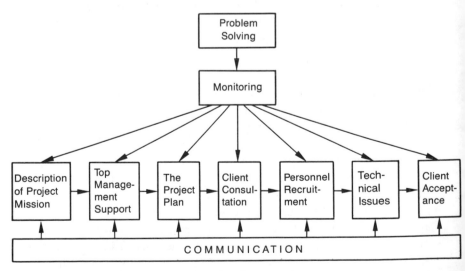

Figure 5.6 Key factors in project implementation

project implementation. These factors, monitoring and feedback, communication, and trouble shooting, must all be present at each point in the implementation process.

In conclusion, no project effort should be initiated without full clarification among the parties as to the possible major constraints to the particular project. As will be discussed in the following paragraphs, these constraints should also be re-evaluated regularly to see if new conditions require new changes. Or if not, even to terminate the project effort if goal fulfilment means breaking important constraints such as budgetary limits, impossible deadlines or other absolute resource limits.

5.3.3   The Project's Milestones

As already contended, to understand the advantage of efficient project planning, we must first of all clarify the main purpose of the project. In general, this means concentrating on the following three issues when making the plan.[20]

1. To make it a basis for directing the course of movement toward an agreed objective.
2. To produce a means of combining tasks and resources – in both a short and a long term perspective.
3. To construct a tool for informing and motivating on future events and activities; what, who, when and where.

Naturally, all three points differ in importance, accuracy and detail depending on the type and size of the project. If the project is simple and lean, and the time span is short, the good knowledge of the output expected from the effort may be enough to start off the project work. But if matters are complicated, if the resource allocation has to match time and money in an intricate way, and if there are other objectives in the short-term perspective than in the long run, then the project would most probably benefit from a well-planned procedure.

Similarly, if everybody knows what to do, and all involved are well-informed and highly motivated, a tiresome planning procedure may destroy the enthusiasm and ruin momentum. But if a better understanding of what is really expected is highly important, and a good plan is felt to motivate individuals to increased willingness to do their best, a plan that is well thought through often proves to be the favourable instrument for personal inspiration and better goal achievement.

Conclusively, if the project goal can be reached without planning, we need not plan but simply go ahead! But if we feel that the course of action is better understood and promoted by some initially confirmed steps of action, the whole project process should be thoroughly planned accordingly.

We should also note that planning always provides a unique possibility to experiment with organizational resources without exposing them to the risks of real-life problems. It is far less expensive to mend a mistake in the planning stage than to correct a real-life error. In effect, rational project planning often depends more on the structure and maintenance of information systems than the use of technical network analyses, and the job of the planning expertise therefore requires a deep understanding of how information and communication will move around in the project and accordingly the human dynamics of the project environment.[65]

The process of planning is virtually the process of resource allocation. And planning is therefore a dynamic process by which contributing and affected groups reach agreement. This consensus is recorded in plans and revised plans that provide the framework for decision making for some time ahead. It is therefore naive to regard project planning as simply an abstract, intellectual exercise divorced from the human side of the project organization. Managing a project is to "lead" people, and the human and technical aspects are inseparable, making the human dimensions a legitimate concern of leadership. In this way project planning aims both to support informed decision making and to stimulate creative problem solving throughout the project life.

The Need for Proper Planning Tools

The merits of project planning have been so widely extolled that few project leaders will normally express their doubts. However, public sentiments do not necessarily translate into private realities. As already discussed in chapter 3, project planning as such took off following the development and application of network analysis on the Polaris project in the 1950s. Until the advent of critical path methods, there was no generally accepted procedure to aid in the management of task efforts such as projects. Each manager had his own scheme which often involved the use of simple bar charts, originally developed by Henry Gantt around 1900. The field now is really the result of contributions from management consultants, computer companies and planners themselves, and it is impressive to see the accuracy and complexity modern project plans can handle. But these advancements do not always make the best contribution to project success. Many consultants have made a good business out of the installation of sophisticated planning systems, which are later shown to be only methodological sleights of hand and are no substitutes for vision and leadership.[66] System analysts and programmers have similarly developed network algorithms which work well in theory but may fail completely in real-life situations.[66] The suspicions of many project managers about project plans are therefore not unfounded.

The crux is to plan at the *right* level of detail. And the "right" level is the amount of detail that can be *feasibly monitored*. Information, therefore, is the main source and dictates the detail of a project plan. Structuring and maintaining information systems becomes then the chief task of the project leader or those given the authority to do the project planning for him or her.

Planning by Milestones

As already contended, project work deals with an uncertain and partly unknown future. One way to avoid too much guesswork is to plan only for a future which with reasonable exactness can be foreseen. And depending on the parameters chosen, one can establish intermediate goals which are reasonably attainable for those involved yet still in line with more long term project objectives. This way of doing "step-wise" project planning, is often referred to as "milestone planning". The milestone issue is in many ways a product of the need for intermediate goals in more long-lasting work endeavours.

Thinking through the checkpoints and events and beginning to list activities will typically generate additional events and milestones not thought of at first. Defining checkpoints and activities in this way is often a back-and-forth process. As already pointed to in the preceding paragraph, we should begin with the larger perspective of the goal, for instance, the overall mission of the whole effort, and then become increasingly more precise when it comes to the objectives closer at hand, then define the necessary milestones, then describe the events, and finally give an exact presentation of the required activities. In effect this means that we work backward from the goal of the project to the first step necessary to take to get to that goal. As illustrated in figure 5.7, goals, objectives, checkpoints, and activities then become highly interrelated and portray the crucial steps in the project journey.

Figure 5.7 The project's milestones

The appropriate project plan becomes after this the fundament on which the right project organization is built and on which the stepwise project execution depends.

5.3.4   The Project's Organization

The purpose of project organizations is to make temporary contrivances aimed at structuring and leveraging the work of people. Historically, projects were structured as functional arrays. The reason was that when new projects were introduced one avoided the creation of a new organizational type. The functional project organization meant minimum threat to existing structure and culture, and the project could safely be run without any major reallocation of existing resources.

A response to the flaws of the functional approach came with the "project-islands" approach[67] in which project personnel were detached from the remainder of the company in separate units. A separate project-only organization supported a temporary, goal-oriented fabrication, it rapidly became popular with project managements.

With reference to the history of the project organization (chapter 3), we could perhaps say that from this emerged a sort of "compromise" organization, combining in one organizational type the best from the former two directions of organizing project work. In essence, this is the "matrix" organization, in which the project partly belongs to, partly is detached from the project's base organization.

Today project organizations find many forms, of which the *matrix* organization and the *network* organization seem to be the most popular.[1] The theory behind the matrix approach is perhaps the most interesting since it tries to catch the best of two worlds. From the functional world we gain specialization, division of labour, immediate application and reduction of personnel, consistence within the project effort and the possibility of the transferral of knowledge from one project to another by the persons involved. From the temporary approach we have better possibilities for goal fulfilment, the advantages of a cross-disciplinary utilization of resources, and the flavour of uniqueness, creativity, and apprehensible communication.

The network phenomenon, which is perhaps the most modern organizational trend for projects, looks at organizations from another angle. It does not attempt to structure people into an organization, but to exploit the natural structures that exist among people. Often networks consist of a grouping of separate links between people throughout an existing organic structure, such as a project. Perhaps the best way to describe the network organization is that it is the collection of friendships, acquaintances, favours, debts, grapevines, cliques, mutual interests and social ties.[67] We must here distinguish the network *organizational* structure from the network *planning* method earlier mentioned. To avoid confusion we should perhaps refer to the *social* network organization when talking about this way of organizing project work.

The Problems of Organized Problem-solving Efforts

However, we must not be blind to the many problems embodied in the organizing of problem-solving efforts as well. The initial reason for trying out different organizational structures in projects came when it was realized that what were advantages in the traditional functional approach often collided with project needs. Those who still insisted on managing projects similar to ongoing organizational structures often had the opinion that projects should be treated as if they were operations. Which meant a focus on *tasks* rather than *goals*. Moreover, the functional "tree" is based on the segregation of specialists into distinct "boxes", with very few crossings over organizational boundaries. In addition to this process orientation, the functional organization is also characterized by what might perhaps be termed "tunnel" vision among its supporters. They seek to define each box, or person, within the organization by rigid rules and responsibilities. Often the outcome is organizational disputes, boundary squabbles and territorial suspicions.

These problems, however, do not imply that the matrix organization and social network organization are free from flaws. For the matrix organization, a handicap is the division of loyalty among personnel and conflicting objectives and methods among the different axes of the matrix. Often this leads to intractable positions taken by both sides in a dispute. This is earlier (chapter 4) referred to as "idiosyncratic relations" or "organizational gridlock".[67] Another problem is caused by the temporary nature of the matrix organization, which leads to temporary lines of communication, temporary authorities, temporary procedures and short-term relationships. Matrix organizations are not only contrived but self-destroying.

The Leadership Role in Organized Settings

A last issue, but by no means the least of issues, is that of *leadership*. It seems that the shorter the project period[20] or perceived project period,[1] the smaller role leadership and mutual interests will play. This may well explain the tenuous and tentative nature of project planning work, and why planning often gets off to a slow, shaky start.

Social network dangers are that they are based on the concept of free and open access to information. Those projects which can not tolerate this, for bureaucratic or security reasons, are unable to use this organizational structure as a working method. As suggested by Gilbreath,[67] there is also a tendency to emphasize "what you do" in a network rather than "who you are". Those who prefer to be identified by where they work or who they are with or whom they supervise will not praise the network approach. And perhaps what is most problematic is that the network organization is often unable to assign total responsibility to any one person or group. Network participants consult, advise, touch base and connect, but seldom lead, or take the consequences of leadership. These disadvantages should therefore be carefully thought over if we decide to use the unstructured potential of this organizational type in project efforts.

Essentially, the real culture of project leadership refers to actual behaviour – those things and events that really exist in the life of an organization. The introduction of project leadership into an existing culture will soon experience changes in attitudes, in values, in beliefs, and in the management system. Thus, a new cultural context for the sharing of decisions, results, rewards and accountability will emerge.

As already suggested in the earlier chapters of this book, we should perhaps in most projects limit the organizational alternatives in project settings to three different "models" of project organizations (chapter 3.4.3):

1. The "fully incorporated" or "steering authority" project organization.
2. The "split authority" or "matrix" project organization.
3. The "full authority" or "project island" project organization.

Their "physical" location in relation to a "base" organization can be illustrated as in figure 5.8.

Briefly, we can identify the first organizational location by its single-professional staffing and often relatively simple goal description. In the second type the project participants are not permanently allocated to the project tasks, and the project manager or leader shares the authority over project resources with line management. In the third type the project is free to live its "own life" and the only demand is that it reaches its goal within the given limits of time and resource expenditures.

All three forms are fully acceptable, depending on what kind of project we intend to execute and what type of personnel is allocated. It is the skill of the project leader in organizing his or her resources in the best way which in the end portrays his or her leadership professionality.

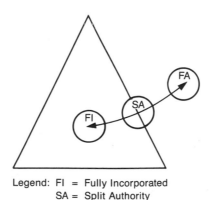

Legend: FI = Fully Incorporated
SA = Split Authority
FA = Full Authority

Figure 5.8 Three possible project organizations

5.3.5   The Project Activities

Successful project execution is complex and difficult. Project leaders must pay attention simultaneously to a wide variety of human, financial, and technical factors. Contrary to line management, projects are often developed by a team of individuals who create a series of complex tasks requiring high levels of coordination.

Fortunately these tasks are not necessarily spread out in an equally complex manner over the whole life span of a project. As earlier contended, the concept of a project life cycle provides a useful framework for looking at project dynamics over time. In a study of 69 Norwegian projects,[1] all of them with considerable variations in terms of time, money and personnel involvement, all the project managers were able to identify four distinct project phases of activity. Their average relative size were as shown in figure 5.9.

The relative dimensioning of the four phases was done by calculating "task production" as the primary measurement scale. This is a generally agreed approach in project efforts,[50, 51] in the sense that by measuring the "provision of work to be done" it is easy to compare the running activity with both the planned activity per time unit and the degree to which the final project goal measured in total "task" units is accomplished.

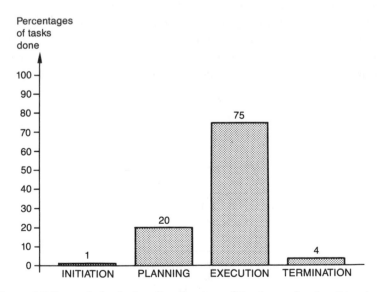

Figure 5.9 Recorded relative distribution of "task production" in projects in Norway in 1988–90

This is also the essence of the method of the Work Breakdown Structure (WBS) in which projects are broken down into suitable packages which again are divided into elements or manageable tasks.[52] Having identified the tasks, they can be executed by people who have the capability to complete them. In this way, work responsibility in projects will be knowledge-based at every level. The number of tasks and work packages employed in a given project depends on its size, its complexity and whether or not particular aids, such as, for instance, computer software programs, are used for the control of costs, time, and other resources.

The Dimensioning of Project Phases

The above average figures considerable differences in magnitude regarding tasks produced within each phase. As may be expected, there is a very limited task production in the project initiation phase. This does not imply, however, that the importance of the phase is insignificant, since at this stage the basic project idea is chosen, the first framework of the project plan made and often the potential project leader contacted and assigned to the project effort. Also the consumed calendar time in this phase may be quite extensive. The termination phase is also quite limited in terms of task production, but as with the project initiation phase this phase should be of great importance, since at this stage the ultimate project goal is supposed to be reached and all the concluding efforts done. As much as 3/4 of the whole project effort goes though into the project execution phase, leaving 1/5 of the task production to the planning phase.

By way of contrast, in a study of R&D projects only, Cleland and King[10] found the relative distribution of the "number of managerial and technical personnel" between these four phases to be 15–114–102–38. This makes the planning phase apparently larger than the execution phase. Burbridge[14] argues that "with the ever increasing complexity of, and tighter constraints on, major projects the emphasis placed on the conception stage is increasing", and that "15–20% of the total budget may be necessary to spend on assembling and evaluating a novel project". These are interesting propositions and perhaps they point to a necessary change in attitude in the future in terms of which project phase should have the strongest attention.

What we may safely conclude is that all four project phases above should receive their attention; the project initiation phase because of the importance of choosing the right project; the project planning phase because most project performance is usually measured against the planned effort done in this phase; the execution phase because of its consumption of resources and its momentum; and the termination phase due to the importance of the goal fulfilment activity and the general desire to terminate the process in a sound, rational and rewarding way.

What is clear is that every project relies on the successful conduct of many processes. These processes are not necessarily intended to be perfect, for their role is often a quite pragmatic one, namely to accomplish objectives. As such, many operational principles do not apply to their design or conduct. Whenever possible, however, certain repetitive processes may benefit from operational analyses. The issue is to shorten the gap between activity and results, eliminate non-contributing activity, segmentation, formalized conclusions, capitalizing on human ingenuity, and for some processes outright termination. Because of their need to circumvent process obstacles, today's project leaders need to be innovative, result-oriented, and resourceful when executing project work.

However, it must be quite clear that each major project endeavour or project element contains both general and specific failure factors. The general ones are those similar to other infatuations pertaining to planning, execution and information systems. Specific failure factors include personality dependence, disjointed activity, the burden of tradition, debasement of the human element and the human contribution, procedural adoration, fluff and impotence. However, one very persistent and chronic problem found in the area of process design and implementation seems to be the unnecessary encumbrances tacked on to innocent processes, formalized through the procedure approval process, and made virulent through the continued acceptance of them as if they were inescapable facts of life.

Criteria for Good Project Processes

Gilbreath[67] has debated if there are some particular criteria for good project processes. Seven of them are described below:

1. That the process is easily established and understood. The more complex a process, the more prone it is to misunderstanding and incorrect implementation.
2. That the process makes use of operational aids. A goal should therefore be to segregate repeated processes from unique ones. Processes lending themselves to operational controls should

take advantage of them, for instance by introducing operational analysis methodology.

3. That the process can be modified without project disruption. Each process should be designed to accommodate foreseen changes in the project environment, and to be readily modified if unforeseen changes occur.

4. That the process is goal-oriented. No process should be self-justifying. Like plans and information systems project processes should not be used to justify organizations or sustain personal authority.

5. That the process produces identifiable results. Any process that fails in doing so is an open-ended series of activities. As already contended, one basic project feature is that it has an end. Otherwise the process easily becomes indeterminate and we cannot tell whether it has begun, is taking place, or is completed.

6. That the process is necessary. It is not enough that a project process brings identifiable results, if those results are inconsequential to the project effort and its goal. It pays to design processes such that the end results are identified quickly, before too much time and money is spent unnecessarily.

7. That the process rewards compliance. We must be careful that the project process does not damage project achievements or jeopardize the position or effectiveness of the performers. Often process circumvention leads to a better understanding of why a particular project process is poor.

To this must be added, though, that no process is perfect, and perfection is seldom a project goal: Accomplishment is, however. One way to promote project success is therefore to examine proposed processes or those in use, and determine if any pragmatic improvements can be made. And we should remember that no matter how intricate, failure-resistant and effective a process appears in the design stage, it will be prone to fail if it ignores the human factors. Any process that fulfils a recognized human need is most probably on the right track toward successful implementation.

Conclusively, performing project activities is to turn expectations into accomplishments. Perhaps one of the least understood reasons for project success involves the notion of processes. Particularly if our perspectives are not guided by the pragmatism that often distinguishes project work from operations. We must realize that all processes, like all tools, are important only in that they are necessary to achieve results. No process should be undertaken unless it can be shown to contribute directly to the project's proper mission. Processes involve activities, tasks, functions, resource usage, the exercise of authority and judgement, and express or imply responsibility for their implementation. In this way no project activity can be executed without a clear connection to the "world of decisions".

5.3.6   The Project Decisions

What has become abundantly clear during the modern history of project management is that project *decisions* are at least equally, if not more, important than the project activities in successful project accomplishments. If we take an ordinary project plan and investigate the amount of effort that goes into decision making compared to that exerted in order to improve activity performance, we should not be surprised to find that the effect of a good or wrong decision in the long run far outlives a badly performed job. A poorly effectuated job can generally be re-done, while decisions often are felt as final judgements not so easily repaired.[1] Not that we cannot make new decisions, but often decisions have psychological impacts beyond their immediate time horizon. Too much tottering in the decision-making process on the part of project authorities may lead to feelings of insecurity and frustration among all involved parties, and in the longer run demotivation, ineffectiveness, and perhaps finally unsuitability for the tasks envisaged. Such effects have already been discussed in the earlier chapters of this book, but it is worth stressing that project personnel may be far more willing to engage in rework than repeatedly accept wrong decisions.

For this reason the decision process in projects should be well investigated with regard to the degree to which it could be improved. First of all, the classical three steps in any decision-making process are:

1. What is the *problem?*
2. What are the *alternatives?*
3. Which alternative is *best?*

In a more elaborate framework this sequence is also the core of what is generally referred to as "consequence analysis", which follows the pattern shown in figure 5.10.

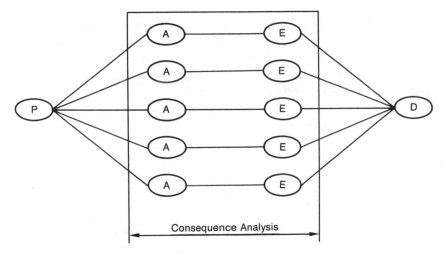

Figure 5.10 The main elements of consequence analysis

where:

P = The recognized Problem
A = The different Alternatives
E = The outcome of the Evaluation of each alternative
D = The best possible Decision resulting from the evaluation process

This is a sequence indirectly acknowledged by many, in the sense that early particular methods and techniques for better decision making in organizations were launched. The rich flora of "operational research" (OR) methods in the 1960s and 1970s confirm this. Particularly useful were techniques such as "decision-trees", "priority-ranking" methods (NPV, ROI), "mini-max" methods, and the like. This is still a rapidly developing area, and the increasing emphasis today on "Decision Support Systems" (DSS), "Expert Systems" (ES) and "Artificial Intelligence" (AI) structures supports this notion.

With the fast development of the project approach as a problem-solving tool in itself, these techniques were found particularly applicable. But history has also revealed that the benefits of using quantitative techniques are often not sufficiently understood by managers, and also that many managers simply lack knowledge of quantitative techniques. In addition comes the fact that required data may be difficult to quantify, and that many managers are quite successful without using any techniques at all!

The Limitations of "Scientific" Methods

What has become quite clear is that "scientific" methods alone cannot answer every decision problem in projects. Projects also have a "soft" side dominated by the human component, which follows different rules for "optimal solutions" and different rules for effective conduct. This dual system of emphasis is illustrated in figure 5.11.

As the figure is intended to describe, the "structural" system is run through a sequence of activities starting out with the project goal, affected by the physical resources made available, measured by the intermediate results obtained and controlled by the observed discrepancy between the intermediate results and the final goal description. As long as a discrepancy is observed, the process continues towards it final goal fulfilment. This system finds its counterpart in a "cultural" system starting out with a recognized desire, manipulated by the human resource input, measured by the degree of need satisfaction, which generally is more "evaluated" than "measured", and which in turn either fulfils the initial desire or does not.

Both these processes are typical feedback processes, they work in

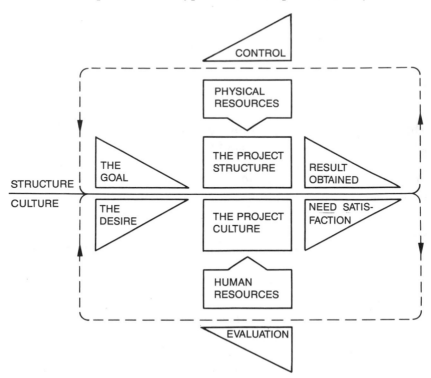

Figure 5.11 The dual side of project leadership

parallel, and are the key elements in the complete project decision structure.

The "Risk" Notion

The lesson to be learned from this is that effective project work needs both good knowledge of how tools and structure function, and a good understanding of how the human mind works. But this perspective alone is often not enough to really make the decision process in projects successful. The additional issue increasingly recognized is the influence of *risk* on project performance. The important notion is what makes people willing to take risks? Since decision making in project environments is always risky – due to the uniqueness of the project work itself – this has become a crucial area of importance.

When managers refer to risk analysis, they usually refer to "decision analysis".[70] For this reason a first step is to determine the manager's own "utility function" for resource spending. Utility models are particularly useful when the decision maker is seeking a decision that achieves several different objectives simultaneously. When this is the situation different kinds of weighted factor scoring models should be recommended. This is an approach which has proved useful for a wide range of project-related decisions.[71, 72]

Simulation combined with sensitivity analysis is another useful form for evaluating the risk of a project endeavour while still in the conceptual stage.[2] Using the net-present value approach, one would support a project if the net-present value of the cash flow, including the initial cash investment, is positive and represents the best available alternative of funds. By altering different value parameters, the sensitivity of different resource allocations can be tested, and thereby the risk involved with different alternatives. Precautions should be taken, however, that we do not utilise the "full-cost" philosophy at this stage. The full-cost approach to estimating cash flows forces the inclusion of arbitrary determined overheads in the calculation. These overheads are by definition often not affected by the change in product or process and thus are not relevant to the decision and the risk involved. Normally the only relevant costs are those that will be changed by the implementation of the new process or product.

This brings in the aspect of the former mentioned DSS-analysis in which we are given a picture of the proposed change in terms of the cost and time involved. The uncertainty associated with each individual element of the process can then be included. Simulation runs will indicate the likelihood of achieving various levels of savings. Investigation of the simulation model will also expose the major sources of uncertainty in the final cost distribution. If the project itself is near the margin of acceptability, the uncertainty may be reduced by doing some preliminary research aimed at reducing uncertainty in the areas of cost estimation where it was highest. The preliminary research can be subjected to a cost-benefit analysis when the benefit is reduced uncertainty.

As already contended, the uniqueness of project work implies a balance between *risk* and *challenge*. In all the above calculations we should therefore also include the implications different kinds of solutions may have on the human component. In a simplified way we could perhaps demonstrate the interrelationship between risk and challenge as proposed in figure 5.12.

The model suggests that when uniqueness is a basic project characteristic, this automatically stimulates two fundamental needs in human beings, namely the need for security and the need for growth. Alderfer[73] argued, for instance, that Murray and Maslow's need hierarchies were basically composed of three components; the need for "growth", the need for "relatedness" and the need for "existence".

In general, we can conclude that both risk and challenge are important factors for the well being of the human component in project work. Or, to regard it in another perspective, projects without a certain amount of risk

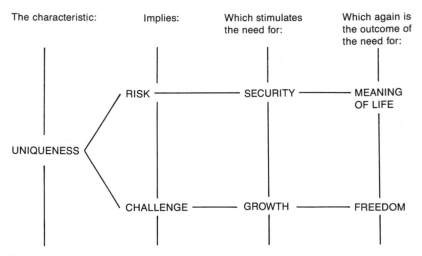

Figure 5.12 A possible connection between task uniqueness and human needs

or challenge should perhaps be adjudged. That project work by this also supports the need for "freedom" and "meaning" makes it even more worthwhile to engage in.

Decision Makers and Decision Supporters

A last issue connected to decision making in projects is here related to recent studies of project work in Norway.[69] It was found that criticism of decisions in many projects was particularly "one-sided". By interviewing people at different levels of authority both in private and public organizations, the tendency to blame one's own superiors for inadequate decisions was uncovered. Since this seemed to be a major criticism at almost every organizational level, one immediate conclusion was that only the most incompetent people occupied the top echelon positions in these organizations! While this corresponds well with the popular "Peter Principle" in which everyone in the end is promoted to his personal level of incompetence, this should not to be assumed to be a true law of conduct among intelligent people. And further investigation of this phenomenon also revealed that there was a different effect prevailing, namely that the decision makers often lacked good enough information for them to make sensible decisions!

In a growing "information culture" this naturally poses new and intriguing questions and gives rise to a number of theories. One is that perhaps the rapidly increasing amount of available information makes the sorting of it an impossible task and produces puzzlement and passivity among leaders.[74] Another possibility could be that in a typical welfare society such as that found in Norway, leaders become so "democratized" that they slip into a sort of "over-kindness" which prevents them from demanding good enough decision support documentation from their own subordinates. For two interrelated levels of responsibility in an organization this can be illustrated as in figure 5.13.

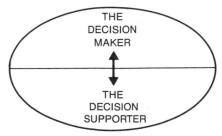

Figure 5.13 The two main decision-making bodies in organizational structures

If the decision supporter conveys incomplete or confusing information through reports or oral contribution, the decision maker easily feels insecure and tries to avoid taking the decision.

The following could be a typical case demonstrating this effect:[1]

One Friday afternoon the project leader rushes into the office of his nearest subordinate asking him to finalize by Monday morning a paper he is preparing. He adds that the paper contains important data which both of them must analyse in order for him to decide the next course of action in the project. The subordinate loyally does so, spending the whole weekend writing up findings and ranking the alternatives. On Monday morning he delivers the requested material and, catching the project leader on his way out of the office, sees him glance through the paperwork saying: "Good. Super – Eh, I'm sorry but I am already late for a meeting. I'll get back to you."

A week passes and nothing happens. Early next week the subordinate sees his boss in the corridor and tells him he is still waiting for his decision. And he also adds that he cannot proceed further without a proper answer. The project leader again excuses himself, looks at his watch, refers to a new meeting he has to attend, and disappears again.

Another three days pass, and the subordinate bumps into his boss once again. This time he demands a decision, claiming that he regards the situation where his boss completely ignores taking vital decisions as totally frustrating!

This time the project leader reacts, feeling the criticism was just, and together they walk into the boss' office to solve the problem.

It is only at this stage that the project leader discovers, after reading the papers through again, *why* he has not made the decision in the first place. And the reason is simply that the paper is not good enough. It is incomplete in several respects, heavily biased towards the subordinate's own favourite alternative: all the positive outcomes of the decision are described in detail, while the negative ones are either only given a brief mention or not mentioned at all. All these things he saw already the first Monday morning, but he was not even aware himself that this was also the reason he had avoided the decision. But now he could clearly see that the document was simply unsuitable as adequate decision support material.

And this makes him say: "Yes. Perhaps I am a lousy decision

maker, but the fact is that you are a no-good partner in this process as well. If I don't get better decision support from you, you may never get the decisions you want!"

It took him three weeks to discover this. Some project leaders never discover these things, often because they simply hide themselves in a constant shortage of time and thereby avoid discovering the reasons for their irresoluteness.

The conclusion we can draw from this is that a good decision process in projects is a mutual responsibility for all parties involved. For this reason we tend today to formalize the decision process in projects by appointing special groups or committees having particular responsibilities and duties in relation to the project progress.[20] Typical are steering committees, being in charge of major decisions and of directing the project work according to special policy requirements. Reference groups are also recommendable if different kinds of opinions are sought as decision support and the project team itself is not able to, for technical or bureaucratic reasons, to create those appropriately. Also line management could well be included in the project work, particularly those who "lose" important knowledge-workers to the project and must therefore fulfil their regular duties with reduced capacity. Capacity lost is also a responsibility to inform superiors about. Other project cooperators or "stakeholders" are project coordinators, project evaluators and project directors. Their roles and responsibilities should be defined properly for each project, taking into account that proper project organization must be composed so that the full responsibility and authority is covered by the appointed bodies in combination. The finesse is to not leave any area of decision uncovered, or not having several bodies cover exactly the same area so that ineffective disagreement and contention develop.

5.3.7   The Project's Techno-economical Control

The ever-present aims of meeting performance, time and cost are the major considerations throughout the project's life cycle. Traditionally, cost has been seen as the most important parameter, but according to recent research in many projects, performance and schedule are equally or even more important than cost.[9] It would therefore be a great source of comfort if one could predict with certainty, at the start of the project, both how the performance, time and cost constraints would be met. In a few cases, such as routine construction projects, we can generate reasonably accurate

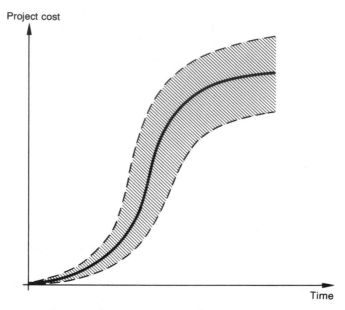

Figure 5.9 Estimates of project cost made at project start

predictions, but in most cases we are unable to do so. The crosshatched portion of figure 5.9 therefore illustrates the way uncertainty in projects in general must be viewed at the beginning of the project effort.

The value of performing milestone control is illustrated in figure 5.10. If new forecasts about project performance, time and cost are made either at fixed intervals in the life of the project or when specific milestones are reached, then there will be less uncertainty about the final goal achievement. In short this is the rationale for having project control systems in general, and is also the basis for all the techniques and methods developed, regardless of their sophistication and advanced computer orientation. Today a considerable number of books describing such techniques are available[2, 3, 10, 20] and it seems in fact that the major problem today is not that we are unable to find control tools but rather how to select the one most appropriate for the project in question.

Common Control Problems

Few project leaders, in effect, would argue the need for controlling projects according to plans. The challenge is to manage the available tools and techniques effectively. In a survey by Thamain and Willemon,[75] it was

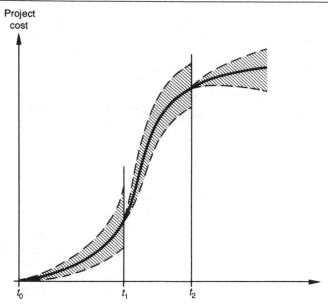

Figure 5.10 Estimates of project costs at different time intervals

found that project leaders list the following reasons as being responsible for poor project performance:

1. Unrealistic project plans
2. Staffing problems
3. Technical complications
4. Customer and management changes
5. Inability to detect problems early

Obviously, some of these problems should be possible to solve by using better technical and economical follow-up systems. One basic problem is to strike a good balance between long-run and short-run control objectives. Not because the blending is difficult, but because the project leader is often preoccupied with urgent short-run problems rather than longer-run problems. A good rule is to place the control as close as possible to the work being controlled and to design the simplest possible mechanism to achieve control.

The Connection between Project Planning and Project Control

We should be aware that planning and control are two sides of the same coin. This is illustrated in figure 5.11.

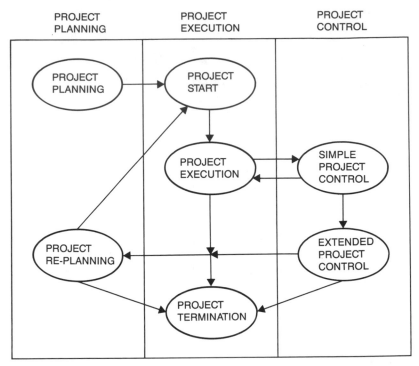

Figure 5.11 The interplay between project planning, project execution and
    project control

The figure illustrates the necessary connection between the project plan on
the one side and the project control on the other. The actual project work
from start to finish occurs in the centre column. The other two columns are
added purely for the purpose of helping the project work to proceed better
and more effectively towards its goal. For this reason none of these two
columns must contain work or procedures that obstruct the main objective
of the project endeavour – which is to reach the goal. While this seems an
indisputable statement, we may in many projects find both plans and
control systems so complicated, so laboursome, and so demanding that
even more effort has to be allocated to manage these systems than to reach
the proper project goal!

   As the figure illustrates, we must naturally be aware that plans and
control instalments must not be too simple either. The initial project plan
is good enough when we find that we are ready to start the project work. It
is a good idea to formalize the project start itself in a recognizable way so

that all involved and affected by the project work are properly informed about the actual change now due to take place. Different actions can support this. Arranging a special "kick-off" meeting may help defeat bewilderment and enhance motivation. Written and oral information may smoothen possible negative reactions among less informed co-workers. Team-building exercises may strengthen the necessary social collaboration amongst project participants.

The full activity of actions and making project decisions follow the start procedure, and the project plan serves as the helpful background for the daily work.

In the "perfect" project the next stop is the project termination. This occurs if no obstacles are observed, all planned activities are performed exactly as envisaged, and the project terminates because the originally desired goal is fully reached.

There are many reasons for regarding this description of project work as a too "perfect" or almost never-occurring one. In the first place, all project work is by definition unique. And uniqueness implies, as already contended, risk and indistinctness. We should therefore at least at some predefined points or milestones in the process induce some simple controlling remedies in order to convince ourselves that the project progresses in a desirable manner. This control has as its main objective to clarify the project's situation in the most simplified and effective way. Just asking people about project statements is quicker than demanding written reports. Rough comparisons are better than detailed diagrams and statistical exactness. The main objective is to arrive at a decision on how to proceed further – either by demanding more detailed control data, or to decide that no more control is necessary and the project work can continue as before. It should even be mentioned that by such a loose control, we also build up confidence at the subordinate level. Being trusted that information given is reliable and need not to be controlled further is a strong motivating factor[1] and should be used deliberately to provide better work relationships and social collaboration. In effect, in every preconceived control effort lies also a suspicion of unreliability!

If, however, the simple control exposes a critical gap between the actual progress and the planned progress, immediate remedies should be implemented. The first one is of course to measure the size of the gap. This can be done in many cunning ways, and the literature and the tools available, particularly those related to data processing devices and statistical measurement methods, are today manifold and generally of a very high standard.[2, 20] In this respect increasing emphasis has been placed on different kinds of "earned value" methods, in which not only the progress in terms of time spent and money used is measured, but also the actual "value" of the work done. This brings in new and interesting dimensions in project control, in the sense that a project which is behind the set schedule may still be well off if the work done is of a particularly high value or has opened up for new and favourable possibilities for the company or organization in question.

The Value of Project Work Performed

The formula for a project's "earned value" can generally be expressed as follows:

Earned Value = (Estimated percent completion per task) X (Planned cost per task)

The earned value thus becomes the amount that should have been spent on each task thus far. This can then be compared to the actual amount spent.

Another worthwhile parameter to calculate is the "critical ratio", which can generally be expressed by the following equation:

$$\text{Critical Ratio} = \frac{\text{Actual progress}}{\text{Planned progress}} \times \frac{\text{Planned Cost}}{\text{Actual Cost}}$$

In essence, the main objective when monitoring projects is to keep project performance, cost and schedule well related. We must also be aware that differences between work scheduled and work planned may develop for several different reasons; for example, official change orders in the work elements necessary to accomplish a task, informal alterations in the methods used to accomplish specific tasks or official or unofficial changes in the tasks to be accomplished. Similarly, cost variances can result from any of the above as well as from changes in input factor prices, changes in accounting methods demanded by the base organization or changes in the mix of input factors needed to accomplish a given task. If the plan is not altered to reflect such changes, comparisons between plan and actual work are not meaningful.

5.3.8 The Project's Social Control

Meeting schedule and cost goals without compromising performance appears to be a technical problem for the project leader. In reality it is only partly technical, because it is also a human problem. As already suggested, a programme like Management By Objectives helps. It gives the team members a chance to monitor their own progress and achievements while allowing full recognition by the project leader. Because the system is participative and makes team members accountable for their specific parts of the overall plan, it not only motivates them but also clearly denotes the degree to which team members are mutually dependent. This strongly reinforces the team feeling. The fear of "letting the team down" is also a strong motivating factor.[2]

Another major element posing a behavioural problem for the project leader is interpersonal conflict. When the project is first organized, priorities, procedures, and schedules all have roughly equal potential as sources of conflict. During the build-up phase, priorities become significantly more important and procedures are almost entirely established by this time. In the main programme phase, priorities are finally established and schedules are the most important cause of trouble within the project, followed by technical disagreements.[2] Obtaining adequate support for the project is also a point of concern. At project finish, meeting the schedule is the critical issue, but interpersonal tensions that were easily ignored early in the project may suddenly erupt during the last hectic weeks of the life cycle. Worry about reassignments exacerbates the situation.

Conflict Handling

Conflict can be handled in several ways, but one thing seems sure: Conflict avoiders do not make successful project managers. Much has been written about conflict resolution and there is no need to summarize that literature here beyond noting that the key to conflict resolution rests on the project leader's ability to transform a win–lose situation into a win–win one. Thamain and Wilemon[68] have written an interesting article on the nature of management of conflict. They also divided project work into four phases, and managed to log the number of conflicts during a sample project. Their results are shown in table 5.12.

Source of conflict	Amount	Project phase			
		Start	Early	Main	Late
Project priorities	102	26%	34%	24%	16%
Administrative procedures	77	35%	35%	19%	11%
Technical trade-offs	86	21%	30%	36%	13%
Staffing	88	25%	28%	28%	19%
Support cost estimates	59	35%	22%	25%	18%
Schedules	120	21%	24%	30%	25%
Personalities	67	25%	28%	22%	25%
Sum and Average figures	599	27%	29%	26%	18%

Table 5.12 Number of conflicts in a sample project[68]

As the table reveals, conflict over schedules and priorities dominate, and most conflicts seem to take place in earlier project phases. These observations have as already contended in chapter 4.3.2 been studied in more depth by model simulations and interview inquiries among central Norwegian project leaders[1].

What became clear was that project managers revealed different reactions and varied ways of motivation and demotivation during project development.

Project Phase Preferences

In short the following conclusions for each project phase were drawn:

> During project *initiation,* "personal" preferences which stimulate curiosity and eagerness to understand, to "stand out", and to be creative seemed to be particularly pronounced among the majority of the project managers. The "leadership"-profile was less expressed, but energy was seemingly concentrated on the "strategic" issue of "showing off" and the "tactical" issue of "competing", presumably in order to get both the managers themselves and their projects well "known" in the environment.

> During project *planning,* "leader"-oriented preferences such as keeping order and ensuring the execution of orders "my way" seemed to dominate. As "leaders" most project managers uses their power and responsibility for the more mundane and

"operational" planning duties. Their complete approach as "individuals" and as "leaders" appeared to be aimed at creating a stable and calm environment, which could be controlled and mastered by systems and structures they felt familiar with in order to make the project a motivating effort for themselves.

During project *execution,* preferences were more diverse. Most project managers sought support for their opinions and work responsibilities in different ways. As "leaders" they tried to "fight" for their cause, or their projects, and were willing to work hard in order to understand and succeed. In many ways this could be described as a "manipulative" type of behaviour, with a strong, indirect will to lead the work in the direction felt to be the most appropriate.

During project *termination,* the preferences had many similarities with those of the initiation phase. As managers the majority of them felt they now had to finish the project in a way that was favourable to themselves, both in the short and long term. They therefore wanted to show their excellence, and "achieve" as much as possible. As "leaders" their attitude was more mixed. The importance of taking leadership and fighting for their project, combined with a strong desire to "show off", resembled their desires in the project initation phase but perhaps with a more "leader"-oriented preference.

The Project Resource Triangle

A special issue of interest is the way project leaders regard their superiors and cooperate with them. Naturally, disagreements may occur at the highest project level. An illustrating example comes from the forthcoming Lillehammer Olympic Games Project 1994.

When Norway was assigned this project after beating tough international competition, the event was regarded as a triumph for the country. Once the first celebrations were over, however, it was soon realized that, to put it mildly, the original budget and the one used to win the competition contained flaws. At least four to five times more money had to be invested. When this became clear, the project had three central actors:

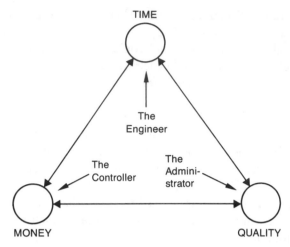

Figure 5.13 The project resource triangle.

(1) the administrative head (who came from a position as a local bank manager),
(2) the financial head (who was appointed by the government), and
(3) the technical head (who got his post through an ordinary applicational procedure).

What became apparent was that these three enactors disagreed on very important issues, namely which constraints were fixed and which were not. The conflict is illustrated in figure 5.13.

The administrative head, the Director of the Games, assumed the *quality* of the Olympic Games to have the highest priority. Norway had been given a unique chance to profile itself internationally as a nation of marvellous winter recreation possibilities, of spellbinding fjords and untouched mountain areas, and as a healthy lung in a world of pollution and contamination. In short: as a small nation with great potential. In his view these qualitative issues had to come first, the price tag later.

The government representative had a completely different opinion (and was a strong proponent for his view as well). He meant the *money-apex* was fixed. First the price tag, then the quality of the Olympic Games had to be adjusted according to the given budget.

Into this fierce competition appears the third actor, the technical director, whose job it was to build the arenas, cater for all the complex communication systems needed, arrange the lodging for thousands of people, etc. The more the administrative head and government representative fought without arriving at clear decisions, the more he despaired because he had to keep the *time-apex*. The start of the Games was in February 1994, not in March or any other later time!

No wonder the conflict ended with total collapse. From the highest authoritative level a new administrative head was appointed, the government representative was allowed to keep his position but was given far less power, and the technical head was awarded a more influential position. Today it is known that the price tag is still in upwards motion, through a mix of direct and indirect costs, that the quality most probably will be highly satisfactory, and that the Games will take off exactly on time!

We should after this be very careful to include all sorts of social interaction parameters in project work, and be fully aware that project control is in many projects perhaps even more important than the traditional technical and economical control occupation.

5.3.9 The Project's Internal Communication

Communication is the activity that takes up most of a project leader's time. Leaders seldom find themselves alone at their desks thinking or contemplating alternatives in solitude. When they are not talking with superiors, peers or subordinates in person, they are usually communicating by telephone or writing memos or letters. According to Hunsaker and Cook,[33] it is unusual for a manager to work without interruption for longer than an occasional half hour two or three times a week.

Still the communication aspect of the project is often the most worrying problem. And one of the reasons for this is perhaps the difficulties that arise due to misinterpretation. This occurs when the receiver understands the message to his or her own satisfaction, but not in the sense that the sender intended it. Although misinterpretations can be a consequence of sender or channel noise,[33] poor listening habits or erroneous inferences on the part of the receiver are often to blame.[76]

As suggested by Hunsaker and Cook,[33] the following six errors seem to dominate in this respect:

1. Different frames of reference.
   A combination of past experience and current expectation often leads two people to perceive the same communication differently. Within even one singular project people with different functions often have different frames of reference. Marketing-people may interpret things one way and production people another. An engineer's interpretation is likely to differ from that of an accountant. Project leaders must work hard to ensure that these disparate frames of reference do not impede effective internal project communication.

2. Problems of semantics.
   Many professional and social groups adopt a kind of inside jargon that provides them with a sense of belonging and may even facilitate communication within the group itself. But sophisticated technical and financial terms can intimidate and confuse outsiders, especially when members of a privileged group use them to protect a professional mystique. To communicate effectively in a project, a sender must refrain from using terms that may be unfamiliar or ambiguous to the receiver.

3. Different value judgements.
   Value judgements are a source of noise when a receiver evaluates the worth of a sender's message before the sender has finished transmitting it. Often such value judgements are based on the receiver's previous experience either with that sender or with similar types of communications. When listeners form value judgements, speakers are usually aware of it through verbal and non-verbal feedback. Subsequently, the senders become guarded and defensive, which often inhibits transmission of their real concerns.

   Value judgements may also arise from a receiver's inference about the sender's intentions. Whereas the sender knows what intention underlies a communication, the receiver must infer what is really meant. Sender credibility is important here, because a receiver's degree of trust and confidence in the sender directly affects his or her reaction to the words and gestures of the message.

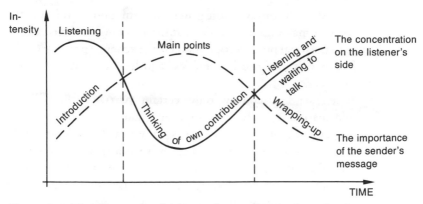

Figure 5.14 The dissonance between the sender's and receiver's concentration in the conversations

4. The inclination to selective listening.

When messages conflict with what receivers believe or expect, they are often prone to selective listening in the sense that we block out the information or distort it to match preconceived notions. At times project executors may become so absorbed in their tasks that when someone initiates conversation, they are not able to disassociate and listen effectively. Not only is it difficult for a preoccupied person to receive the message the sender intends, but it may actually appear that the receiver doesn't care about the sender or the message. This can create negative feelings and make future communications even more difficult. A common pitfall occurs in emotionally charged conversations or philosophical debates when receivers listen only for an opening to speak, rather than pay attention to the content of the sender's message. This is illustrated in figure 5.14.

In the introductory phase the sender will perhaps only disclose general remarks, preparing for his coming, more in-depth views. In this phase the receiver listens quite carefully, trying to find immediate clues to which he will respond. When the sender then enters the phase where he explains his views more thoroughly, the receiver has already stopped listening because he is now preparing his own response. When the receiver then recognizes that the sender is nearing the end of his speech, he begins to listen again, only by this point the sender is finishing off and again conveys more general information. In this way the receiver may miss the sender's entire meaning in their haste to get a personal point across. As such an exchange progresses, the feedback is likely to become less and less relevant.

5. Filtering.

When senders convey only certain parts of the relevant information to receivers, they are said to be filtering the message. Filtering often occurs in upward communication when subordinates suppress negative information and relay only the data that will be perceived by superiors as positive.

Another kind of filtering occurs in times of information overload, or intense time pressure. When project leaders are deluged with more information than they can process effectively, one response is to screen out and never decode a larger number of messages. When time pressures are on, even the information that has been absorbed and processed may not be communicated by the leader to all concerned employees, because there simply isn't enough time.

6. Distrust.

A lack of trust on the part of either communicator is likely to evoke one or more of the barriers already mentioned. Senders may filter out important information if they distrust receivers, and receivers may form value judgements, make inferences, and listen only selectively to distrusted senders. Such situations are complicated by the fact that the distrust itself may have arisen from earlier communications that were impeded by some of the same barriers. In other words, neither party is dishonest, but their poorly developed communication skills have led them to distrust one another.

Another form of organizational distrust[33] has to do with status rather than with ethical assumptions. Lower-status employees tend to be intimidated by upper-status job titles, plush offices, sophisticated modes of dress, and perhaps even by a particular leader's reputation. Rather than take the risk of being judged incompetent or being ridiculed, subordinates may refrain from seeking help or requesting the information they need from a high-status manager. This type of distrust results in no communication at all.

5.3.10 The Project's External Communication

Four basic questions should be asked in relation to the external project communication:

1. Who other than the people directly involved in the project should receive information about it?
2. What are these people's preconditions and limitations in apprehending this information?
3. Which reactions are we aiming at among these people?
4. What kind of information are they perhaps most interested in receiving?

By such a simple analysis we may easily find out that if there are several possible information-receivers, they will most probably require different types of information, and even if the information was the same, they perhaps need to have it presented in a different "wrapping", depending on their hierarchical level or closeness to the project. The top echelons tend to need short, decision-oriented information, peers prefer technically intelligible and adequate information, and interest groups may ask for different kinds of consequence analyses.

Choice of medium is also important. The selection ranges from reports and other publications to newspaper articles and yearbooks, and further to presentations in radio, TV, etc. for larger projects. We must not forget the use of particular meetings, seminars, symposia, and direct personal contacts through telephone, letters, and personal visits. With the increasing number of possibilities other than plain reports now available, we should spend time finding the right one for each particular project situation. An old rule of thumb may be helpful in this process:

The average person remembers:

10% of what he or she *reads*
20% of what he or she *hears*
30% of what he or she *sees*
40% of what he or she *hears* and *sees* simultaneously
70% of what he or she *says*
90% of what he or she *says* and *does* simultaneously

Even though these figures are rough estimates and the ability to absorb information will vary from person to person, the figures clearly point to the advantage of active communication compared to the passive conveyance of reports.

We must also be aware of the way information is brought *into* the project. This process is normally triggered off by the type of antennae-system build around the project. Since project work takes place in a world of turmoil and change, we should regularly investigate which possible terms of reference are changing and thereby perhaps induce a need for project reviews. This is especially important with more long-lasting projects.

This job should be the responsibility of all project participants. But often this may be the particular responsibility of the reference group or appointed team members. We should even think about particular individuals outside the project who could be called upon to reveal special information that is relevant to the project's progress. This may be done in order to secure that the project really reaches a *desired* and *essential* goal when the project effort is over. (A goal which is perfect at project start-up may end up as an uninteresting one and even a completely wrong goal two years later if strived for in solitude.) We must avoid the situation when project leaders neglect to change the project course even when there are clear signs that important preconditions were not thought of or have been changing during the course of the project development, hiding themselves behind an original written goal formulation.

An illustrating example of the problems encountered in locking oneself within an initial project frame comes from a Norwegian aid project in Tanzania.

> Several years ago Norway decided to help Tanzania build up a fishing industry, and it was decided to implement a project on the northern coastline of the country. The area, Mbegani, was a small fishing village with almost no road connection to the rest of the country, particularly not to the nearest city, Dar es Salaam, which was the natural market place for the fish catch.
>
> A Norwegian consulting company was hired to do the job, which was quite sizeable, and they immediately started to define the project in accordance with their own professional standard.
>
> In the end an extremely modern, fashionable complex of buildings, slipways, fish processing equipment, fish-packing plants, research laboratories, and the like was erected. Boat-building facilities, classrooms for educational purposes, dormitories for students and bungalows for expatriate personnel were

also set up. Asphalt roads and sports courts were also included, even a very high-standard motorway extending four kilometres into the bush was built, awaiting the rest of the road network in the country to be developed in this area.

The opening ceremony was splendid, with high-ranking officials from both countries in attendance, and the project was highly praised.

After one year of operation the fatal truth was discovered: there was no fish in the area!

It has been admitted that the whole project was a failure. Several hundred million Norwegian kroner was wasted on a project with no future. Even fish-pond production is impossible, and an attempt to utilize the whole complex as a marine training centre has failed.

The party that is really to blame for this is the Norwegian consulting company supervising job. At a very early stage it must have become quite clear to them that the fish resources were almost non-existent. But either they did not reflect on it, concentrating on their professionality which was to recommend buildings, or they chose to hide this fact so that they could keep a prosperous contract. Either way this lack of noticing the reality of the project's immediate environment must be regarded as an unethical behaviour which should not take place in serious project business.

5.4   References

1 Jessen, S.A. 1990: The Motivation of Project Managers. A Study of Variation in Norwegian Project Managers' Motivation and Demotivation by Triangulation of Methods. Thesis submitted for the degree of Doctor of Philosophy, Henley, The Management College and Brunel University. August 1990.

2 Meredith, J.R. & S.J. Mantel Jr. 1989: *Project Management. A Managerial Approach.* (Second edition.) John Wiley & Sons. N.Y.

3 Gray, C.F. 1981: *Essentials of Project Management.* Petrocelli Books, Inc. Oregon.

4 Miner, J.B. 1980: *Theories of Organizational Behavior.* The Dryden Press, Hinsdale. Ill.

5 Murray, H.A. 1938: *Explorations in Personality.* Oxford University Press. N.Y.

6 Butler, A.G., Jr. 1983: Project Management – Its Functions and Dysfunctions. In D.I. Cleland & R.W. King (eds.): *Project Management Handbook.* Van Nostrand Reinhold Company. N.Y.

7 Slevin, D.P. 1983: Motivation and the Project Manager. In D.I. Cleland & R.W. King (eds.): *Project Management Handbook*. Van Nostrand Reinhold Co, N.Y. 552–566.
8 Baker, B.N. 1988: Lessons Learned from a Variety of Project Failures. *Proceedings of the Ninth World Congress on Project Management 1*. Glasgow. 113–118.
9 Wenstøp, F. & P. Gottschalk 1985: *Kvantitativ beslutningsanalyse*. Universitetsforlaget, Oslo.
10 Cleland D.I. & R.W. King 1983: Life Cycle Management. In D.I. Cleland & R.W. King (eds.): *Project Management Handbook*. Van Nostrand Reinhold Co. N.Y. 209–221.
11 Augustine, N.R. (ed.): 1989: Managing Projects and Programs. *Harvard Business Review*. Mass.
12 Kolltveit, B.J. 1988: *The Technical Concept and Organizational Effectiveness of Offshore Projects*. Henley, The Management College, March. Henley.
13 Anderson, S.D. & R.W. Woodhead 1987: *Project Manpower Management. Decision-making Processes in Construction Practice*. Wiley-Interscience Publication, John Wiley & Sons. N.Y.
14 Burbridge, R.N. 1988: Conception of Projects. *Proceedings of the Ninth World Congress on Project Management 1*. Glasgow. (Unpaged.)
15 Morton, G.H.A. 1983: Project Manager, Catalyst to Constant Change. A Behavioral Analysis. In D.I. Cleland & R.W. King (eds.): *Project Management Handbook*. Van Nostrand Reinhold Co, N.Y. 533–551.
16 Reve, J. & T. Levitt 1984: Organization and Governance in Construction. *Project Management 2, 1*.
17 Harrison, F.L. 1988: Conflict, Power & Politics in Project Management. *Proceedings of the Ninth World Congress on Project Management 1*. Glasgow. 513–520.
18 Andersen, E.S, Grude, K., Haug, T. & J.R. Turner 1987: *Goal Directed Project Management*. Coopers & Lybrand. London.
19 Adams, J.R. & S.E. Barndt 1983: Behavioral Implications of the Project Life Cycle. In D.I. Cleland & R.W. King (eds.): *Project Management Handbook*. Van Nostrand Reinhold Co. N.Y. 222–244.
20 Jessen, S.A. 1992: *Prosjektadministrative Metoder*. Universitetsforlaget, Oslo.
21 Morris, P.W.G. 1988: Initiating Major Projects – The Unperceived Role of Project Management. *Proceedings of the Ninth World Congress on Project Management 1*. Glasgow. 801–813.
22 Lord, A.M. & D. Birchall 1988: The Choice of Management Structure and Staffing the Team during Project Initiation. *INTERNET Proceedings*. 189–196.
23 Ashley, G. 1988: The Art of Management of Human Resources Generation and Implementation of Human Capital. *Proceedings of the Ninth World Congress on Project Management 1*. Glasgow. 87–95.
24 Birchall, D. & J. Dingle 1988: A Fresh Look at Project Preparation. *Proceedings of the Ninth World Congress on Project Management 1*. Glasgow. 329–336.
25 Turner, E.K. 1988: Scope Definition for Bidding Project-Control Services. *International Journal of Project Management 6, 1*, 39–44.

26 Beck, D.R. 1983: Implementing Top Management Plans through Project Management. Abbot Laboratoties, Inc. In D.I. Cleland & R.W. King (eds.): *Project Management Handbook*. Van Nostrand Reinhold Co. N.Y. 166–184.

27 Spirer, H.F. 1983: Phasing out the Project. In D.I. Cleland & R.W. King (eds.): *Project Management Handbook*. Van Nostrand Reinhold Co. N.Y. 245–264.

28 Baker, B.N., Fischer, D. & D.C. Murphy 1983: Project Management in the Public Sector: Success and Failure Patterns Compared to Private Sector Projects. In D.I. Cleland & R.W. King (eds.): *Project Management Handbook*. Van Nostrand Reinhold Co. N.Y. 686–699.

29 Taylor, F.W. 1911: *The Principles of Scientific Management*. (1967) Norton. N.Y.

30 Locke, E.A. 1968: Toward a Theory of Task Motivation and Incentives. *Organization Behaviour and Human Performance*, May.

31 Likert, R. 1961: *New Patterns of Management*. McGraw-Hill. N.Y.

32 Locke, E.A. 1978: The Ubiquity of the Technical Goal Setting in Theories and Approaches to Employee Motivation. *Academy of Management Review 3*, (July), 594–601.

33 Hunsaker, O.L. & C.W. Cook 1986: *Managing Organizational Behavior*, Addison-Wesley Publishing Company, Reading. Mass.

34 Davis, K. & J.W. Newstrom 1989: *Human Behavior at Work*. McGraw-Hill International Editions.

35 Cummings, T.G. 1977: Emergence of the Instrumental Organization. In P.S. Goodman & J.M. Pennings (eds.): *New Perspectives on Organizational Effectiveness*. Jossey-Bass. San Francisco. Cal.

36 Adices, I. 1979: Organizational Passages – Diagnosing and Treating Lifecycle Problems of Organizations. *Organizational Dynamics* (Summer). 3–25.

37 Hersey, P. & K.H. Blanchard 1969: Life Cycle Theory of Leadership. *Training and Development Journal 23*, 2. 26–34.

38 Randolph, W.A. & B.Z Posner 1988: *Effective Project Planning and Management*. Prentice-Hall International Editions. Englewood Cliffs. N.J.

39 Torrington, D., Weighman, J. & K. Johns 1985. *Management Methods*. Institute of Personnel Management and Gower. London.

40 Royston, G.H.D. 1990: Operational Research and the Reform of the UK Health Service. In H.E. Bradley (ed.): *Operational Research 90*. Pergamon Press. Oxford.

41 Tannenbaum, R. & Massarick, F. 1957: Leadership: A Frame of Reference. *Management Science*, (October).

42 Zeldman, M.E. 1980: How Management Can Develop and Sustain a Creative Environment. *S.A.M. Advanced Management Journal*, Winter.

43 Hayes, R. & W.J. Abernathy 1980: Managing Our Way to Economic Decline. *Harvard Business Review*, (July–August).

44 Sounder, W.E. 1974: Autonomy, Gratification, and R&D Outputs: A Small-Sample Field Study. *Management Science*, (April).

45 Mansfield, E. 1968: *Industrial Research and Technological Innovation*. Norton. N.Y.

46 Baker, N.R. 1974: R&D Project Selection Models: An Assessment. *IEEE Transactions on Engineering Management*, (November).

47 Sounder, W.E. 1973: Utility and Perceived Acceptability of R&D Project Selection Models. *Management Science*, (August).

48 Porter, M.E. 1985: *Competitive Strategy*. Free Press, N.Y.

49 Suresh, N.C. & J.R. Meredith 1985: Justfying Multimachine Systems: An Integrated Strategic Approach. *Journal of Manufacturing Systems*, (November).

50 Richardson, G.P. & A.L. Pugh III 1981: *Introduction to System Dynamics Modelling With DYNAMO*. M.I.T. Press, Cambridge. Mass.

51 Roberts, E.B. 1981: A Simple Model of R&D Project Dynamics. In E.B. Roberts (ed.): *Managerial Applications of System Dynamics*. M.I.T. Press, Cambridge. Mass.

52 Cox, B. & M.W. Dale 1987: The Management of Finance. In H. Darnell (ed.): *Total Project Management, Book 2*. The Asset Management Group of the British Institute of Management.

53 Boynton, A. & R.W. Zmud 1984: An Assessment of Critical Success Factors. *Sloan Management Review*, (Summer), 17–27.

54 UNDP 1988: *Guidelines for Project Formulation and The Project Document Format. Programme and Projects Manual*.

55 Slevin, D.P. & J.K. Pinto 1987: Balancing Strategy and Tactics in Project Implementation. In J.R. Meredith & S.J. Mantel Jr. (eds.): *Project Management*. John Wiley & Sons, N.Y.

56 Humble, J. 1976: *Målrettet Ledelse*. Hjemmet Forlag. Oslo.

57 Wenstøp, F. 1987: *Statistikk og dataanalyser*. TANO. Oslo.

58 McGregor, D. 1960: *The Human Side of Enterprise*. McGraw-Hill. N.Y.

59 Stoner, J.A.F. & C. Wankel 1986: *Management*. (Third edition.) Prentice-Hall International. N.Y.

60 Carroll, S.J. Jr. & H.L. Tosi 1973: *Management by Objectives: Applications and Research*. Macmillan. N.Y.

61 "Hartmark IRAS." 1970– : The MBO technique was actively applied in Norwegian companies during the 1970s by Norwegian consulting companies. This author was personally involved in many projects initiated by the MBO approach in the years 1975–1980 as staff consultant in Hartmark–IRAS.

62 Carroll, S.J. Jr. & H.L. Tosi 1968: Managerial Reactions to Management by Objectives. *Academy of Management Journal 11*, 4.

63 Jamieson, B.D. 1973: Behavioural Problems with Management by Objectives. *Academy of Management Journal 16*, 3.

64 Kolb, D.A., Rubin, I.M. & J.M. McIntyre 1984: *Organizational Psychology: Experimental Approach to Organizational Behavior*. (Fourth edition.) Prentice-Hall, Englewood Cliffs, N.J.

65 Morton, G.H.A. 1983: Human Dynamics in Project Planning. In D.I. Cleland & R.W. King (eds.): *Project Management Handbook*. Van Nostrand Reinhold Company,N.Y.

66 Davis, E.W. 1972: CPM Use in Large Construction Firms – A Top Management Survey. In M. Ogander (ed.): *The Practical Application of Project Planning by Network Techniques*. John Wiley & Sons. N.Y.

67 Gilbreath, R.D. 1986: *Winning at Project Management*. John Wiley & Sons. N.Y.

68 Thamain, H.J. & D.L. Wilemon 1975: Conflict Management in Project Life Cycles. *Sloane Management Review,* Summer.

69 The material supporting these suggestions is collected from ongoing studies of project work in smaller communities in northern Norway. This research work is in its earliest stages, but important conclusions seem possible to draw already on the existing material. Why the decision-making process is particularly recognized is due to the fact that in many of these communities the project approach was chosen as a problem-solving instrument due to its apparent better decision-making ability.

70 Hertz, D.B. & H. Thomas 1983: *Risk Analysis and Its Applications.* John Wiley & Sons. N.Y.

71 Townsend, H.W.R. & G.E. Whitehouse 1977: We Used Risk Analysis to Move Our Computer. *Industrial Engineering,* (May).

72 Garcia, A. & W. Cowdrey 1978: Information Systems: A Long Way fron Wall-Carvings to CRT's. *Industrial Engineering,* (April).

73 Alderfer, C.P. 1969: A New Theory of Human Needs, *Organizational Behavior and Human Performance 4.*

74 March, J.G. & J.P. Olsen 1976: *Ambiguity and Choice in Organizations,* Universitetsforlaget, Bergen.

75 Thamain, H.J. & D.L. Wilemon 1986: Criteria for Controlling Projects According to Plans. In S.R. Meredith & D.J. Mantel Jr. (eds.): *Project Management.* John Wiley & Sons, N.Y.

76 Johnson, D.W. 1981: *Reaching out.* (Second edition.) Prentice-Hall. Englewood Cliffs, N.J.

77 The SMG-group and QMT. a.s. 1990: The Complete Project Manager. PrimaVera ed.

6 SUMMARY AND CONCLUSIONS

"He that will not apply new remedies must accept new evils; for time is the greatest innovator"
(Francis Bacon)

6.1 Future Aspects

Since project management organizational forms are among the most adaptable forms we know today, they will most likely become almost universally accepted over the next 10–20 years. But it is after all a modern invention and needs support to succeed. First, the project concept seems to work best when related to some base organization. Therefore, functionalist specialist positions will most likely also remain as an organizational line element. From this mutual dependency we will most likely see an emerging need for new "dual" organizational structures; one which will promote the use of project organizations for solving important unique, one time problems within and between different organizational structures, and one which will credit the use of bureaucratic, well-structured, reliable and long-lasting structures.

This difference in structure and objectives will definitely foster a need for *more professional* project management and leadership. This change in attitude and responsibility is already developing rapidly, and it must be assumed that more emphasis will be placed upon reducing the number of layers of supervisory positions in existence today between the project managers and the upper-level management.

In this process too the role of project management will change. The new role will probably be far more of a "leadership" role than a "managerial" one. Although leadership in many ways is similar to management, there is a difference between the two. As suggested by Cherrington,[1] "for managers to be effective, they need to be good leaders. However, not all leaders are good managers!»

In essence, leadership is more narrowly defined, it refers to *influencing* the behaviour of others. In other words, leadership is the *incremental* influence one individual exerts over another, above or beyond mechanical compliance with routine directives.[2]

Leadership therefore occurs when one individual influences others to do something voluntarily rather than because they were required to do it or because they fear the consequences of non-compliance.[3] By this definition almost everyone in an organization can be a leader. And this is also the reason why project leadership will be the future way of leading in our organizations, since projects may take place at any level and in many forms in future organizational life. And it serves to emphasize an important organizational outcome: the creation of an energetic and highly committed work force that is successfully adapting to the demands of a changing environment and competently producing viable products or services.

We must in this respect be aware that although most of the literature on leadership emphasizes the influence of the leader on the group, the influence of the group upon the leader should not be overlooked. The relationship between the leader and the group implies a reciprocal influence. Groups have the capacity to influence the behaviour of their leaders by responding selectively to specific leader behaviours. The influence of a leader can also be constrained by many external factors, such as organizational policies, group norms, and individual skills and abilities. Other variables have been found to neutralize or substitute for the influence of a leader, such as the skills and abilities of followers and the nature of the task itself.

6.2   The Project Approach as a Cultural Phenomenon

As already suggested, the project approach has developed as a mixture of two organizational trends. The first in which the project concept has continually been formed as a protest or reaction to recognized inadequacies in the recommendations of "new" organizational thinking in our western cultures in modern time. The other trend is early application of new organizational theories to see if they work. In this way, the current project approach may perhaps best be described as a "rational, open system" thinking, while leading theorists recommend the "natural, open system" thinking models as the best for organizational well-being today (see also chapter 4).

Another way of looking at the project approach as a cultural phenomenon was done by this author in which the earlier described project characteristics were compared with Gert Hofstede's research on cultural differences.[4] According to him, four different dimensions of cultural differences in a world-wide perspective could be recognized, namely:

- Uncertainty avoidance
- Power distance
- Individualism
- Masculinity

By simple measurement techniques (squaring differences, adding them and square-rooting the sum) seventeen different countries were compared with regard to their deviation from an "ideal" project form in the different project phases. The result is shown in table 6.1.

COUNTRY	REGION	PROJECT INITI- ATION	PROJECT PLAN- NING	PROJECT EXECU- TION	PROJECT TERMINA- TION	TOTAL SCORE
1. Germany	N-Europe	10	1	1	2	(12.93)
2. Italy	S-Europe	5	2	2	1	(15.71)
3. France	S-Europe	1	6	6	3	(18.31)
4. USA	USA	2	7	7	4	(19.57)
5. Netherlands	N-Europe	7	5	5	5	(19.65)
6. Norway	N-Europe	–	3	3	6	(20.35)
7. Great Britain	N-Europe	3	9	9	7	(20.95)
8. Arab Countr.	Middle-East	4	8	8	–	(22.19)
9. East Africa	E-Africa	8	4	4	–	(22.38)
10. Sweden	N-Europe	–	–	–	9	(23.32)
11. Denmark	N-Europe	–	10	10	–	(23.92)
12. Japan	N-Asia	–	–	–	8	(24.68)
13. Thailand	SE-Asia	–	–	–	10	(25.18)
14. West Africa	W-Africa	–	–	–	–	(26.77)
15. Philippines	SE-Asia	6	–	–	–	(27.92)
16. Yugoslavia	E-Europe	–	–	–	–	(29.00)
17. Malaysia	SE-Asia	8	–	–	–	(31.97)

Table 6.1 Ranking of countries according to their potential project adaptability

As the scores indicate, the project approach is a typical westernized problem-solving approach, fitting the way people in such countries think and behave. Among the "top ten" countries 80% are European with Germany as a leader. On the basis of this we could perhaps suggest that the German methodological and effective approach lies behind the rules and roles earlier advocated for project work. However, we must also notice that when project initiation is focused, where creativity, innovation and audaciousness is the prime concern, other cultures score high. Examples are East-African countries, Arab countries and South-East Asia. Perhaps the best project work demands a collaboration between different nations and cultures, a possibility hitherto unrecognized but one which perhaps gives the project approach an even more prosperous and rightful international dimension.

Conclusively, as the art of project leadership stands today, we can point to the following points as the most typical advantages of it:

1. The designation and use of a project leader provides a focal point for leading, monitoring and controlling the work that has to be done.
2. The project approach answers the need for developing a complex product or system within a specified period of time, within predetermined cost and performance parameters.
3. Numerous components, sub-systems and systems can be developed in parallel with various groups or entities within or outside the company.
4. The working toward definite goals, the charisma of an effective project leader, the technical challenge and the potential benefits if the project succeeds can provide a high level of personal morale and camaraderie. Personnel tend to identify themselves with the project and its success.

6.3   Areas of Project Management

The scope of project management has continuously been widening since it first evolved as a new way of solving problems some 40 years ago. It may be assumed today that the concept will be particularly powerful in areas that experience the fastest rate of change. According to Gordon,[5] the following five areas will macro-economically be the most "restless" ones in the future:

1. The unemployment rate
2. The inflation rate
3. Production growth
4. The interest rate
5. The foreign exchange rate

Project work will most probably take its place supporting or preventing undesired developments within these change areas. Projects which reduce unemployment will be initiated both by governments and within industries experiencing the hardship of staff reductions. High inflation rates and changing interest rates will promote short term efforts and investments and thereby favour the fast and immediate R.O.I. often sought by project endeavours. Production growth in changing environments demands new products and new market areas which promote the flexibility of the project approach. The influence of international trade and policy will enhance "international project management" crossing national borders. This will demand fast and effective team-building combining different cultural backgrounds.

Other trends strongly supporting project developments are the increasing speed in technological advancements, the shortening of the product life cycle, the greater demand for new product introduction, the trend towards "people management" rather than "task" management and the need for new organizational thinking related to the need for solving the problem at hand instead of organizational tradition and indolence. In a project simulation program developed by the QMT group in cooperation with the SMG group,[6] project work was classified as illustrated in figure 6.1.

As the diagram suggests the term "project management" should perhaps only be used when we introduce a "new product". Though we may question if this definition perhaps limits the potential of the project

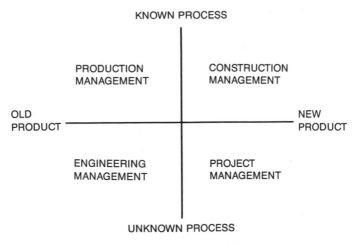

Figure 6.1 Four dimensions of problem solving

approach too much, it clearly points to the importance for the project leader to master uniqueness and creativity in project endeavours.

In this situation we must assume that the "project leadership" role will be increasingly important. As suggested by Kertzner,[7] the following leader-skills will be particularly important in the future:

1. Producing an "end result" within constraints of available resources and performance requirements. This will require a "global view" of the project objectives and accurate planning of how success will be achieved.
2. Leadership aspects of directing the project team effort, but recognizing that the reporting of results and control feedback will be highly automated and will require relatively less attention.
3. Decision making based on the use of all pertinent data, but observing that this will still involve uncertainty within an uncontrolled environment.
4. Negotiations for needed resources and resolution of conflicting demands on those resources. In fact, the interface requirement will take on larger proportions of the conflict between computer control and human initiative. Resolution across the man-machine interface will be particularly demanding.

The anticipated role of the future project manager will largely be related to operational planning of unique projects. While the computer can make real contributions in all programme development, it will probably not be capable of identifying all relevant alternatives, testing them against the broader environment and charting an operational plan to achieve the unique objectives of a "one shot" project. The project leader's "system view" of the world will permit evaluation of the true alternatives and coaching of the project team to execute the selected action plan.

But these developments also place stress upon the project concept as such. It is very likely that the goals and objectives of a given project team will change during its life time, even though the original plan was for a relatively short-lived project. Contingency planning in this environment will become an absolute necessity and it is possible that new courses in this discipline will emerge in specific environments.

An interesting trend today is that colleges and universities are increasingly teaching graduate and undergraduate interdisciplinary courses in project management. There will most probably also be massive further-education programmes in the areas of project and product management. Companies will become not just international, but supranational. Concurrent with the emergence and growth of the new supranational company will also come a blurring of the distinction between government and business. One manifestation of this lack of distinction is the profit-oriented, nationalized company. Within the supranational company, the project leader's task will become increasingly complex and difficult as he or she tries to coordinate the activities of many people, speaking many languages, in several countries, with different skill levels in what will become increasingly international projects.

We may safely conclude from this that the project concept is a highly viable one and will be the future method of solving almost every operational problem identified within existing organizational structures. The crux is to transform these problems to goal-directed, one-time, and resource-limited endeavours. This will then challenge the individual, the organization, and it may even challenge the established cultural methods of measuring success. If such new measurements benefit mankind, they should be given as much support as possible.

6.4   References

1 Cherrington, D.J. 1989: *Organizational Behavior*. Ally & Bacon. Mass.
2 Katz, D. & R.L. Kahn 1978: *The Social Psychology of Organizations*. John Wiley & Sons. N.Y.
3 Meredith, J.R. & S.J. Mantel Jr. 1989: *Project Management. A Managerial Approach*. (Second edition.) John Wiley & Sons. N.Y.
4 Hofstede, G. 1985: The Interaction Between National and Organizational Value Systems, *Journal of Management Studies 2, 4*.
5 Gordon, J.G. 1987: *Macroeconomics*. Little, Brown & Company. Boston. To.
6 Graham, R. 1990: The Complete Project Manager. A simulation program developed by the SMG Group, London, and QMT a.s., Norway.
7 Kertzner, H. 1990: Project Management in the Year 2000. In J.R. Meredith & S.J. Mantel Jr. (eds.): *Project Management*. John Wiley & Sons. N.Y.